Hidden Wars

OXFORD STUDIES IN GENDER AND INTERNATIONAL RELATIONS

Series editors: Rahul Rao, University of St Andrews, and Laura Sjoberg,
Royal Holloway University of London

Windows of Opportunity: How Women Seize Peace Negotiations for Political Change
Miriam J. Anderson

Women as Foreign Policy Leaders: National Security and Gender Politics in Superpower America
Sylvia Bashevkin

Gendered Citizenship: Understanding Gendered Violence in Democratic India
Natasha Behl

Gender, Religion, Extremism: Finding Women in Anti-Radicalization
Katherine E. Brown

Enlisting Masculinity: The Construction of Gender in U.S. Military Recruiting Advertising during the All-Volunteer Force
Melissa T. Brown

The Politics of Gender Justice at the International Criminal Court: Legacies and Legitimacy
Louise Chappell

The Other #MeToos
Iqra Shagufta Cheema

Cosmopolitan Sex Workers: Women and Migration in a Global City
Christine B. N. Chin

Intelligent Compassion: Feminist Critical Methodology in the Women's International League for Peace and Freedom
Catia Cecilia Confortini

Hidden Wars: Gendered Political Violence in Asia's Civil Conflicts
Sara E. Davies and Jacqui True

Complicit Sisters: Gender and Women's Issues across North-South Divides
Sara de Jong

Gender and Private Security in Global Politics
Maya Eichler

This American Moment: A Feminist Christian Realist Intervention
Caron E. Gentry

Troubling Motherhood: Maternality in Global Politics
Lucy B. Hall, Anna L. Weissman, and Laura J. Shepherd

Breaking the Binaries in Security Studies: A Gendered Analysis of Women in Combat
Ayelet Harel-Shalev and Shir Daphna-Tekoah

Scandalous Economics: Gender and the Politics of Financial Crises
Aida A. Hozić and Jacqui True

Building Peace, Rebuilding Patriarchy: The Failure of Gender Interventions in Timor-Leste
Melissa Johnston

Rewriting the Victim: Dramatization as Research in Thailand's Anti-Trafficking Movement
Erin M. Kamler

Equal Opportunity Peacekeeping: Women, Peace, and Security in Post-Conflict States
Sabrina Karim and Kyle Beardsley

Gender, Sex, and the Postnational Defense: Militarism and Peacekeeping
Annica Kronsell

The Beauty Trade: Youth, Gender, and Fashion Globalization
Angela B. V. McCracken

Global Norms and Local Action: The Campaigns against Gender-Based Violence in Africa
Peace A. Medie

Rape Loot Pillage: The Political Economy of Sexual Violence in Armed Conflict
Sara Meger

Critical Perspectives on Cybersecurity: Feminist and Postcolonial Interventions
Anwar Mhajne and Alexis Henshaw

Support the Troops: Military Obligation, Gender, and the Making of Political Community
Katharine M. Millar

From Global to Grassroots: The European Union, Transnational Advocacy, and Combating Violence against Women
Celeste Montoya

Who Is Worthy of Protection? Gender-Based Asylum and US Immigration Politics
Meghana Nayak

Revisiting Gendered States: Feminist Imaginings of the State in International Relations
Swati Parashar, J. Ann Tickner, and Jacqui True

Out of Time: The Queer Politics of Postcoloniality
Rahul Rao

Gender, UN Peacebuilding, and the Politics of Space: Locating Legitimacy
Laura J. Shepherd

Narrating the Women, Peace and Security Agenda: Logics of Global Governance
Laura J. Shepherd

Capitalism's Sexual History
Nicola J. Smith

The Global Politics of Sexual and Reproductive Health
Maria Tanyag

A Feminist Voyage through International Relations
J. Ann Tickner

The Political Economy of Violence against Women
Jacqui True

Queer International Relations: Sovereignty, Sexuality and the Will to Knowledge
Cynthia Weber

Feminist Global Health Security
Clare Wenham

Bodies of Violence: Theorizing Embodied Subjects in International Relations
Lauren B. Wilcox

Hidden Wars

*Gendered Political Violence
in Asia's Civil Conflicts*

SARA E. DAVIES
AND
JACQUI TRUE

OXFORD
UNIVERSITY PRESS

Oxford University Press is a department of the University of Oxford. It furthers
the University's objective of excellence in research, scholarship, and education
by publishing worldwide. Oxford is a registered trade mark of Oxford University
Press in the UK and certain other countries.

Published in the United States of America by Oxford University Press
198 Madison Avenue, New York, NY 10016, United States of America.

© Oxford University Press 2024

All rights reserved. No part of this publication may be reproduced, stored in
a retrieval system, or transmitted, in any form or by any means, without the
prior permission in writing of Oxford University Press, or as expressly permitted
by law, by license, or under terms agreed with the appropriate reproduction
rights organization. Inquiries concerning reproduction outside the scope of the
above should be sent to the Rights Department, Oxford University Press, at the
address above.

You must not circulate this work in any other form
and you must impose this same condition on any acquirer.

Library of Congress Control Number: 2023049370

ISBN 978-0-19-006417-4 (pbk.)
ISBN 978-0-19-006416-7 (hbk.)

DOI: 10.1093/oso/9780190064167.001.0001

Contents

List of Tables and Graphs   ix
Acknowledgments   xi
List of Abbreviations   xiii

Introduction: Conflict-related Sexual and Gender-Based Violence as a "Hidden War"   1

1. Reframing Sexual and Gender-Based Violence in Conflict   14

2. Rethinking Methodologies for Sexual and Gender-Based Violence in Conflict   35

3. Interrogating Rumors: Beyond the "Rape as a Weapon of War" Narrative in Burma   55

4. Probing Silences: Sexual and Gender-Based Violence in Conflict and Peace in the Philippines   84

5. Deconstructing Victory: Narratives of Absence of Conflict-Related Sexual and Gender-Based Violence in Sri Lanka   111

6. Comparing Regional Patterns and Trends in Conflict-Related Sexual and Gender-Based Violence across Asia   139

Conclusion: Exposing Hidden Wars and Interrogating Silences to End Impunity   158

Notes   169
References   175
Index   207

Abbreviations

ACLED	Armed Conflict Location and Event Data Project
ADB	Asian Development Bank
AGIPP	Alliance for Gender Inclusion in Peace Processes
ARMM	Autonomous Region in Muslim Mindanao
ARSA	Arakan Rohingya Salvation Army
ASEAN	Association of South East Asian Nations
BARMM	Bangsamoro Autonomous Region in Muslim Mindanao
BBS	Bodu Bala Sena
BIFF	Bangsamoro Islamic Freedom Fighters
CBA	Comprehensive Bangsamoro Agreement
CDM	Civil Disobedience Movement (Burma)
CEDAW	Convention on the Elimination of All Forms of Discrimination Against Women
CIDKP	The Committee for Internally Displaced Karen People
CPA	Centre for Policy Alternatives
CPP	Communist Party of the Philippines
CRSV	Conflict-Related Sexual Violence
CSO(s)	civil society organization(s)
CTF	Consultation Task Force on Reconciliation Mechanisms (Sri Lanka)
DHS	demographic and health survey(s)
DILG	Department of Interior and Local Government (Philippines)
EAO(s)	ethnic armed organization(s)
EU	European Union
FHH	female-headed households
GBV	gender-based violence
HRW	Human Rights Watch
ICC	International Criminal Court
ICJ	International Court of Justice
IDPs	internally displaced persons
IGOs	intergovernmental organizations
INGOs	international nongovernmental organizations
IPV	intimate partner violence
IS	Islamic State
ITJP	International Truth & Justice Project
KHRG	Karen Human Rights Group
KIC	Karen Information Center

KWO	Karen Women's Organization
LLRC	The Lessons Learned and Reconciliation Commission
LTTE	Liberation Tigers of Tamil Eelam
MARA	monitoring, analysis, and reporting arrangements
MCW	Magna Carta of Women
MILF	Moro Islamic Liberation Front
MNLF	Moro National Liberation Front
MOA-AD	Memorandum of Agreement on Ancestral Domain
NAP	National Action Plan
NATO	North Atlantic Treaty Organization
NCA	Nationwide Ceasefire Agreement (Burma)
NGO	nongovernment organization
NLD	National League of Democracy (Burma)
NRC	Norwegian Refugee Council
NSAGs	Non-State Armed Groups
OHCHR	UN Office of the High Commissioner for Human Rights
OIC	Organization of Islamic Cooperation
OSCE	Organisation for Security and Co-operation in Europe
PDVA	Prevention of Domestic Violence Act
PSF	Peace Support Fund
SCR	Security Council Resolution
SDCC	Shari'a District Courts
SGBV	sexual and gender-based violence
SHCC	Shari'a circuit courts
SHRF	Shan Human Rights Foundation
SNLD	Shan Nationalities League for Democracy
SPDC	State Peace and Development Council (Burma)
SRSG	Special Representative of the Secretary-General
SWAN	Shan Women's Action Network
UCDP	Uppsala Conflict Data Program
UN	United Nations
UNDP	United Nations Development Programme
UNFPA	United Nations Population Fund
UNGA	UN General Assembly
UNHCR	UN High Commissioner for Refugees
UN HRC	UN Human Rights Council
UNOHCHR	United Nations Office of the High Commissioner for Human Rights
UNSC	UN Security Council
UPDJC	Union Peace Dialogue Joint Committee (Burma)
USA	United States of America
USDP	Union Solidarity Development Party (Burma)
UWSA	United Wa State Army

We are very grateful to Angela Chnapko and the anonymous reviewers for their excellent advice.

Finally, we are grateful to our wonderful families who love, support, and encourage us. Our feminist husbands (Alex and Mike) and feminist sons (Isaac, Hugo, and Seamus) made sure we had the mental and physical time to work on this book together. Thank you.

Acknowledgments

In 2012 we were awarded our first grant from the Australian Research Council to examine Preventing Sexual Violence and Gender-Based Violence in Conflict. In the proposal we stated that we wanted to determine the preconditions for widespread and systematic sexual and gender-based violence in a society. In this book we present over ten years of research dedicated to examining the preconditions in societies where it is dangerous to report this violence and the violence is therefore hidden, and also where it may be controversial to refer to these situations as conflicts.

We are grateful to the Australian Research Council Discovery Project Award scheme for providing us with the opportunity to conduct research in the countries we present in this book as case studies. Our visits to these countries permitted us to meet incredible individuals and their organizations that bravely work every day to support victims-survivors' families, to investigate and report cases of conflict-related sexual and gender-based violence, and to dispense care and services. We met some who engage with and train the perpetrators in the hope that this is the first step to ending this violence. All these individuals demonstrated immense bravery. They were generous in their time with us. We are humbled by their integrity, dedication, and hope.

We acknowledge the research assistance and support over the years of Elliot Dolan-Evans, Sarah Hewitt, Sara Meger, Phyu Phyu Oo, Yolanda Riveros-Morales, and Maria Tanyag. The coding process was managed with patience and good humor. We sincerely appreciate the assistance of Daniela Di Piramo for patiently getting us over the finishing line with the formatting of the manuscript.

We appreciate the wonderful researchers around the world who are as passionate and committed to this research as we are and with whom we have had engaging discussions at International Studies Association and Sexual Violence Research Initiative conferences and Women, Peace and Security workshops.

Table and Graphs

Table

2.1	Coding SGBV Reports	50

Graphs

3.1	Total Conflict-Related SGBV Reports in Burma, 1998–2016	57
3.2	Total Fatalities by Conflict Type vs. Total SGBV Reports in Burma, 1998–2016	76
3.3	Total Victims-Survivors per SGBV Report in Burma, 1998–2016	76
3.4	Reported Perpetrators of SGBV in Burma, 1998–2016	77
3.5	Reported Armed Perpetrators of SGBV in Burma, 1998–2016	78
3.6	Sources of SGBV Reports in Burma, 1998–2016	78
3.7	Reported SV and Reported GBV in Burma, 1998–2016	79
3.8	Reported Victims-Survivors by Gender in Burma, 1998–2016	80
3.9	Reported Locations of SGBV Crimes in Burma, 1998–2016	80
4.1	Total Conflict-Related SGBV Reports in Philippines, 1998–2016	100
4.2	Total Fatalities by Conflict vs. Total SGBV Reports in Philippines, 1998–2016	100
4.3	Reported SV and Reported GBV in Philippines, 1998–2016	101
4.4	Reported Perpetrators of SGBV in Philippines, 1998–2016	102
4.5	Reported Armed Perpetrators of SGBV in Philippines, 1998–2016	102
4.6	Reported Gender of Perpetrators in Philippines, 1998–2016	104
4.7	Reported Victims-Survivors by Gender in Philippines, 1998–2016	104
4.8	Reported Victims-Survivors by Age in Philippines, 1998–2016	105
4.9	Reporting Sources of SGBV in Philippines, 1998–2016	106
4.10	Reported Locations of SGBV Crimes in Philippines, 1998–2016	107

5.1 Reported SV and Reported GBV in Sri Lanka, 1998–2016 128
5.2 Total Conflict-Related SGBV Reports in Sri Lanka, 1998–2016 128
5.3 Total Fatalities by Conflict vs. Total SGBV Reports in Sri Lanka, 1998–2016 129
5.4 Reported Locations of SGBV Crimes in Sri Lanka, 1998–2016 129
5.5 Reported Perpetrators of SGBV in Sri Lanka, 1998–2016 130
5.6 Reported Gender of Perpetrators in Sri Lanka, 1998–2016 131
5.7 Reported Armed Perpetrators of SGBV in Sri Lanka, 1998–2016 131
5.8 Reporting Sources of SGBV in Sri Lanka, 1998–2016 132
5.9 Reported Victims-Survivors by Gender in Sri Lanka, 1998–2016 133
5.10 Reported Victims-Survivors by Age in Sri Lanka, 1998–2016 133
6.1 Total Conflict-Related SGBV Reports for Three Countries, 1998–2016 141
6.2 Total SGBV Reports for Three Countries by Source, 1998–2016 143
6.3 Total SGBV Reports by Victims-Survivors Gender for Three Countries, 1998–2016 144
6.4 Total SGBV Reports by Victims-Survivors Age for Three Countries, 1998–2016 144
6.5 Total SGBV Reports by Location for Three Countries, 1998–2016 148
6.6 Total Reported Perpetrators of SGBV for Three Countries, 1998–2016 149
6.7 Total Reported Armed Perpetrators of SGBV for Three Countries, 1998–2016 150
6.8 Total Reported Perpetrators of SGBV in Burma, 1998–2016 151
6.9 Total Reported Perpetrators of SGBV in Philippines, 1998–2016 151
6.10 Total Reported Perpetrators of SGBV in Sri Lanka, 1998–2016 152
6.11 Total Reported Gender of Perpetrators for Three Countries, 1998–2016 153

VAW	violence against women
WHO	World Health Organization
WLB	Women's League of Burma
WLHRB	Women's Legal and Human Rights Bureau
WPS	Women, Peace and Security

Introduction

Conflict-related Sexual and Gender-Based Violence as a "Hidden War"

Sexual and gender-based violence (SGBV) has always been part of warfare. In Asia, testimonies of egregious rape and sexual violence extend back to the Rape of Nanking (Chang 2012); to the experience of Korean comfort women in World War II (Yoshimi 2002), South Asian women in the India/Pakistan Wars of Partition, and the 1971 Bangladesh war (Da Costa and Hussain 2010; Mookherjee 2015), and to the forced marriages and sexual slavery during the Cambodian genocide (Tyner 2018). With the recognition of SGBV as international crimes and threats to peace and security by the 1998 Rome Statute of the International Criminal Court (ICC) and the 2000 UN Security Council Resolution 1325, scholars and researchers have struggled to explain why and when this violence occurs.[1] Their explanations have been based on official (state) reports, unofficial reports (from civil society), and media reports, but what happens when we take silence or non-reporting seriously? How do we know what we know about this type of violence, which is accepted, underreported, and often hidden?

Surveys commissioned by The Asia Foundation (2017) suggest that SGBV is one of the deadliest violence types in Asia. SGBV is undoubtedly part of conflict dynamics, but it also exists before and after armed conflict. This book advances a novel way of understanding SGBV by exploring the relationship between structural gender inequality with the patterns of reporting and nonreporting in protracted civil wars in Asia.

Despite the growing field of scholarship on conflict-related SGBV, gaps remain in our knowledge about its prevalence and patterns, especially in the Asian region. Asia has some of the most protracted conflicts in the world (Parks, Coletta, and Oppenheim 2013), but the complexity of subnational conflicts in Asia often masks the gendered dimensions of political violence.

Redressing the lack of knowledge (and action) on conflict-related SGBV in Asia, this book provides a framework for examining the social and political conditions that enable and constrain reporting across phases of conflict in the Asian context. We show how the conditions of reporting affect the impunity for this violence as well as national and international responses to prevent and end it.

Hidden Wars is concerned with understanding the relationship between availability of SGBV reports and structural gender inequality in three conflict-affected societies: Burma, the Philippines, and Sri Lanka. Our study is based on extensive field research and analysis of a new dataset on SGBV in each location. Psychological, public health, and criminology research shows that structural gender inequality is the most significant risk factor for SGBV (Heise and Kotsadam 2015). We argue that the presence and types of SGBV in a conflict often reflect highly politicized and gendered environments. Scholars and policymakers acknowledge reporting gaps and silence pose major difficulties for identifying and responding to SGBV, but rarely note data limitations resulting from the politicized context of reporting SGBV affects data collection on the ground. The full extent of conflict-related SGBV is effectively hidden within and across many conflicts within Asia. Our book seeks to address this and theorize the reporting conditions for SGBV in low-intensity conflict environments like those predominant across Asia.

Background

Over the past two decades the study of conflict-related SGBV has yielded crucial new insights. We now know that SGBV, particularly rape, is sometimes ordered under a clear command chain, but at other times, its occurrence appears to be random and opportunistic (Baaz and Stern 2013; Wood 2008a). Sometimes the pattern is widespread but not systematic and sometimes the pattern is small but systematic (Leiby 2012; Ferrara 2014). Under international law, evidence of even one incident may be sufficient proof of a systematic pattern of violence (Mibenge 2013; Seatzu 2021). What "counts" as an SGBV crime is determined by existing gendered norms, social stigmas, and political contexts within individual countries (Cohen and Hoover Green 2012; Ní Aoláin, O'Rourke, and Swaine 2015). These contexts influence who is willing and able to report crimes and how they are categorized and recorded (Sjoberg 2016; Hoover Green 2018). Our awareness of SGBV is thus deeply rooted in unconscious gendered bias and discrimination (Davies and True 2015; Baaz and Stern 2018). This leaves us with several unanswered questions: Why and when is SGBV distinguished from other acts of torture and violence (Baaz and Stern 2013; Gray, Stern, and Dolan 2020)? Why is it still assumed that the majority of victims-survivors are always women (Sjoberg 2016; Kreft and Schulz 2022)? Who has access to report these crimes (Nordås and Cohen 2021)? And how intense does a conflict need to be for conflict-related SGBV to be counted (Cohen and Nordås 2014)? In this book, we argue that the answer to these questions lies in both how we conceptualize SGBV, what data we collect, and where we collect this data.

Reports provide a particular narrative of who commits SGBV and who is subjected to it. But the reports frequently overlook the structural context of inequality and discrimination in which the violence occurs. This context is almost always gendered and racialized. As a result, reports do not present a neutral or unbiased picture of the overall pattern of SGBV. Rather, they present particular parts of the problem. In some situations, for example, it may be more "acceptable" for some ethnic and politically active women to report sexual violence, while other groups of women affected stay silent (Davies and True 2017a). Similarly, in environments where homosexual sex is criminalized, men may never come forward to speak about sexual violence against them for fear of prosecution (Dolan 2014). Children may have no outlet available to report the SGBV they experience in conflict. In addition, some forms of SGBV may be so entrenched within a local conflict that they are accepted by those people subject to this violence and never reported—for example, retribution rape and marriage between clans or rape of Indigenous women by migrant colonizers (see Davies, True, and Tanyag 2016). Paradoxically, one indication that SGBV may be widespread in a society is the presence of gender norms that prohibit or constrain its reporting or recording (Davies and True 2015). Reports of SGBV do not take place outside of these contexts, which goes a long way towards explaining why SGBV in Asian conflicts has received comparatively little scholarly attention.

SGBV is under-reported everywhere in the world due to difficulties with reliable data in dangerous and unpredictable conflict conditions. Despite the low-intensity conflict status for most of Asia's conflicts over recent decades (Aspinall, Jeffrey, and Regan 2013; Bellamy 2017), consistent and reliable data are especially scarce in Asia, where demographic and health surveys are comparatively infrequent and national reporting systems are relatively underdeveloped. In Asia reporting of SGBV both in conflict and peacetime conditions is affected by the low level of public awareness; the scarcity of institutions to report to in rural, conflict, and displacement settings; the lack of protection for victims-survivors or others reporting SGBV due to ineffective or gender-biased law enforcement and justice systems; and institutional incapacity to record and analyze SGBV data (see Chapter Two, this volume).[2] These problems compound the under-reporting of conflict-related SGBV in Asia compared to more rigorous efforts to gather better data through surveys or incident reporting in other conflict situations in other regions (Nordås and Cohen 2021). Thus, it is crucial to address the social and political causes of this under-reporting at the same time that we seek to improve the tools for data collection and analysis.

Our book argues that scholars, advocates, and policymakers should pay attention not just to the information contained within reports but to the phenomena and processes of reporting as well as the institutions and mechanisms that facilitate or block it. That is, in order to improve our understanding of SGBV we need to improve our knowledge of what enables and constrains the reporting of this type of violence. Furthermore, we need to critically examine how conflicts themselves are defined and presented as "violent": "battle deaths" is a well-recognized indicator of conflict intensity, but it is not the only form of violence that can affect the rights, dignity, and safety of local populations. "Gendered political violence" is what we define and observe in this book. Failure to report and recognize this violence in situ permits responsible states to avoid prosecution and prevention through deterrence, to invest in and deploy early-warning prevention programs and conflict prevention initiatives, as well as to support gender parity in peace processes.

Conflict-Related Sexual and Gender-Based Violence in Asia

SGBV has been documented in several conflicts in Asia since 1945,[3] and is frequently heightened in conflict-affected situations (Buss 2014; True 2012; The Asia Foundation 2017). Women's and girls' severe lack of access to social and economic resources in conflict-affected and displacement situations affects their vulnerability to violence, and strong gender codes and homosexual laws prevent the documentation of violence perpetrated against boys and men. However, differences are discernible in SGBV patterns across countries, based on official and unofficial reports.

Mapping SGBV, as defined, is difficult in Asia due to the limitations of existing data. First, few datasets are designed to record SGBV in peacetime, let alone during conflict, and those datasets are not comprehensive but rather focus on one particular type of SGBV. For example, country-level demographic and health surveys include questions only about intimate partner violence, often exclusively for married women, and in fewer than half the countries in Asia. Second, there are significant issues with the quality of available data, given the significant under-reporting by victims-survivors in societies that have, until recently, failed to recognize SGBV as a criminal offense or a public policy problem outside of conflict situations. As such, data may not reflect which groups of women and men, boys and girls are most vulnerable to SGBV or the specific obstacles to reporting violations they may face.

Indeed, political bias and gender bias inform the decision to report some forms of SGBV as an act of political violence (vs. others) and often determine what reports are issued detailing SGBV across particular phases of a conflict. In this book, we argue that greater attention must be paid to the gendered political environment that determines which actors report SGBV, what types of violence are reported and recorded (including how).

Our Approach

In this book, we walk a middle path between scholars who see SGBV perpetrated during conflict as a distinct type of violence to be explained and scholars who view SGBV as part of a continuum of gendered violence that is often exacerbated during conflict but must be analyzed in relation to similar violence occurring before and after conflict and in peacetime (Baaz and Stern 2013; Cockburn 2011; Leatherman 2011; True 2012). Based on the research presented here, we argue that SGBV is a significant problem on the ground in Asia's civil conflicts research but we do not yet fully understand its nature and scope to be able to concur with either of those scholarly perspectives. However, we believe that both lens can help us see how forms of violence are connected, from the interpersonal to the intergroup and overtly "political" types of violence. The power of SGBV compared with other types of violence lies not in the physical acts of violence themselves, but in the shame and social stigma that victims-survivors suffer (Henry 2011; Skjelsbæk 2011). Physical, psychological, sexual, or economic SGBV intends to denigrate and silence the victims-survivors and, by association, their families or communities. It both exploits and reinforces stereotypes and oppression based on gender, ethnicity, class, caste, sexuality, or other identities. SGBV can be a war crime, but also an act of genocide (Allen 1996). Thus, SGBV and conflict play into and affect one another.

Some scholars however argue that "rape in wartime looks qualitatively different in many ways than rape during peacetime" (Cohen 2016: 195; also Wood 2006). Baaz and Stern in their study of the Democratic Republic of Congo agree insofar as they argue that the "rape as a weapon of war" narrative recognizes that rape's occurrence during war is necessarily "shaped by the situational and interactional nature of warfare" (2013: 110). But understanding rape as (only) an act of war still depends on particular frames and causal relationships between gender, ethnicity, politics, and military relations (2013: 63).

Building on this multidisciplinary body of scholarship, we argue that in order to understand the patterns of SGBV we need to trace their relationship to the other types of violence within civil wars. In particular, we must understand the environment in which this violence is taking place—especially the gendered social relations in the conflict region before, during, and after the "reporting events." We may also need to pay further attention to the multiple actors and institutions that may report SGBV in conflict situations and the impact of their presence on the patterns of reporting.

Our approach to the study of conflict-related SGBV is distinct as are the cases in the underexamined Asian region we have selected to analyze in depth. Like others, we seek to understand the prevalence and patterns of SGBV in conflict. However, we argue that in order to deepen our understanding of their causes we must first engage with *how we know* what, when, and where SGBV is present. Knowledge production—including the institutional mechanisms for reporting SGBV and the methodologies for collecting and analyzing SGBV data—are inseparable from the problem, as well as the solution to this violence. Qualitative and quantitative studies point to a "tip of the iceberg" (Palermo, Bleck, and Peterman 2014) phenomenon in fragile situations, where there is a high prevalence but low levels of actual reporting of SGBV.

The framework we present for analyzing SGBV in this book is applied to three protracted conflict situations in Asia: Burma,[4] the Philippines, and Sri Lanka from 1998 to 2016. We selected three countries where there is knowledge of SGBV taking place but dramatic variation in the conflict intensity (from low to high),[5] variation in populations affected and targeted for SGBV, and assumptions about in which locations SGBV is prevalent. Comparison across these cases enables us to show the relevance of contextual gender analysis to the production of knowledge about SGBV, as well as to the explanation of its causes and effects.

Outline of the Volume

Our book is in two parts with six chapters followed by a conclusion. Part One consists of two chapters that set out the theoretical and methodological framework for the study, while Part Two comprises four chapters that apply this framework to three country case studies and the comparative analysis of these cases. The Conclusion updates the reader on the current situation in the three countries, the implications of this research for the Asia-wide region, and directions for future research to build on this book.

Part One

In Chapter One, "Reframing Sexual and Gender-Based Violence in Conflict," we set out the theoretical background and framework for this study. Sustained feminist civil society activism in the 1990s enabled witness testimony of acts of sexual and gender violence in the International Criminal Tribunals on Former Yugoslavia and Rwanda. As a result, these acts of violence were defined as international crimes in the 1998 Rome Statute and a mandate to intervene in situations where widespread and systematic acts of SGBV may be occurring, as followed in UN Security Council Resolution 1325 (2000) and Resolution 1820 (2008) (see Davies and True 2017b). In Chapter One, we examine the evolution of explanations of SGBV and argue that there is a relative absence of analysis of SGBV in low-intensity conflict environments due to a failure to take into account the complexity of violence in that context. We lay bare the current challenges of mapping SGBV in conflict globally, and in Asia specifically. We do not deny the usefulness of macrodata sets, but we do make the case for more attention on region-specific and context-specific understanding of conflicts and their patterns of violence, in order to understand why a vast array of SGBV acts are perpetrated, in what context, and with what effects. We present the case for an in-depth comparative examination of SGBV reporting practices in three low-intensity conflicts in Asia.

Chapter Two, "Rethinking Methodologies for Sexual and Gender-Based Violence in Conflict," establishes the methodological approach we adopt to study conflict-related SGBV in low-intensity conflicts building on and learning from previous studies. We suggest there is a need to address the "tip of the iceberg" (Palermo et al. 2014) phenomenon. It is rarely interrogated to understand its implication: that incident reports fail to indicate the magnitude of the problem.

If SGBV reports do not reflect the scale, intensity, or diversity of crimes, and reporting is not a panacea but a politicized practice, then how do we know the magnitude of the problem and its patterns? What is happening in conflicts without a knowledge base, and what priority should we give to the meaning of reports that are often the sole source on SGBV in some conflict situations? In Chapter Two, we suggest a reflexive methodological ethic of probing, triangulating, and cross-referencing longitudinal data collection to meaningfully address the gaps and silences in the data. Feminists know that silence does not mean absence (of violence). Rather, silence often masks the violence and ensures that the acts can continue. It allows some stories to be told, while others cannot be told—and we as scholars and global media interlocutors have a politicized desire to listen to certain stories and ignore others. This dynamic is visible in the contemporary #metoo movement generated by social media networks.

We suggest the need to investigate the gendered, political, and politicized conditions in which SGBV is reported and, even more significantly, is not reported. We consider the trends of reporting in oppressive environments where SGBV is thought to be occurring. With respect to low-intensity conflicts that experience violence for protracted periods we seek to theorize SGBV reporting conditions in these "high-" and "low-" conflict environments.

In Chapter Two, we present how we coded open-access reports on SGBV in Burma, the Philippines, and Sri Lanka, from government, media, and nongovernment sources (including UN agencies and offices) from 1998 to 2016. We explain why we paid attention to a much broader category of locations, perpetrators, SGBV crimes, age and gender of victims-survivors, and reporting timelines in order to identify patterns within the conflict dynamics of each country over the same period of time.

Part Two

This second part of the book presents our analysis of the three conflict-affected settings in Asia. In consecutive chapters, we ask the same questions of each conflict case, based on our study of official, unofficial, and media SGBV reports between 1998 and 2016. Our analysis examines this reporting set against qualitative research, including fieldwork, conducted in each country between 2015 and 2017. To learn more about the processes of reporting and how they may affect the number and types of reports (on which we based our analysis of reporting patterns), we interviewed a range of civil society, national, and international grassroots, NGO, government, and international organization representatives within each country.

To qualify and contextualize data on all forms of reported SGBV in conflict-affected Asian contexts, we map the social, political, and institutional barriers to reporting, and the prevailing degree of gender discrimination and inequality. Our field-based study of the conflict situations helps to interpret and explain the variation in our database in the reports of specific kinds of SGBV committed by the military, nonstate armed groups, and civilians across the cases.

Each case study chapter in this part of the book is structured to address the following questions:

- What explains the reporting that does exist, and what are the conditions that lead to the reporting of SGBV?
- Do reporting trends reflect the conflict trends—the crimes, perpetrators, and relationships established in the political science literature to date?
- Does reporting replicate preexisting understandings of gendered power. Is the focus on armed/military issues as well as the visibility of traditional institutions of violence?
- Finally, how far and in what context is the power to report in local conflict-affected areas compounded by political tensions and pervasive gender discrimination?

As mentioned earlier, we examine SGBV reporting between 1998 and 2016 in three Asian countries, all with a history of protracted conflict both before and during the time in which reports are collected.

Chapter Three, "Interrogating Rumors: Beyond the 'Rape as a Weapon of War Narrative' in Burma," investigates a country that has experienced multiple, protracted conflicts since independence in 1948 and the military coup in 1962; during the period of study, Burma continued to experience significant political reform that started in 2010 and was attempting to broker the largest national ceasefire agreement (2015).

The majority of reports on SGBV in Burma are attributed to the Tatmadaw state military, which has been presented as soldiers raping (ethnic-minority) women for opportunistic and military advantage. In the early phases of reporting, the Tatmadaw were portrayed as soldiers operating in jungle territory who rape and pillage with absolute impunity. Recently, the reporting has begun to show the Tatmadaw as using SGBV, particularly rape, to achieve tactical advantage—to cleanse populations (the Rohingya Muslim population in the Rakhine state) and to terrorize populations into submission to the peace process (i.e., Kachin ethnic group).

Chapter Three examines why these narratives have come to dominate our understanding of SGBV prevalence during the Burma civil conflict; we closely analyze the relationship between SGBV reporting cycles and conflict phases, as well as political developments, in the civil conflict between 1998 and 2016.

Chapter Four, "Probing Silences: Gender-Based Violence in Conflict and Peace in the Philippines," explores the location of the Mindanao separatist conflict in the Autonomous Region of Muslim Mindanao (ARMM) as the focus for SGBV reports. During the 1998–2016 period, the Bangsamoro Ceasefire (1997) and Peace Agreement (2014) were adopted. As we reveal in this chapter, regardless of the phases of battles associated with the separatist conflict during this period, the region has been continually vulnerable to high levels of clan violence and interracial and interreligious divides often fueled by SGBV. These localized forms of violence are frequently cyclical and revenge-retribution attacks, with women identified as the "commodity" to be negotiated, abducted, and attacked. Crucially, Mindanao reveals that strong SGBV legislation and practices within a country have minimal impact and force in locations of protracted conflict. The absence of SGBV reporting in the conflict-affected areas—despite its location next to "peaceful" areas where high rates of SGBV were being reported—did not raise questions.

The Mindanao case is rarely, if ever, considered as a site to understand the relationship between conflict and SGBV. However, the political rivalries within the region, coupled with local clan-level violence and organized crimes, disclose high volumes of anecdotally "accepted" SGBV. This case reveals the need to re-examine the methodology we use to count sexual violence in low-intensity conflict settings, and to also consider how internal political impediments to reporting determine what cases of SGBV receive international attention.

Chapter Five, "Deconstructing Victory: Narratives of Absence of Sexual and Gender-Based Violence in Sri Lanka," examines that nation's conflict in the North and North-Eastern Provinces against the separatist Tamil Tigers, was at times as bloody and intense as the Burma conflict. We trace reporting patterns between 1998 and 2016, which include the brokered ceasefire between the government and Tamil rebels in 2002, the ceasefire breakdown in 2006, and the significant battles that took place in the North and North-East Provinces until the end of the twenty-seven-year conflict in 2009, when the Sri Lanka Government declared victory. We continually code SGBV subsequent to the end of this conflict, where the country has been subject to a UN Human Rights inquiry and the government has yet to institute any formal transitional justice processes.

Similar to Burma and the Philippines, we find that the reporting conditions for SGBV are influenced by the political context and narratives told to date. There is a nationalist struggle for Sri Lankan identity, with women often presented as the warriors or the victims-survivors in these narratives. Unlike the two other cases, there was a clear Sinhalese victory over the Tamil minority and an end to battles in the North since 2009. However, "victors' justice" did not end the violence. Moreover, the reporting of SGBV itself has faced intense politicization during the postwar years. In the immediate postconflict years, reporting was seen as a divisive and highly dangerous activity. In more recent years, reporting SGBV experiences during the war and within the war-affected communities has become more accepted and even less dangerous—but the narrative usually must adhere to victors' justice terms and conditions. There is still a climate of impunity for SGBV committed during and after the conflict.

Moreover, the political and nationalist struggles are far from over in Sri Lanka. Evidence gathering, witnesses, telling stories—the act of documentation itself—have become part of the women's empowerment movement but also part of nationalist and, increasingly, religious nationalist movements.

Similar to the Philippines, Sri Lanka has a progressive autonomous women's movement and a developed economy that favors women's participation in the economy, but the conditions available to report and document are still highly contested.

Chapter Six, "Comparing Regional Patterns and Trends in Conflict-Related Sexual and Gender-Based Violence across Asia," brings together the major insights of the study. In this last chapter, we consider our findings across the three cases to interrogate reported and nonreported violence and to explore the effects of conflict dynamics as well as patterns of SGBV before, during, and after conflict.

We highlight four common trends within and across the three sites of our study, which we argue has implications for SGBV data collection in conflict situations, reporting SGBV in conflict situations, and the constitutive relationship between conflict and SGBV. We argue that the four common trends should be further examined in other low-intensity or protracted conflicts (or both) for further validation. For example,

1. Observation of an escalation of SGBV reports when there is international access to conflict areas, which can amplify the number of reports as well as the potential politicization of these reports.
2. Consistently low reports may be the result of no state provision of services or institutions for reporting conflict-related SGBV, which is emblematic of state denial of conflict and low prioritization of gendered political violence.
3. Little reporting of SGBV perpetrated by nonstate armed actors does not mean no prevalence.
4. How a conflict ends may sustain conflict-related SGBV and impunity.

In our Conclusion, we suggest that our study of SGBV reporting in low-intensity conflict situations reveals a politicization of SGBV that includes deliberate ignorance of its occurrence and refusal to report, but also conversely, extreme efforts to document and report to advance particular group struggles. Furthermore the label 'low-intensity' can be misleading. Each conflicts has experienced cycles of severity. Reliable SGBV data collection in these circumstances is difficult to obtain and vulnerable to allegations of politicization. This results in all sides mistrusting and misusing reports for political advantage. What is clear from our findings is that low-intensity conflict environments permit the state, but also humanitarian and military actors, to avoid responsibility for data collection on SGBV. There is limited discussion of when reports do not take place to "protect" peace accords, protect combatants over victims-survivors, or maintain humanitarian access, or because the reporting of particular crimes is too "sensitive" or "risky" and the victims-survivors' own safety cannot be guaranteed. Only when we have seriously analyzed the particular discriminatory gendered contexts of a conflict-affected situation can we know how far and in what ways impunity for SGBV crimes affects reporting, by whom, and when.

Our attention to what data are collected, who reports this data, and when they are reported in low-intensity conflict environments sheds new insight into which SGBV reporting methods can be prioritized and improved in order to hold responsible actors like states and international organizations accountable for action to prevent these crimes. This study, we hope, also makes an important contribution to the design of future research on SGBV reporting—to pay more attention to reporting silences and gaps.

1
Reframing Sexual and Gender-Based Violence in Conflict

This book advances a novel understanding of sexual and gender-based violence (SGBV) by exploring the patterns of reporting and nonreporting in protracted civil wars in Asia. Despite the growing field of scholarship on conflict-related sexual violence, there are significant gaps in our knowledge about the prevalence and patterns of SGBV, especially in the Asian region (Davies and True 2017a; Koos 2017). Surveys commissioned by The Asia Foundation (2017) suggest that SGBV is one of the deadliest violence types in Asia. SGBV is part of conflict dynamics, as well as preconflict and postconflict political violence. Redressing the lack of knowledge and action on SGBV in low-intensity conflicts in Asia, this volume provides a framework for examining the social and political conditions that enable and constrain reporting across phases of conflict. We show how the conditions of what gets reported in which context affects national and international recognition of where SGBV occurs and, in turn, the necessary responses to prevent and end this violence.

In this chapter we examine the evolution of SGBV and suggest that there is a relative absence of analysis of SGBV in low-intensity and protracted conflict environments. This argument is of particular significance for the Asian region. Most of the research and knowledge on SGBV documents its occurrence, prevalence, perpetrators, and victims-survivors in situations where there are or have been high-intensity conflicts[1]—intrastate or interstate— and genocide. Primary understanding of SGBV depends upon prior identification of a situation that is conflict-affected. Since the 1990s—a decade that saw growing research and activism on conflict-related sexual violence— protracted or low-intensity conflicts[2] have made up the majority of conflicts within the Asian region (Gleditsch et al. 2002; Lewis 2019). This has meant, for example, that reports of SGBV occurring within Burma, the Philippines, Timor Leste, North Korea, and postconflict Cambodia and Sri Lanka have not received nearly the same amount of study as other locations, such as

Liberia and the Democratic Republic of Congo, where media reports of sexual violence captured public attention during cycles of high-intensity interstate and intrastate conflict (see, e.g., Autessere 2014; Cohen and Hoover Green 2012; Meger 2016). We argue that attention to SGBV in low-intensity, protracted conflict situations merits further study. For example, in the case of one low-intensity, protracted conflict situation in Burma, widespread acts of genocide and ethnic cleansing, including SGBV, against the Rohingya and other minority populations were documented in 2017 and 2018. However, as we discuss in Chapter Three of this book, a pattern of well-established SGBV had been a feature of political violence within Burma long before the 2017 genocide.

All high-intensity conflicts have low-intensity origins (Greig 2015). Understanding SGBV in high-intensity conflicts requires attention to the "small" cases and questioning "incidental" reports of its practice in low-intensity conflict environments. Prevention of both SGBV and conflict also depends on this knowledge base and research to build it. There is a need to construct a theory regarding the trends and patterns of SGBV across different phases of conflict, degrees of intensity of conflict, and types of conflict. The gendered conditions under which this violence is prioritized, understood, documented, and reported requires knowledge of the region-specific and context-specific instances of SGBV that may challenge macro trends and patterns. We do not deny the usefulness of macrodata sets, but our role as feminist researchers is to explain and prevent violence. Without more attention to these SGBV crimes in low-intensity, sometimes protracted conflict environments—and the conditions in place to report these crimes—we cannot understand the array of SGBV acts that are perpetrated. And without this attention to low-intensity conflict situations, we cannot understand how to anticipate the escalating political violence relationship to SGBV even if we understand that political violence is gendered in its motives, forms, and impacts (Bardall, Bjarnegård, and Piscopo 2020).

This chapter proceeds in three sections. The first examines the evolution of a collective understanding of conflict-related SGBV across policy, advocacy, and scholarly communities. The second section considers how this understanding has given rise to political and social science theories on the causes and types of sexual violence informed by (primarily) high-intensity conflict environments. These theories tend to find that violence is distinguished by its organized (policy), hierarchical (military), and/or collective (social) motivations amongst perpetrators (Baaz and Stern 2013; Nordås and Cohen 2021). Most studies draw on conflict situations—and sometimes genocides—where these crimes are occurring amidst a variety of other types of violence by multiple actors (Meger 2016: 62; Johansson and Sarwari 2019: 471–472; Skjelsbæk 2018: 503). Motivations vary considerably, even within a single conflict (Kreft and Schulz 2022). Is it worth, we ask, specifically examining situations where SGBV is occurring in low-intensity conflict environments? The threshold for what counts as SGBV has led to two primary understandings of the conditions that give rise to SGBV: war and the militarism context driving this violence (*inter alia*, Asal and Nagel 2021; Nagel 2021; Wood 2006; 2018), and opportunistic acts in lawless environments where there are highly gendered social, political, and economic conditions (inter alia, Agerberg and Kreft 2020; Kreft 2020; Solangon and Patel 2012). This book suggests that we need to identify a middle path that addresses SGBV as *gendered political violence* (Baaz and Stern 2013; Yadav and Horn 2021). The concept of gendered political violence not only recognizes that SGBV is an act of political violence as defined in the 1998 Rome Statute, but it understands this political violence to be the product of discriminatory societal norms around gender that affect the identities of perpetrators and victims-survivors, the structural conditions enabling violence, and the state and social institutions normalizing the violence by failing to effectively prevent or respond to it. While SGBV as gendered political violence often targets individual women and girls, it is especially used to exclude and marginalize minority groups, as we explore in this book (Davies and True 2015: 508).

In the final section, the chapter turns to Asia as a significant location to test and refine the empirical and theoretical middle path not yet taken. These crimes have occurred and are still occurring in several situations and contexts in Asia, allowing us to study SGBV as an act of gendered political violence that deliberately discriminates by target, location, and stigma.

The Evolution of Conflict-Related SGBV

The 1998 Rome Statute of the International Criminal Court (ICC) was the first international instrument to include widespread and systematic sexual and gender-based (Oostervald 2005) violence (SGBV) as crimes against humanity, crimes of genocide, or war crimes committed in international and noninternational armed conflicts (Coundouriotis 2013). In 2014 the Office of the ICC Prosecutor adopted a Public Policy Paper on Sexual and

Gender-Based Crimes, which sought to elaborate on the terms "sexual" and "gender-based violence" (Altunjan 2021; Oostervald 2018). First, it is important to explain the distribution and features of crimes under these two terms: sexual violence *and*—distinct but related—gender-based violence. Gender-based violence or crimes (under ICC terminology) are those crimes committed against persons, whether male or female, because of their sex and/or socially constructed gender roles. Gender-based crimes do not always manifest as a form of sexual violence. They may include nonsexual attacks on women and girls, and men and boys, because of their gender. Crimes under gender-based violence include acts of persecution based on gender that may fall under a crime against humanity, an act of genocide, or a war crime, whereas sexual crimes fall under the subject-matter jurisdiction of the ICC as listed under articles 7(1)(g), 8(2)(b)(xxii), and 8(2)(e)(vi) of the statute. These crimes specifically include rape, sexual slavery, enforced prostitution, forced pregnancy, enforced sterilization, or any other form of sexual violence (Office of the ICC Prosecutor 2014: 5).

In addition to the much wider array of SGBV crimes covered in the Rome Statute is a much broader definition for when they need to occur to be recognized as crimes. This definition is often overlooked, but these crimes can occur inside or outside the theatre of war: sexual and gender-based violence may be used instrumentally and rationally without being "strategic" in the sense of a commanded military tactic (i.e., it may be a practice even if not issued as policy [Wood 2014: 471]). In order to be considered a crime under the jurisdiction of the ICC, sexual violence need not be widespread or systematic, rather it may be an act of sexual violence that forms part of a widespread and systematic attack on a civilian population (Office of the ICC Prosecutor 2014: para. 32, p. 18).

Along with the Rome Statute, SGBV crimes are covered in UN Security Council Resolutions 1325 (2000) and 1820 (2008). At the adoption of Resolution 1325 in 2000, the UN Security Council called for an "immediate and complete cessation by all parties to armed conflict of all acts of sexual violence against civilians," considered crimes under the 1998 Rome Statute.[3] Resolution 1820 declares sexual violence a threat to international peace and security. In that resolution and the subsequent UN Security Council resolutions on sexual violence (1888, 1889, 1960, 2106, 2122, and 2467), the UN and member states are expected to adopt a series of measures to prevent and protect populations from these crimes, including UN missions adopting early-warning matrices for populations experiencing SGBV, reporting perpetrators and situations to the UN Security Council, and the Security Council itself attaching sanctions to individuals and armed groups suspected of these crimes.[4] In addition, the introduction of the Joint Memorandum of Understanding(s) between the UN Office for the Special Representative on Sexual Violence and military forces provides the steps required of listed armed groups to ensure that soldiers do not participate in, order, or condone acts of SGBV.[5] Through a combination of these prevention and protection responses, the expectation is that the UN will be able to identify situations where SGBV is occurring, to publicly "name and shame" perpetrators, and to list situations in the annual Secretary-General reports on "situations of concern for sexual violence" (reported since 2012) (Heathcote 2012). Indeed, Resolution 1820 (2008) and Resolution 1960 (2010) called for the UN Office of the Special Representative on Sexual Violence to report to the Security Council through the UN Secretary-General all suspected or confirmed incidences of widespread and systematic SGBV in conflict-related situations.[6]

Two key shifts arrived with UN Security Council involvement in the Rome Statute's definition of widespread and systematic SGBV: an exclusive conflict focus (and sometimes postconflict) and a threshold emphasis. First, there has been less investigatory focus on the situations and crimes of SGBV occurring outside the "theatre of war" (Meger 2021: 118; Kochanski 2020: 506–507). From 2000 onward, sexual violence in the UN Security Council Resolutions refers to its occurrence in the context of armed conflict. The mandate of the UN Office of the Special Representative on Sexual Violence, created in 2009 under Resolution 1888, cemented this narrower focus in both the office and its annual reports for the UN Secretary-General:

> Engage in advocacy efforts, inter alia with governments, including military and judicial representatives, as well as with all parties to armed conflict and civil society, in order to address, at both headquarters and country level, sexual violence in armed conflict, while promoting cooperation and coordination of efforts among all relevant stakeholders, primarily through the inter-agency initiative "United Nations Action Against Sexual Violence in Conflict." (Resolution 1888: para. 4)

The conflict emphasis can limit the UN Security Council, the Special Representative annual reports, and the academic gaze to situations where there is UN Security Council—and therefore political—consensus that the situation experiencing sexual violence is a recognized conflict (that merits UN Security Council attention, and, secondary to that, ICC investigation). This limitation also extends, for example, to sexual exploitation and abuse committed by peacekeepers in UN peacekeeping missions (with an entirely separate reporting process; see Olsson et al. 2020).

The second shift that emerged is the sexual violence 'threshold' and when acts of gender and sexual violence warrant reporting (Baaz and Stern 2013; Cohen and Nordås 2014; Ní Aoláin, O'Rourke, and Swaine 2015; Altunjan 2021). Returning to the Office of the ICC Prosecutor guidance, SGBV crimes can occur inside and outside of conflict; the crimes may contribute to widespread and systematic crimes (i.e., the "number" threshold); and the crimes may be instrumental or do not need to also be part of strategy (policy) to merit investigation. How should these elements influence observers in the field (sites of violence), decision-makers in New York (site of the Security Council), or The Hague's (site of the ICC) recognition and reporting of SGBV? This book is primarily concerned with the reporting "threshold" question, given the emphasis that reporting should come from conflict or postconflict situations.

How do those who report and raise the alarm, whether local or international actors, balance concern for victims-survivors' safety (small numbers could mean individuals are more readily identifiable) with accusations that they are "selectively highlighting sexual violence to garner public attention to a crisis" (Cohen and Hoover Green 2012)? How does the presence or absence of international actors—UN agencies in particular—affect reporting patterns?[7]

Despite the limited mandate of the UN Office of the Special Representative on Sexual Violence, the first UN Secretary-General report in 2012 (S/2012/33) (UNSG 2012a) included a broad category of situations of concern for, as well as instances of, sexual and gender-based violence. This report came under heavy criticism from two permanent UN Security Council members (Russia and China) and one non-permanent member (Egypt). Since then, annual reports have focused on "conflict" and "postconflict" as the primary criteria for receiving and documenting such violence (UN SRSG 2013; UNSG 2013; UNSG 2014; UNSG 2015; UNSG 2016; UNSG 2017; UNSG 2018; UNSG 2019; UNSG 2020; UNSG 2021; UNSG 2022b; UNSG 2023) but there has been no threshold placed on the number of attacks necessary to merit reporting (Davies and True 2017a). For example, the annual reports (2012–2023) have primarily referred to numbers of SGBV crimes committed in conflict situations, but the attacks reported within these situations range from three to the hundreds. The limit on reporting a wider array of SGBV situations to the UN Security Council remains membership consensus—that the situations reported meet "conflict," "postconflict," or (increasingly) "violence extremism" designations accepted by the permanent membership.

A threshold on the number of attacks required to report has not yet appeared in discussions within the UN Security Council on conflict-related sexual violence or the ICC. The problem with both the UN Security Council and the ICC is the political threshold and the anticipation of resistance to raising situations that are "low-intensity." The point here is that there is a threshold custom when it comes to reporting sexual violence in conflict; the threshold may be either that the situation needs to be in a "conflict" that has the attention or consensus of the UN Security Council, or the threshold may be the number of attacks that need to be reported per year. Prevalence and thresholds are increasingly discussed in the academic literature and are subjects we return to in the next chapter, on methodology (Palermo, Bleck, and Peterman 2014; Cohen, Hoover Green, and Wood 2013; Cohen and Nordås 2014; Nordås and Cohen 2021). In that chapter, we examine the risk of reporting bias where emphasis on conflict (usually high-intensity conflict) to detect sexual violence may lead to oversight of politically violent situations in which SGBV is occurring to achieve political ends. In the next section, we examine contemporary theoretical insights into the patterns of SGBV in conflict and other politically unstable situations.

Theories and Patterns: What We Know and What We Don't Know

As with all early-warning analyses to prevent conflict and genocide (Stanton 2014; Von Joeden-Forgey 2012; Zartman 2015), protection from, and prevention of, widespread and systematic sexual and gender-based violence (SGBV) requires engagement with the "contributing political, social and economic context" that provides signals of trouble ahead (UNSG 2009: 6). We argue, however, that most research on SGBV in conflict has tended to focus on the trouble rather than the signals.

In the 1990s, literature often referred to sexual violence in conflict, specifically rape, as a "tool of war." This research was linked to the findings from the wars in the former Yugoslavia and the Rwandan genocide: that

SGBV crimes in these conflicts were not subsidiary but central to the desired outcomes of the conflict (Skjelbaek 2001; Nowrojee 1996; Salzman 1998; Schwartz 1994; Mackinnon 1994). This focus led to some controversy amongst feminist advocates (Engle 2020; Stern 2019). However, knowledge and evidence from ethnic conflict and genocide in the early 1990s resulted in the inclusion of sexual and gender-based crimes in the 1998 Rome Statute as war crimes, crimes against humanity, and acts of genocide. In the 2000s, advocacy, especially within the UN Security Council, foregrounded crimes of SGBV as security "threats," specifically as threats to the maintenance of international peace and security (Engle 2020). This required highlighting the tactical operation of sexual violence and defining sexual violence as a rational instrumental tool of war—that is, based on the deliberate order by a military leader to secure or govern territory. The problem with emphasis on sexual violence as "strategic" is that it has been rare to identify situations where such a precise order had been issued, or where sexual violence has occurred at the recognized scale and intensity to politically necessitate, for example, an operation to restore peace and security because of this violence (Altunjan 2021). One possible exception has been the sustained peace operations' engagement in sexual violence prevention in the two-decades-long UN peace operation in the Democratic Republic of Congo (Lotze 2020). Lotze (2020: 538) notes that the mission initially approached all SGBV acts committed by state and nonstate forces as strategic, but this understanding changed over time and altered the missions approach to preventing SGBV. Furthermore, as noted earlier, the absence of a UN peacekeeping mission deployment or ICC indictment does not indicate an absence of SGBV at the scale to necessitate a peacekeeping operation. Dara Kay Cohen (2016) argues that her research on patterns of rape prevalence in civil wars between 1980 and 2009 reveals there that is no "rape in war" norm. Government troops and rebel soldiers are rarely ordered to rape. The acts of sexual violence that Cohen (2016) documents in El Salvador, Sierra Leone, and Timor Leste occur due to the social networks and socialization of the soldiers and rebels. That is, sexual violence wells up from below rather than being commanded top down. As a result, recent studies of SGBV in conflict situations have turned to identifying the pivot points—that is, why do some actors rape in war and some do not, and in which wars does rape occur and in which wars is it absent (Cohen, Hoover Green, and Wood 2013; Wood 2014; Cohen 2016; Asal and Nagel 2021; Binningsbø and Nordås 2022: 1068–1069)?

The recognition of sexual and gender-based violence as international crimes has provided a definition to facilitate the documentation and investigation of these crimes. Scholars meanwhile continue to struggle to explain why and when this violence is used in conflict, and what is unique about its occurrence (Henry 2016; Wood 2018; Danielsson 2019: 6–10; Nagel 2021). In the field of political science and international relations, typologies of SGBV in conflict situations have been developed to address these questions (Boesten 2017; Wood 2018). This violence includes opportunistic-, instrumental-, and gender-targeted persecutions (Baaz and Stern 2013; Chappell 2014; Cohen 2016; Kirby 2015; Mibenge 2013; Swaine 2017; Zalewski et al. 2018). These crimes are perpetrated by one or more sides (ethnic, political, religious, or criminal groups) that are in conflict (D'Costa and Hossain 2010; Al-Ali 2018: 20). The perpetrators may be state or nonstate actors. They may be men or women, soldiers, militias, and civilians. The victims-survivors may be adults or children.

An analysis of all articles, books, and review articles on the topic of "sexual violence in conflict" published in social sciences journals and books between 1998 and 2016 (the period of our study) reveals that the majority of the 418 publications identify three main types of conflict in the understanding of sexual violence patterns: civil war, war (interstate conflict), and ceasefire peace process (Web of Science 2019). The majority of studies and datasets, however, tend to select cases of sexual violence within only one of these types of conflict—that is, they study patterns of sexual violence in civil wars or offer a comparative study of civil wars and interstate conflicts (Cohen and Nordås 2014). In fewer than twenty of the selected cases, there was no official or recorded conflict but there was state fragility: South Africa (apartheid era), Kenya (2008 elections), and Egypt (protests in 2011) were the few cases where publications studied the patterns of gender violence as "conflict-related" but not during actual conflict. Studies of sexual violence during public protests, locations of violent extremism and terror attacks, and one-sided violence against civilians (e.g., genocide) were all single-case explorations.

Here we examine attempts to explain the occurrence of SGBV across two decades of research that have focused on explanations for the onset and preponderance of sexual violence in numerous conflict situations. The focus in this volume is on literature that tries to make sense of patterns of SGBV. We identify three main theoretical explanations: opportunistic, instrumental, and gendered, and examine each in turn.

One of the first attempts to understand *variation* in use of sexual violence in armed conflict was Elizabeth Wood's 2006 study of eight cases ranging from the Second World War to the El Salvador civil conflict and the US-led war in Vietnam. Wood asked, if sexual violence is a "strategic tool"—that is, an effective weapon in waging war—why don't all armed groups use it consistently? She drew on existing studies to compare "non-event" cases where allegations of the perpetration of sexual violence by at least one armed group involved in the conflict was noticeably absent. Wood defined "absence" as the rare or minimal reporting of sexual violence. She tested a number of existing hypotheses and found little support for the type of conflict, the instrumentality (rational choice) of SGBV to the group, the militarization of masculinity, and preexisting uneven gender relations as causes of wartime sexual violence. For each potential explanatory factor, Wood used the method of falsification, pointing to an anomalous case that she claimed disproved the classic hypotheses (2006: 325).[8]

Based on her falsification of potential explanations, Wood (2006) argued that the most compelling explanatory relationship was the individual opportunity to commit such violence facilitated by the lack of a hierarchical command structure and explicit norms against sexual violence within armed groups. Wood's study spurred a debate within the fields of political science and international relations about the primary drivers of sexual violence in armed conflict between those scholars who argue that SGBV is largely opportunity-driven (Butler, Gluch, and Mitchell 2007) and those who argue that sexual violence is instrumental for groups seeking control within a conflict (Farr 2009).

Kathryn Farr (2009) extended Wood's (2006) study, suspecting that there may be differences in the use of SGBV across types of conflict and perpetrator. Farr compared war rape in twenty-seven armed conflicts reported by Project Ploughshares in 2007. Farr, like Wood (2006), did not refer to the 1998 Rome Statute's definition of sexual and gender-based violence, but noted that there are few studies of "extreme war rape," defined as "regularized, war-normative acts of sexual violence accompanied by intentional serious harm, including physical injury, physical and psychological torture, and sometimes murder" (2009: 6).

Farr's study was notably one of the few at this time that examined sexual violence, including gender-based violence, as part of a broader pattern of political violence against a particular group. Similar to Bastick, Grimm, and Kunz (2007), Farr was less concerned with the falsification of sexual violence in war and more concerned with understanding the prevalence and prominence of "particular rape sites, perpetrator groups, and victim targets" (2009: 10). From her twenty-seven cases, Farr (2009) identified four war rape patterns: field-centered/opportunistic, field-centered/woman-targeted, state-led/ethnic-targeted, and state-led/enemy-targeted.

Farr's analysis revealed variation in the reporting of conflict-related sexual violence, as well as different motivations and targets depending on the phase of the conflict and combatant grievance. For example, in Liberia and the DRC, strong rebel groups were fighting to gain control over valuable resources in a country: SGBV tended to be highly prevalent and perpetrated by rebels and state agents in the location where fighting was occurring (field-centered/opportunistic). Thus, rape occurrence could have a strong opportunistic component, but it could also have a "strategic" purpose—for instance, expulsion of populations. Field-centered/woman-targeted rape occurred more often in conflicts such as Afghanistan and Iraq, where state and rebel groups both were perpetrators. Farr found here that women were specifically targeted in these conflicts for "deviant" social behaviors, including dress, appearance in public, political activism, and so on. State-led/ethnic-targeted rape was perpetrated in contexts like Chechnya and Burma, where a powerful, controlling state attempted to quash a smaller secessionist or minority-representing group. In this category, rape victims-survivors were often targeted based on ethnicity. Of note, Farr's study revealed that gender norms within these societies appear to further inform the selection of victims-survivors for this particular form of violence. Gender identity, not biological sex, was the selection criteria in most of the situations she investigated. Finally, in Farr's findings, state-led/enemy-targeted rape tended to target victims-survivors based on ideological affiliations with rebel groups and activism critical of the state. In this situation, large and powerful rebel groups appear to have committed little SGBV, while state security forces tended to employ SGBV as a means of torture or repression (e.g., in Colombia and Sri Lanka).

As Farr (2009) herself acknowledged, these findings were limited to situations already embroiled in violent conflict. What was not clear in her study is whether the motivations for different groups to deploy sexual and gender-based violence against different victims-survivors underwent important shifts depending on the phase of conflict—before, after, and during armed fighting. Across the twenty-seven cases, nearly all combatants at some stage engaged in practices of sexual violence, but the reported crimes and locations differed considerably. Furthermore, with a minority of exceptions, most of the sexual crimes were not gender-neutral; there were gender-based motivations in the selection of victims-survivors and in the type of violence used. The instrumental argument at this point has acknowledged the potential for opportunity to influence the perpetration of SGBV, but for Farr sexual violence more often than not appears to be premised on instrumental objectives attached to the conflict. What Farr does not examine is the degree to which sexual violence is instrumental, which is no doubt difficult to discern without in-depth field research.

In a 2013 article and 2016 book, Cohen published her examination of rape in civil conflicts based on the Fearon and Laitin (2003) civil war dataset. Cohen (2013; 2016) introduced a sexual violence scale of intensity (0–4) based on a single reporting source (US State Department annual reports) and found the socialization of armed groups to be the most significant explanation for the perpetration of rape. In Cohen's research, insurgencies that forcibly conscript combatants, fight over lootable resources, and "aimed at the center" (that is, were not secessionist) were more likely to perpetrate rape in civil conflicts. State armed forces were also more likely to commit rape when they pressganged their fighters and ordered rape as part of "scorched-earth" policies. Cohen found no evidence of a relationship between sexual violence and ethnic hatred, ethnic cleansing, or genocide, nor any relation to gender inequality or discrimination (though we suggest that existing gender inequality discrimination measures are not sufficiently comprehensive to be "ruled out"; see Davies and True 2015). Cohen (2016) agreed with Wood (2014) that "opportunistic" arguments do not always hold because opportunities were available to all to rape in some situations, and yet not all chose to do so.

The combatant socialization theory that Cohen (2013; 2016) suggested is that sexual violence, on a widespread or systematic scale (rape can be widespread but not systematic, and vice versa), is explained by recruitment practices, unit cohesion, and recruitment pool. Cohen does not describe socialization in instrumental terms, but the benefits of socialization are instrumental for the group. Strengthening unit cohesion and morale, particularly if a side is losing or the recruits are forced, requires combatant socialization practices to instill unit cohesion and loyalty. Cohen argues that gang rape "increases mutual esteem," and sexualized group violence especially serves to break social taboos and communicate norms of virility and masculinity (2016: 191). Her finding is that a permissive environment for rape perpetrators is a more significant factor than the presence of gender inequality, ethnic grievances, or the genocidal intent of the regime, although all these same factors may be part of that permissive environment. This result has been corroborated by Cohen and Nordås's (2014) statistical research design and analysis that uses an expanded database of the Uppsala Conflict Data Program and additional reporting sources (Amnesty International and Human Rights Watch reports in addition to US State Department annual reports). In their 2021 study, they examine the state of the field and note a multiplicity of explanations for the duration, phase, and type of "wartime sexual violence." They conclude that the "cohesion, ideology, governance, and training" are critical for analyses of armed actors' behaviour as perpetrators, and further inquiry into "closing the impunity gap" to "deter future acts of sexual violence" is needed (Nordås and Cohen 2021: 203, 207).

At this point, the theoretical explanation for sexual violence spans from a deliberate instrument of war that is ordered and then carried out with efficiency and purpose to an opportunistic act in the absence of professionalism and accountability; more recently, a nuanced understanding of sexual violence in conflict focuses on perpetrator group dynamics as practices that can be mitigated, if albeit largely ignoring the relational dynamics and conditions of victimization. The instrumentality identified here is gain-of-function from the combatant. Cohen (2016) identifies particular incentives that have led to some combatants tolerating, permitting or encouraging rape to strengthen unit cohesion. We might also observe that gender inequality may not predict the occurrence of sexual and gender-based violence, but this violence is not gender-neutral. There are clear "gender-based motivations, gender-based impacts, and gender-based implications" that explain SGBV (Sjoberg 2016: 130). As Lotze (2020: 542) suggests,

> Deeper understanding of vulnerability may be required. Although it is recognized that CRSV [conflict-related sexual violence] is not solely a women's issue as men and boys are both victims of and deeply affected by such violations, for male survivors, sexual violence remains shrouded in cultural taboos. In 2018, in over 60 countries no provisions for male victims existed within the scope of national sexual violence legislation, leaving male and boy victims particularly vulnerable to accusations of homosexuality, in particular in countries where this is criminalized. Lesbian, gay, bisexual, transgender and intersex individuals who are victims of violations are often vulnerable to stigmatization, exclusion or criminal persecution if they come forward.

Variations of the different types of sexual violence deployed in the phases and intensity of political violence and conflict, including situations prior to armed conflict, have been relatively neglected. Taboos, attitudes, values, beliefs, sexuality, and interests do not arise "naturally" nor are they gender-neutral. There is a gender-subordination practice that underpins SGBV (Sjoberg 2016; Schulz 2020). Indeed, a recent article by Guarnieri and Tur-Prats (2023) has sought to demonstrate that prior gender norms are causal for both the strategic and expressive use of sexual violence. Gender subordination is indicative of the socioeconomic power one group seeks to wield over another and on whom they are committing these acts of violence (Ellsberg et al. 2020). We can observe gendered patterns of hierarchy and subordination in conflict. This *gendered political violence* context may not predict but it does explain SGBV: it assists with understanding who is identified as the appropriate victim-survivor and who is empowered as the appropriate perpetrator of violence in that conflict (Grey and Shepherd 2013).

This question helps us to understand that the practice of rape may be opportunistic and it may be instrumental, but in both instances it is tolerated (opportunistic) or incentivized (instrumental) because the victim(s)-survivor(s) and perpetrator(s) are part of a sex and gender story in each conflict (Baaz and Stern 2013; Sjoberg 2016).

SGBV is not gender-neutral (Baaz and Stern 2013). The targeting of victims-survivors is gendered political violence. Sexual violence is instrumental and opportunistic in conflict because gender subordination is at the root of the perpetrator(s)/victim(s)-survivor(s) relationship. Gender-based violence is not tangential to conflict outcomes. Gender-based violence achieves political ends: it can enable territorial control (Nagel 2021), create fidelity to armed groups (Hedström and Olivius 2021), and sustain the political economy of war (Hudson and Matfess 2017; Hutchinson 2020; True 2012). The question is why this victim-survivor, why this perpetrator, and what does subordination of one group achieve for the other? It may be opportunistic, which tells us the status of social gender within that group (Wood 2015); and it may be instrumental, with the intention to seize control over bodies and reproduction (Asal and Nagel 2021).[9]

As we discuss in the next chapter, SGBV remains a silent and hidden crime. In situations where groups of peoples face discrimination, targeted violence, and conflict, nonreporting of SGBV will be the norm for a range of reasons that include trauma experienced by victims-survivors, the politics and dangers associated with reporting SGBV, the lack of robust institutions to report to, the broader culture of impunity for reporting, and the practical difficulties encountered in examining and compiling reports on SGBV in the field.[10] Such non-reporting underlines the challenging conditions to understand when SGBV occurs and the need to understand the gendered subordinating power of violence (Clark 2014).[11]

Contrary to the view that feminist perspectives cannot appreciate men and boys as victims-survivors of sexual violence (Quijano and Kelly 2012: 483–484), a gendered analysis of SGBV identifies why sexualized violence would be effective in societies where it is culturally taboo (Schulz 2020). Indeed, a gendered analysis leads us to ask why silences exist in the reporting of violence against boys and men (Lewis 2014; Touquet and Schulz 2021). Taboos and silence also raise the question of whether—when we claim SGBV did "not" occur—we are sure that we have uncovered the political, social and cultural barriers to reporting that informed this finding (e.g., Wood 2006; 2009; Peterman et al. 2011; Human Security Report Project 2012; Boesten and Henry 2018; Davies and True 2017b; Barbour 2020; Ju 2023). Perhaps less so in the 2020s—but certainly in previous situations where the most vulnerable had no access to humanitarian actors or digital technology—few people or organizations on the ground were equipped to witness and report these crimes, let alone have institutions to report to (Sooka et al. 2014). But it would be a mistake to presume that in the 2020s barriers to reporting have been overcome. In the case of Ethiopia's civil war, Afghanistan's return to Taliban rule, zero-Covid in China, the arbitrary detention of the Uyghur population in China, the information blackout in North Korea, Russia's annexation and then invasion in Ukraine, Burma's military coup, and the Islamic Republic of Iran's crackdown on revolutionary protests, authorities and militaries tightly control humanitarian access, execute prolonged internet blackouts, or both. Such efforts to suppress information and access are purposive: when experiences of sexual violence are circulated, there is a deliberate intent to suppress the report(s) or present these reports as "fabrication," "hype," and random rather than widespread acts (Chinese Human Rights Defenders 2022; HRW 2021; The Irrawaddy 2022; Mahderom 2022; Wamsley 2022).

Repositioning gender into the study of widespread and systematic SGBV enables a more fine-grained and dynamic understanding of the gendered structural conditions that affect the incidence and reporting of SGBV crimes (True 2012; Guarnieri and Tur-Prats 2023). We need greater sensitivity to gender inequalities within and across groups and to the dramatic shifts in gender discrimination over a short period of time, particularly if accompanied by dramatic shifts in discrimination against other groups at risk of exclusion, such as ethnic or sexual minorities (Davies and True 2015). The reported incidence of mass SGBV may not correlate with standard measures of gender equality. These measures are often static, largely cross-sectional, national statistical indicators of women's rights or gender equality (see Liebowitz and Zwingel 2014), which mask the inequality and discrimination experienced by particular groups of women and girls and in the subnational contexts in which civil conflict often takes place. The quality of national indicators on gender equality is even weaker in protracted conflict contexts and subnationally, as we reveal in the case of the Philippines. In sum, national gender equality statistics or analyses may not serve as the best proxies to establish the relationship between the presence of SGBV in conflict and the socioeconomic patterns of gender inequality.

In most studies, sexual violence—primarily defined as "rape"—occurs when perpetrator dynamics fuel these crimes; according to this frame, they are opportunistic crimes or "a long-running feature of life" in that armed group (Wood 2020). Mass sexual violence is an instrumental strategy deployed against civilians for a purpose, whether combatant socialization or enabling the acquisition of resources, land, and power (Loken 2017; Krüger and Nordås 2020; Whitaker, Walsh, and Conrad 2019). Recent studies have been vital in identifying patterns of sexual violence and documenting cases of sexual violence as mass atrocity crimes. However, some political and reporting practices can distort collective knowledge of SGBV patterns. Ju (2023), for example, has queried a presumption in recent studies and their datasets that no mention of sexual violence indicates its absence, a "zero observation," revealing that many government and rebel actors go to great lengths to conceal sexual atrocities. This insight reveals how little we know about the relationship between the reports received of such violence, the relationship between reporting and political violence, and the role of societal gender stereotypes, stigma, and politics in facilitating or obstructing these reports. We consider whether a relationship exists between the presence of humanitarian actors and the provision of reports—which means, in turn, that we know more about sexual and gender-based violence in situations where there is humanitarian (and media) access rather than more about SGBV in all situations.

Drawing on these theories and gaps in our knowledge of SGBV, we seek to extend and challenge prevailing assumptions about the relationship between opportunity, instrumentality, reporting, and gender, especially when studying the prevalence of SGBV in protracted, low-intensity conflict settings.

SGBV in Low-Intensity Conflict Settings: The Importance of Asia

Human rights violations in low-intensity conflicts have continued to occur across Asia.[12] Much has been written about the peaceful coexistence that the region has achieved in the aftermath of China's civil war, the partition of India and Pakistan, the independence of Bangladesh, and the Indochina Wars. While regional and international wars of high intensity (over one thousand battle deaths per annum) have not occurred in the Asian region into the 1990s, 2000s, and 2010s at the same scale as they have in sub-Saharan Africa and the Middle East, protracted and violent conflicts have still taken place in this region. The political instability and civil conflicts experienced in the region today can be traced to Asia's recent history of colonization, independence wars, and Cold War proxy conflicts. The continued existence of state fragility, organized state-led and nonstate combatant-led violence, one-sided mass atrocities, and violent extremism in the Asian region always pose risks for the civilians who live with this low-level instability. As the 2017 Rohingya genocide and the 2017 Marawi Siege both reveal, sudden surges in violence have a history and a future legacy. They do not appear out of nowhere. When closely studied, these episodic surges in violence often reveal a continuum of communal-level violence or "frozen," fragile societies where violence simmers.

SGBV has been documented across Asia throughout the twentieth and twenty-first centuries.[13] Testimonies of egregious rape and sexual violence include the 1937 Nanking Massacre in China (Chang 2012) and the experience of the mostly Korean, but also Chinese, Taiwanese, and Indonesian girls and women forced into sexual slavery as "comfort women" or "military sexual slaves" from 1932 to 1945 for Japanese soldiers (Yoshimi 2002; Hata 2018; Min 2021). This system of sexual slavery involved thousands of women for over a decade; those who did not die of injuries, disease, and execution lived for years without recognition of their forcible recruitment and enslavement (Coomaraswamy 1996; Stetz 2019; Myadar and Davidson 2020; Hongxi 2020). South Asian women in the 1947 Indian Wars of Partition experienced the partition through their bodies—thousands were raped, forcibly abducted, married, and tattooed with political slogans on their bodies (Menon and Bhasin 1998; Butalia 2000; Utne 2021). In 1971 the Bangladesh Liberation War from Pakistan (also labeled the Bangladesh genocide) led to thousands of women and girls being forcibly detained and raped by Pakistani forces within their barracks (D'Costa and Hossain 2010; Mookherjee 2015; Ghatak 2022). The Khmer Rouge regime during the Cambodian war and genocide, 1975–1979, forced marriages to take place to increase the agrarian workforce, and Khmer cadres encouraged husbands to rape their wives if they refused (Kasumi 2008; Tyner 2017; Denov et al. 2022). For years, crimes of sexual violence, torture, and slavery were not associated with the Cambodian genocide because the regime had Code 6, whereby sexual relations outside of marriage could be punished by executing both partners. The result was that forced marriage was practiced to overcome this law, rapes were followed by execution, and there was enduring silence by the women who survived these crimes (Lei Win 2013; Jacobs 2020).

In the 1945–1975 Indochinese wars—involving (initially) France, then the United States and Australia across Vietnam, Cambodia, and Laos—there were reports of sexual violence being committed, especially by the American forces deployed in Vietnam (Wood 2008a). As noted earlier, Wood identified these crimes as opportunistic rather than orchestrated, gender-based crimes. Lawson (1989) explains how the image of the American soldier in Vietnam was one of impunity and "inevitability" that bad things happen in war: American soldiers raping "foreign" women and girls are part of what happens in war (for example, the gang rapes that occurred in the 1968 My Lai massacre committed by an American unit that killed 504 civilians led to only one prosecution). The "othering" of Vietnamese women during the Indochina wars continued the pattern during French colonial rule when gendered atrocities against men and women were justified as acts of racial superiority (Rydstrom 2015). During the 1965–1966 Indonesian coup—which some allege was genocide—Komnas Perempuan (2007) recorded testimonies from 122 victims-survivors and witnesses on how the military and police openly committed acts of sexual violence against ethnic Chinese women and communist sympathizers. Torture in prisons was commonplace, with women exposed to strip searches and rape. Many women were pressured into prostitution for soldiers, even forced marriage to survive the aftermath of the genocide.

Case Study Selection

The commonalities amongst these recent historical experiences of sexual violence across the Asian region are striking: rape in detention and rape to elicit silence and obedience, as well as instances of opportunistic rape. In 2020 the Armed Conflict Location and Event Data (ACLED) project recorded five types of political violence (sexual, abduction, mob, attack, and explosions) directed against women across each region (Africa, the Middle East, Latin America and the Caribbean, South Asia, Southeast Asia, Caucasus and Central Asia, Southeastern and Eastern Europe, and the Balkans). ACLED recorded the Southeast Asia region as having the highest reported prevalence of sexual violence as political violence against women (Kishi 2020). There is a history of racial and gender profiling in widespread or systematic SGBV practices in Asia. Groups are selected and then targeted for this violence with the intention of gender subordination—forced marriage, sexual slavery, and forced pregnancies. Finally, there is widespread impunity for and silences around these crimes. The majority of research on SGBV in the region refers to the labor required to uncover these stories—in particular, overcoming the reticence, the silences, and the reluctance of victims-survivors and witnesses to discuss these crimes (Butalia 2000; Kasumi 2008; Pohlman 2015; Traunmüller, Kijewski, and Freitag 2019; Cho 2020; Meger 2021). Government support for victims-survivors is rare and often politicized (D'Costa and Hossain 2010; Hedström and Olivius 2021).

The contemporary political story of Asia is about its rising prosperity and relative peace (Palik, Rustad, and Methi 2020). The conflicts still occurring in the region are described as "low-level" conflicts, with fifteen state-based conflicts in six countries. The majority of fatalities over the previous decade (2009–2019) are mostly attributed to the conflict in Afghanistan, and the region has the greatest number of ceasefires concluded between 1989 and 2018. The end of the Sri Lanka civil war in 2008–2009 saw its highest peak of civilian and battle deaths in the twenty-year conflict. The genocide and ethnic cleansing of the Rohingya population in Burma in 2017 recorded the nation's highest intensity of violence in over thirty years. Political violence on a scale seen in the Middle East or sub-Saharan Africa is now rare in this region. Yet this can create, we suggest, the (mis)perception that SGBV must therefore be a less prominent feature of political violence in the region.

In the remainder of this book, we set out our methodology and then examine three contemporary and protracted low-intensity civil war conflicts: in

Burma, the Philippines, and Sri Lanka. We examine each conflict for SGBV reports between 1998 and 2016. Each country was experiencing its civil conflict during this period, at the same time the 1998 Rome Statute was introduced and came into force, and while the Women, Peace and Security Resolutions 1325 (2000), 1820, and 1888 (2008 and 2009) were adopted. These instruments provided the definitions and guidelines to commence reporting arrangements on conflict-related SGBV. Our interest is in observing how conflicts in the Asian region adapted in real time to international calls for monitoring and reporting conflict-related SGBV.

Our selection of "Asia" case studies is not exhaustive.[14] We were interested in heuristic cases (George and Bennett, 2005: 75) that met the following criteria: (1) low-intensity protracted civil conflicts that span the majority of the reporting period we examine; (2) conflicts that experience cycles of low-, mid-, and high-intensity battle deaths (transition from conflict to war and back to conflict) during the period of study; and (3) conflicts where we could conduct exploratory research, that is, undertake field research to conduct interviews with actors who report SGBV (which informs the qualitative analysis presented in each case study chapter) and complete primary data collection on reporting (see next chapter). We undertook field research in all three locations between 2015 and 2019. Such in-country research was important to establish who was doing the reporting and to probe how reporting decisions were being made. We excluded from the study Afghanistan, the Kashmir border, and North Korea due to safety considerations.

Sexual violence is under-reported everywhere in the world, but reliable data are especially scarce in Asia, where demographic and health surveys are comparatively infrequent and national reporting systems are relatively underdeveloped. Due to these wars being "low-intensity," there is not the same presence of international humanitarian actors who observe and report these crimes (Cohen, Hoover Green, and Wood 2013; Davies and True 2017a). What is known about gender-based violence in the region is that there are high levels of acceptance of this violence from both male and female survey respondents (Fulu et al. 2013). In situations of high-intensity conflict, gender inequality is often seen as too pervasive and diffuse to predict the likelihood of SGBV. In these three cases, however, we have significant variations in gender-equality trends within each country. We seek to understand, therefore, whether the occurrence, presence, and types of SGBV in conflicts reflect their context-specific gendered environments. SGBV in Asian conflicts has received comparatively little reporting and little scholarly attention until now.

Conclusion

This book investigates how sexual violence in conflict is reported in situations where there has been low-level conflict intensity before and after intense violent episodes. It is informed by a growing concern among scholars and advocates that the focus on rape and other forms of sexual violence in conflict situations may diminish the importance of other types of SGBV, including SGBV outside of conflict situations. We argue that the widespread and systematic "threshold" for SGBV has been misapplied. SGBV can occur outside of conflict, and it need not occur on a massive scale. Thus, we need to bring back the study of gender relations and integrate it with the opportunity and instrumentality arguments that seek to explain the nature, causes, and types of SGBV in politically unstable situations. Asia as a region has a history of sexual violence, in and outside of conflict, that aims to subordinate particular groups into racial and gendered roles, thus diminishing their political power. This book closely examines three cases that test and contribute to our knowledge of whether victims-survivors selection is targeted or opportunistic, whether SGBV escalates before the onset of conflict and thus could be an early-warning indicator, and finally, whether there is an actual political opportunity to report the crimes of perpetrators during and after conflict.

2
Rethinking Methodologies for Sexual and Gender-Based Violence in Conflict

In Chapter One we highlighted the absence of reports on sexual and gender-based violence (SGBV) in low-intensity conflict situations as a field worth further investigation. In this chapter we suggest that in order to deepen our understanding of gendered political violence we must first engage with how we know what, when, and where SGBV is present. Knowledge production, including the institutional mechanisms for reporting this violence and the methodologies for collecting and analyzing reporting data, are inseparable from the conceptualization of the problem of SGBV and the solutions that respond to it in conflict situations (Wood 2014; Sjoberg 2016; Campbell 2018; Gray and Stern 2019; Nordås and Cohen 2021). Feminist scholarship reveals the gendered nature of all knowledge and data on conflict-related SGBV (Kirby 2013; Kreft and Schulz 2022; Kreft 2022). In this chapter we ask how situations of endemic gender discrimination affect our knowledge of where violence is taking place, and who the perpetrators, targets, and victims-survivors of it are in low-intensity conflicts in Asia.

This chapter has three main parts. First, we explain why existing methods for understanding and preventing SGBV often do not apply to Asia. We investigate the social and political conditions in which SGBV is reported and, even more significantly, is not reported. Second, we explore how the silences can be identified and investigated given the blind spots of existing SGBV reporting and data collection methods. We suggest the need for methodological approaches that can shed light on the contexts of SGBV within specific phases and locations of conflict. Third, we illustrate our methodological approach to identifying and analyzing SGBV in Asian contexts of low-intensity conflict. We highlight the importance of feminist analytical reflexivity in addressing the limitations of our approach and what it implies about the silences and absence of reports in particular areas and phases of conflict.

What Is the Problem: Why Don't Existing Methods Work?

Knowledge has proliferated on SGBV in conflict since the first UN Security Council Resolution focused on the prevention of this violence in 2008 (S/Res/1820). Yet, at the same time, qualitative and quantitative studies of SGBV point to a "tip of the iceberg" (Palermo, Bleck, and Peterman 2014) phenomenon in fragile and conflict situations. That tip can be seen in the high prevalence but low level of actual SGBV reporting that particularly characterizes conflict settings, even in UN peacekeeping missions (Lotze 2020). Nonreporting is a major problem for identifying and responding to SGBV in politicized conflict contexts where reporting SGBV on the ground (and, therefore, data collection) is frequently difficult.

Consider the conditions necessary to support reporting. Victims-survivors need access to clinics to seek treatment—or police stations to report their experience. In conflict situations, it is rarely safe to approach a police station (if one exists), let alone access a health clinic for treatment. The 2022 UN Secretary-General Report *Women and Peace and Security* (S/2022/740) outlines the difficulty with data collection: in Afghanistan, 51 per cent of women's organizations—the only source of first-response services for sexual violence—have had to close since the Taliban's takeover in 2021. Around the world, especially in conflict situations, attacks against women human rights defenders are "extremely under-reported and anonymized in official United Nations statistics," and these women are "much more likely than men to be targeted with sexual and gender-based violence" (UNSG 2022a: 3).

In the same year, the UN Secretary-General 2022 report on conflict-related sexual violence (S/2022/272) again referred to the dangerous reporting conditions that affect how we know about SGBV (UNSG 2022b). Moreover, service providers were subjected to threats and attacks, causing the closure of essential services—including emergency post-rape care and sexual and reproductive health care—for victims-survivors of sexual violence. Long-standing barriers to reporting and accessing services, such as stigma, fear of retaliation, and weak rule-of-law institutions, further exacerbated by the ongoing pandemic (UNSG 2021), were heightened by conflict and political crisis. Globally, despite deepening constraints, victims-survivors and service providers continued to report sexual violence crimes. The 2022 report is limited to incidents of "conflict-related sexual violence" that were verified by the United Nations. While it conveys the severity and brutality of recorded cases, it "does not purport to convey the full scale and prevalence of these crimes" (UNSG 2022b: 4–5).

Scholars and policymakers are aware that reporting silence is a major problem. The *UN Framework on the Prevention of Conflict-Related Sexual Violence* (UN 2022a: 6) states that "the rate of case reporting is understood to be orders of magnitude lower than the actual prevalence rate." Nordås and Cohen (2021: 204) note that quantitative and qualitative studies of sexual violence carry the risk of data bias and limitations due to under-reporting and stigma. We argue that while scholars accept this fact, its implications for our understanding of the patterns of this type of violence—and how they affect and are affected by conflict—are not interrogated. Incident reports by themselves cannot indicate the magnitude or other patterns of SGBV to inform prevention strategies. Moreover, some of our global assumptions about SGBV and its relationship with conflict and violence may be flawed. There is no doubt about the documentation of widespread and systematic sexual violence recorded in Bosnia-Herzegovina, Rwanda, the Democratic Republic of Congo, Iraq, South Sudan, and Syria, and in more recent situations such as Ethiopia and Ukraine. However, there is great potential for error in what counts as SGBV, who is a victim-survivor, and when it is "conflict-related." For example, intimate partner violence experienced in conflict may or may not be reported as conflict-related (which may alter our knowledge of escalation and prevention; see Ekhator-Mobayode et al. 2022). Furthermore, sexual violence against boys and men is vastly under-reported (which may alter our knowledge of prevalence and nonevents; see Chynoweth 2017; Kreft and Schulz 2022).

Moreover, current SGBV research and policy frameworks may not reflect the low-intensity conflict dynamics in Asia as discussed in Chapter One. In particular, this is the case where SGBV may fluctuate in response to escalating/deescalating violence, and victims-survivors may be targeted in smaller numbers. For example, intimate partner violence in displacement camps may be conflict-related while military officials in small communities may perpetrate "stranger rape," whether in uniform or not (Baaz and Stern 2009). If SGBV reports do not reflect the scale, intensity, or diversity of crimes, and reporting is a politicized practice, then how do we learn more about SGBV in conflict? What approaches and methods can we use? This is the situation in the cases we examine in this book. It is important to understand what might be happening in such conflicts, but we are without a substantive knowledge base.

There are significant barriers to building that knowledge in low-intensity conflict settings in Asia, including the lack of awareness of SGBV in general, and in fragile or militarized situations where armed groups are present. Existing knowledge of conflict-related sexual violence in civil wars in Africa and the Middle East may not be as relevant to ongoing low-intensity conflicts in Asia. The Uppsala Conflict Data Program (UCDP) definition of "minor conflict" requires more than twenty-five direct "battle deaths" due to conflict annually. But such a threshold may not be met in all years in low-intensity conflicts where conflicts may be long-lasting, as in the cases of Sri Lanka, the Philippines, and Burma that we examine in this book. Additionally, the widespread perception or belief by governments in Asia that they are not in conflict or conflict-affected situations is also a significant barrier to greater knowledge, systematic data collection, and study. For these governments, outwardly recognizing civil or communal conflict in public or multilateral fora is seen as an admission of weakness—that the country is not stable or sovereign—which in turn could undermine domestic political authority and legitimacy.

A narrow understanding of the situation as conflict is not just battle deaths–related, therefore, but political. Even at the height of atrocities being committed in Burma and Sri Lanka, the UN Security Council never adopted a resolution addressing either situation (risk of veto was the reason provided, but this did not stop the United States, the United Kingdom, and France's attempts at the same time for resolution in Libya, for example). The Philippines' conflict situation has never even been discussed in the UN Security Council. This reluctance to refer to conflicts in Asia appears to be linked to multiple causes, including the persistence of the "peaceful Asia" narrative (Kivimäki 2014)—which neglects ongoing atrocities and conflict in Afghanistan, China, the Philippines, Burma, North Korea, and Sri Lanka—and the vanguard state theory (Southgate 2019), which identifies how states form strong regional blocs that collectively agree to nonviolation of sovereignty norms. The implication of the nonrecognition of conflict in the region is the reality that the collection of data through SGBV reporting and recording of incidents is also a political act. Nonrecognition or "low-intensity status" of conflict suits the government and military, most often in control of the victory narrative in each of the conflicts mentioned, by ignoring or rejecting allegations of SGBV crimes committed by their forces and in their territory. Indeed, as we discuss throughout this book, all the conflicts we examine at some stage provided not only immunity for their soldiers but extended immunity for SGBV crimes to paramilitary and nonstate armed actors.

Foundational research by scholars and practitioners over the past decade has opened up the empirical study of the patterns of SGBV. Cohen and Nordås (2014) and Nordås and Cohen (2021), for instance, have analyzed and coded types of "sexual violence" in US State Department, Amnesty International, and Human Rights Watch reports from civil war–affected countries over a thirty-year period (1989–2019).[1] The not-for-profit media organization Women's Media Centre has created an online database of testimonials from women and men victims-survivors across selective historical and contemporary conflicts called Women Under Siege.[2] The Armed Conflict Location and Event Data Project (ACLED) collects (traditional and social) media reports on "political violence targeting women," which includes the event type "sexual violence." This dataset covers all countries reported as conflict situations where this violence has been occurring in a civic/public space, but the dates of coverage are not uniform (i.e., data date back to 1997 for the African region but only back to 2018 for parts of Asia).[3] There remain, however, gaps even in these comprehensive datasets. First, a lack of data for some countries or time periods may be evidence *not* of the absence of SGBV, but rather of an oppressive political context (e.g., Burma) that makes it difficult to document such violence and potentially life-threatening to report it (Oo and Davies 2021). In low-intensity conflicts such as the Philippines and Northern Ireland, for example, patterns of sexual violence may be present but not reported as conflict-related (Swaine 2015: 774; Davies, True, and Tanyag 2016: 465). There may be no international humanitarian actors present to report these crimes back to headquarters, and in some settings (not all), local civil society actors may be more selective and judicious in their reporting unless they are affiliated with a particular "side" (Kreft 2020; Oo and Davies 2021; Hedström and Olivius 2021). These acts may take place in the "private" sphere of the displacement tent, or they may not be recorded because humanitarian workers fear for the safety of those willing to report. If we accept that the absence of reports does not indicate the absence of SGBV, why silencing exists in one scenario and not another needs to be probed in each context.

In addition to the issue of unreported SGBV, the focus in recent research has been on the causes of sexual violence, which excludes other types of gender-based violence covered in the Rome Statute of the International Criminal Court (ICC) as war crimes (Office of the ICC Prosecutor 2014).

This scholarship asks whether rape in war is the product of individual or group perpetrator choices, building on existing disciplinary research on civil war (Wood 2006; Cohen 2013). The gendered nature of sexual violence, particularly its connection to specific preexisting gender norms and hierarchies within and across conflict groups, has implications for how this violence is reported. Why is analysis of gender and of situations with low or no reporting so important for our understanding of SGBV in conflict in Asia, and why don't existing methods work to interrogate these gaps?

Limited Awareness of the Problem

Due to historical impunity for acts of SGBV and the low level of public awareness of these crimes, we are only beginning to understand the scale and full range of types of SGBV in Asia. Lack of awareness of this violence is rooted in systemic gendered discrimination that feeds into a pattern of under- or nonreporting of this violence to authorities, due to the uncertainty of who to report to, along with societal stigmatization of victims-survivors. This under-reporting has resulted in few datasets designed to record SGBV in stable periods in Asia, let alone during conflict periods, and those that do record SGBV are not comprehensive but often focus on one particular type of GBV. For example, country-level demographic and health surveys (DHS) do not ask the same questions or sample the same populations—for example, Burma and Sri Lanka DHS only approached partnered women, and Burma only asked questions about domestic violence. In our case studies only the Philippines had repeat DHS data during our 1998–2016 time period.

Pervasive, preexisting gender, ethnic, class, caste, and other types of oppression associate sexual violence with shame that accrues to (usually but not always female) victims-survivors rather than (typically but not always male) perpetrators. These cultures of stigma are widespread in traditional ethnic and religious communities in Asia. Victims-survivors frequently do not report SGBV to avoid dishonoring themselves and their family (WIN 2019). As a 2013 multicountry study on men and violence of nine rural and urban sites in six countries in Asia reveals, SGBV is pervasive despite variation across contexts and is seen as normal or as a male entitlement.[4] The study singled out "the sense of sexual entitlement" that fuels men's acts of physical and sexual violence against women with almost no legal consequences, reflecting deep-seated gender inequalities in the law and justice system (Fulu et al. 2013: 3).

Few international human rights mechanisms are available to civil society groups in Asia to challenge governments for their failure to address SGBV. Fewer than half of the countries in the Asia-Pacific have ratified the 1998 Rome Statute of the International Criminal Court, compared with 63 per cent in Africa and 82 per cent of Latin American and Caribbean states (Waller, Palmer, and Chappell 2014: 360). The (first) Regional Action Plan on Women, Peace and Security which recommends the creation of monitoring, analysis, and reporting arrangements for conflict-related SGBV, was only recently adopted (November 2022) and applies only to the member states of Southeast Asia (ASEAN 2022). The Asian region has one of the lowest rates of National Action Plans on Women, Peace and Security (LSE 2019). Amongst the conflict situations we study in this book, only the Philippines has adopted a National Action Plan that includes the ambition to monitor and report conflict-related SGBV (see Chapter Four, this volume). Amongst the three cases we examine, only the Philippines has baseline data on domestic violence reports. Given this regional social context and state of knowledge, we need to uncover the reports that are available on SGBV for these conflicts, but also acknowledge that reporting data may not be accurate reflections of the actual patterns of SGBV in Asian civil conflicts.

Under-reporting and Lack of Data

SGBV is under-reported everywhere in the world due to gendered stigma, but reliable data are especially scarce in Asia, where demographic and health surveys are comparatively infrequent, national reporting systems are relatively underdeveloped, and there is a minimal international humanitarian presence. For example, thirty-two out of thirty-seven countries in the Asia-Pacific have completed at least one Violence Against Women prevalence survey (UNFPA 2022). However, only eleven countries have repeated the survey more than once between 2000 and 2022 (the Philippines is one of these eleven countries). The Philippines and Burma have not collected data on nonpartner violence, and Sri Lanka collected this data once in 2019 (ten years after the end of its conflict) (UNFPA 2022). These prevalence surveys are usually administered as demographic health surveys or as WHO global studies of domestic violence. The vast majority are national, not subnational, an important distinction given the subnational conflicts in the three cases we examine here.

The scarcity of trusted local institutions to report to or their inaccessibility in conflict, displacement, and rural settings also affects our knowledge of the patterns of violence. Poor protection for victims-survivors or others reporting SGBV due to ineffective or gender-biased law enforcement and justice systems, and institutional incapacity to record and analyze SGBV data, are also major issues (even first responders may not collect this data to ensure the safety of patients; see Davies 2019). Existing research highlights how, with rare exceptions (Lake 2014; Kreft 2020), victims-survivors are generally not willing to share or officially report their SGBV experiences (Buss 2014). This reticence is heightened in situations of ongoing political violence where women's bodies are frequently the sites of struggle over the social, cultural, and biological reproduction of groups (Schott 2011; Oo and Davies 2021). These problems compound the under-reporting of SGBV even with concerted efforts to gather better data through surveys or incident reporting in conflict situations. Thus, it is crucial to identify the social and political causes of this under-reporting at the same time as we seek to improve the tools for data collection and analysis.

We show how the social and political conditions that enable and constrain reporting across phases of conflict in the Asian context affect the impunity for this violence as well as national and international responses to prevent and end it. Existing reports provide a particular narrative of who commits and who is subjected to SGBV. This narrative can become path-dependent with little deviation in content over time. We need to be conscious of reporting bias: reports do not present a neutral or unbiased picture of the overall pattern of SGBV. Rather, they present particular parts of the problem. In some situations, for example, it may be more "acceptable" for some ethnic and politically active women to report sexual violence while other groups of affected women stay silent (Davies and True 2017c). As a result, what is reported may not be a representative sample from which we can deduce patterns.

Neglect of Gender Analysis Excludes Victims-Survivors

Even with concerted efforts to gather better data through surveys or incident reporting in conflict situations, bias, accuracy, and errors can slip into official reports (Hoover Green and Cohen 2021). Desk-based and field-based research carry the risk of being incomplete and biased without "methodological innovations—together with a disciplined awareness of the breadth and variety of gendered conflict experiences" (Hoover Green 2018: 325).

When there are few reports or some reports are deemed unreliable, scholars need to understand why. We argue that researchers need to investigate silence or the absence of SGBV reports or data as suggestive indicators of gendered political violence. Paradoxically, as we have argued, one of the starkest indications that SGBV may be widespread in a society is the presence of gender norms that prohibit or constrain its reporting or recording (Davies and True 2015: 509). In low-intensity conflicts, with phases of high and low "active" conflict periods, SGBV reports may be a casualty of reporting path dependency where some types of violence or incidents of violence are reported and others are not.

Analysis of SGBV in conflict settings can reinforce preexisting understandings of gendered power with the focus on armed or military issues and the visibility of these traditional institutions that conduct violence. Reporting trends tend to reflect the dominant crimes, perpetrators and victims-survivors, and relationships highlighted in the global discourse on conflict-related sexual violence to date. Du Toit and le Roux (2020) contend, for instance, that a persistent bias exists against male victims-survivors in the emerging field of studying SGBV in conflict. These researchers argue that continuities exist between sexual violence during conflict and times of peace, but also between female and male victimization: "The very same template used to politically subjugate women as inferior to men under 'normal,' peacetime, patriarchal conditions, is also used to subjugate some individual men as subordinates under specific conditions such as armed conflict" (Du Toit and le Roux 2020: 121).

Improving the tools for data collection and analysis cannot occur in isolation from efforts to address the causes of SGBV under-reporting. Given the significant under-reporting by victims-survivors in societies that have only recently recognized types of SGBV as a criminal offense, official reports (from governments, UN, and international rights agencies) are but one source to indicate the patterns of violence. The variety of gendered political violence experiences means that official reports may not reflect which groups of women and men, boys and girls are most vulnerable to SGBV or the specific obstacles to reporting violations they may face.

What happens when we take silence or nonreporting seriously, which is necessary in contexts with limited awareness, data, and reporting of

SGBV, such as in Asia's civil conflict settings? How do we learn about this violence, which is notoriously condoned, accepted, under-reported, and underappreciated? Scholars may need to look to other methods to understand where SGBV is occurring and who is most likely to be affected, a topic we turn to next.

Identifying Silences

Silences in reporting can be identified and investigated with qualitative methodological approaches that can shed light on SGBV within locations that are vulnerable to conflict. Feminist methodology can improve positivist data collection methods and recommend strategies for improving estimates (as is done with maternal health service uptake in conflict and postconflict situations where accurate data collection is not possible, see Chi et al. 2015). Also, inspired by data collection approaches to detect early-warning reports of infectious disease outbreaks, internet surveillance epidemiology approaches such as ProMED and HealthMap have provided guidance on how to approach open-access data collection—news articles and open-access nongovernmental organization reports—as sources for documenting SGBV events (Bhatia et al. 2021). We wanted to know what SGBV crimes are reported, if any, in these protracted conflicts, and which crimes are the most regularly reported.

As such, the purpose of this research is not only to reveal patterns and anomalies in SGBV but to prioritize new investigation methods and to highlight the limitations of existing analysis because of the exclusion of some communities from the production of institutional knowledge.

Feminist scholars know that silence does not mean absence of violence (Parpart and Parashar 2019). If SGBV is used to politically repress already oppressed populations, the value of such violence is in producing silence about where it occurs and who is targeted. The "effectiveness" of SGBV is that it is intended to "engender total submission by humiliating the community as well as the individual" where deep-seated gender norms produce particular narratives of acceptable violence and of how women and girls, men and boys, should appropriately manage injuries and behave in the private versus public spheres (Boesten 2022). In an environment such as Burma, where official reporting of SGBV and violence against women (VAW) is already restricted or minimal due to poor domestic practices and constraints on international organizations, the risk of such violence remains high for potential victims-survivors, communities, and those doing the reporting (as we discuss in Chapter Three in this volume).

The exception to silence is when the violated "purity" of women and girls is publicly reported with the intent of effecting political agitation between rival groups (Clark 2014: 468). Here the effect of gender norms is not only to ignite violence but also to produce bias in the documentation of SGBV. This leads to the second concern: that reporting SGBV has political power in the political-ethnic struggle. In the cases of Burma and Sri Lanka, the majority ethnicity is privileged. In the Philippines, minority ethnicity and religious status are protected. The use and regulation of bodies for sexual reproduction means that, paradoxically, women have a subordinate but central position within these ethnic and religious groups (see Korac 1998). For example, the state regulation of marriage, birth, and birth spacing targets women's roles as biological reproducers for the state's project, which privileges the dominant Burmese ethnicity (Hedström 2016). Until the end of the conflict in 2009, among the minority ethnic Tamil group, young women could be fighters, but their "ultimate" destination was motherhood—to symbolically and materially support the armed struggle in Sri Lanka (see Hedström 2022: 68; Gowrinathan and Mampilly 2019: 9). In Mindanao, Moro women are the object of political violence; the purity of their bodies reflects the family's honor (Sifris and Tanyag 2019: 411). Armed groups target girls and women in rival groups to instigate "clan" wars or *rido*. Women have reported that they often stay silent because reporting SGBV would be tantamount to a declaration of war (Sifris and Tanyag 2019: 411). Such gendered representations of women and men fuel the notion that women's bodies are legitimate sites of political violence and coercive control. The absence of reports of SGBV within a region occupied by a nonstate armed group, for example, may indicate the absence of violence but it may also indicate the absence of the opportunity to report safely.

A reflexive ethic of contextualizing, probing, triangulating, and cross-referencing different qualitative and quantitative data can meaningfully address silences and biases in the data with guidelines for low-intensity conflict settings. We need to understand the environments in which SGBV typically takes place and take into account the gendered social relations in the conflict region before, during, and after violent events to understand the quality and depth of reports on SGBV events and the barriers to reporting these events.

Identifying Locations of Restricted Reporting

Integral to contextualizing data or the lack thereof is research that examines the processes of reporting, including the institutions and mechanisms that facilitate or block it. We need to improve our knowledge of what enables and constrains the reporting of this type of violence. If SGBV is used to politically repress already oppressed populations, the value of such violence is precisely in producing silences about where it occurs and who is targeted. Like media commentators and the public, as scholars we ignore certain stories and listen to others, especially those involving "ideal victims-survivors" who have some social power and are less likely to be marginalized by multiple structures of oppression. According to Christie (1986: 18), an "ideal victim" is a person or category of people "who—when hit by crime—most readily are given the complete and legitimate status of being a victim." Such a person or category must be "strong enough to be listened to, or dare to talk, but at the same time weak enough not to become a threat to other important interests" (Christie 1986: 21). We need to be wary of data and reporting that are focused on ideal victims-survivors only and ask questions about other possible victims-survivors from less "ideal" groups.

As researchers, therefore, we need to identify locations where SGBV reporting is restricted or minimal due to poor domestic practices and constraints on international humanitarian actors. In these locations the risk of violence remains high for potential victims-survivors, and those doing the reporting. Locations with low SGBV reports may also be contexts with genuine grievances against the state. For instance, there may be few reports of nonstate armed groups committing SGBV crimes where those groups are connected to an insurgency vis-à-vis the state and the state is a known SGBV perpetrator. For example, in Burma, the state's failure to address sexual violence committed by government forces also permits nonstate armed groups to get away with this violence. Reporting SGBV is risky for individuals or organizations based in these communities and has minimum reward under the current immunity conditions for both military and nonstate armed groups (Macgregor 2015).

We need to pay attention to the multiple institutions and actors who may report SGBV in conflict situations and the impact of their presence on the patterns of reporting. Previous research reveals how difficult it is to achieve protection for SGBV victims-survivors in conflict situations. There may be few pathways to facilitate reports without further harming the safety of civilians. The risk of (unintended) harm is often greater than the perceived benefit of reporting from the perspective both of victims-survivors and humanitarian agencies on the ground (Schopper 2014; OCHA 2015). For example, we were told of the struggle in Burma between the need to report ongoing sexual violence and the harm that reporting could bring to different environments:

> Reports like that [a military rape in a village that gained international attention] actually increased the insecurity for survivors on the ground. . . . When we see reports like that come we see a drop in survivors reporting.[5]

Seeing Connections in the Data

The failure of political institutions and their agencies to record and prosecute SGBV is inseparable from the lack of research evidence on this violence due to little or no data and difficulties in obtaining them. Public and private cultures of silence, impunity, and shame have both stopped marginalized victims-survivors from reporting this violence and led to scant analysis of this violence. Gender-sensitive methodology, however, can help us to connect interpersonal to intergroup and overtly political types of violence and to elevate the status of available qualitative data and indicators of violence rather than assuming the absence of good SGBV data. The content of actual SGBV reports can provide important information on these connections, yet most organizations and researchers do not conduct content analyses of the data contained within reports. Content analysis also has the benefit of not relying on victim-survivor testimony, which can compound trauma and may not be essential for understanding SGBV's causes and consequences (Boesten and Henry 2018). In the next section, we outline our case selection and methodological approach to identifying and analyzing SGBV in Asian contexts of low-intensity conflict.

Selecting Comparable Cases in a Diverse Region

Theories on where and why conflict-related SGBV occurs have been developed largely on the basis of a single case or a small number of cases, with limited use of sources in global regions outside of Asia or including only one case study from Asia. Our study is focused on the Asian region, a diverse and expansive area in which we have selected three comparable cases of protracted civil conflict: Burma, Sri Lanka, and the Philippines. These cases are similar with respect to the presence of multiple ethnic and religious groups within the state and with postcolonial territorial contestations since independence. These cases also reflect differences in terms of the motivations for conflict with the existence of multiple subnational conflicts, dynamics of ethnonationalism, and religious extremism or separatism. We could have chosen other cases in the Asian region to explore, such as Nepal, Indonesia, or Afghanistan. However, these three cases were deemed the most feasible and most comparable.

All three country cases have experienced low-intensity conflict (battle deaths annually of twenty-five to one thousand) over the 1998–2016 period, with some variation in the number of conflict-related SGBV reports. For instance, both Burma and Sri Lanka were listed on the UN Secretary-General's list of situations of concern for conflict- and postconflict-related sexual violence during 2008–2021, while Mindanao in the Philippines was never listed.

Using the in-depth case study method, we do not seek to explain a definitive outcome of interest—conflict-related SGBV and why it occurs or not—since conflict-related SGBV is known to be under-reported in all cases, possibly even more so in low-intensity conflicts. Rather, we aim to understand why and how conflict-related SGBV is reported or not; moreover, we want to test our theoretical assumption that the conditions for reporting are a major factor, amongst other factors, that affect our knowledge of conflict-related SGBV in Asia. Comparative analysis in this study helps us to untangle when reporting is meaningful and to clarify which factors and their combination are associated with the reporting or nonreporting of SGBV crimes in low-intensity conflict settings.

Interrogating Silences with Mixed Methods

Our approach to interrogating SGBV silences involves analyzing patterns, gaps, and absences in the contents of official (government and intergovernmental) and unofficial (nongovernmental and media) reports. This methodology purposively contextualizes SGBV data within conflict dynamics, political struggle, and local understandings of gender relations, while examining how these dynamics affect the opportunity for victims-survivors and others to report SGBV.

We coded and analyzed the content of SGBV reports for Burma, the Philippines, and Sri Lanka using the detailed ICC definition of SGBV, including the elements of these crimes. This definition enables actors to document and report SGBV as crimes of international concern—which made particular sense in these three Asian contexts, given that the paucity of domestic legislation available to guide reports on SGBV crimes has led to local reliance on international definitions to call for investigations and legal reform (Faxon, Furlong and Phyu 2015: 468).

A report was coded when at least one listed SGBV crime was mentioned or the term "sexual violence" or "gender-based violence" was present. Reports on domestic violence or violence against women were coded separately. We followed the guidance of the Office of the ICC Prosecutor (2014L 22) and the Office of the High Commissioner for Human Rights (OHCHR 2014) on the sources of information that may be taken into account and designated as official (government and international organization reports) versus unofficial (media and civil society or nongovernment organization reports) when building a profile of SGBV reports.

We paid attention to a broad range of SGBV locations, perpetrators, and types, seeking to determine whether victims-survivors were adult males, adult females, or children (reported as boys, girls, children). We documented reporting timelines in order to identify patterns within the conflict dynamics of each country over the same period of time. To facilitate longitudinal analysis, we created a database to code all reports of "sexual violence" and "gender-based violence" by year. Several further dimensions of each SGBV report were individually coded as shown in Table 2.1: the type of SGBV reported; the perpetrator(s) reported and whether they involved government or nonstate armed groups, identifiable by uniform or not; whether a group was targeted; the site of the violence; and the timing of the report (lagged or in the same year).

Three sources were used to collect SGBV reports: the UN document reference site UNHCR RefWorld; Factiva, a DowJones news aggregator site; and Universal Human Rights Index Search. Each of these searches produced, on average, 1000 reports from governments, intergovernmental organizations (IGOs), nongovernmental organizations (NGOs), and media. Our dataset coded 5496 reports of SGBV in the three Asian low-intensity conflict countries from 1998 to 2016.

The collection of reports allowed us to identify who routinely reports SGBV, who is routinely reported as a perpetrator, and who is routinely

Table 2.1 Coding SGBV Reports

Variables	Coding questions	Coding Entries (Y/N for Italic entries below)
1. Reporting Source	Who is reporting these crimes?	*Official Source* Governments - National government - Other governments, e.g., US State Department country reports on human rights violations by security forces - National human rights institutions - Regional organizations, e.g., European Union, European Parliament, ASEAN, OSCE, NATO, international organizations - UN Security Council - OHCHR including treaty committees, HRC - UN Secretary-General reports and Special Representative annual reports *Unofficial Source* - International and national NGOs / civil society organizations - International NGOs field reports, e.g., Amnesty, Human Rights Watch, Oxfam, Save the Children, International Alert, International Crisis Group. - Local NGOs / political actors / civil society (field reports), Burma Women's League, National Democracy Union in Burma, etc. *Media Source* -Reports from newspaper source(s)
2. Location	Where are these crimes being committed?	*Home; Village; Roads; Prison; Jail; Military compound (state); Military compound (non-state armed group, NSAG); Border Checkpoint; Refugee/IDP camps*
3. Political Violence	What is the situation (of violence) where these crimes are committed?	*Minor conflict* (over 25 to 999 deaths); *War* (over 1000 deaths)

Table 2.1 Continued

Variables	Coding questions	Coding Entries (Y/N for Italic entries below)
4. SGBV crimes	Which crimes were committed?	*Gender-based violence* Crimes committed against persons, whether male or female, because of their sex and/or socially constructed gender roles that 'results in or is likely to result in physical, sexual, psychological, or economic harm or suffering, including threats of such acts, coercion or arbitrary deprivation of liberty, whether occurring in public or in private life.' (UNGA 1993).
		For the purposes of this dataset, coding for gender-based violence excludes sexual violence. Reports refer to attacks on women and girls, and men and boys, because of their gender: i.e. attacks or arrest for homosexuality; forced nudity or strip searches at checkpoints; forcible removal of children from parents.
		Sexual violence Crimes listed in 1998 Rome Statute as acts of violence that constitute acts of genocide (Article 6), crimes against humanity (Article 7) and war crimes (Article 8).
		The Rome Statute and the ICC Elements of Crimes list crimes of sexual violence which may occur during conflict and in the absence of conflict. Acts include: rape, sexual slavery, enforced prostitution, forced pregnancy, forced abortion, enforced sterilization, or any other form of sexual violence.
5. Perpetrators	Who is reported as mostly committing these crimes	*Armed group**—state or non-state armed group (NSAG) *Civilian*—individual or group of civilians *Unknown*—not stated or unknown
		*If *Armed* we would further establish:
		State (military, police, paramilitary); *NSAG* (non-state armed group)—title of group will be listed, i.e. LTTE (Sri Lanka), CPP (Mindanao) or referred to as 'armed rebels' or 'rebels' or 'ethnic armed groups'; *Unknown*

(continued)

Table 2.1 Continued

Variables	Coding questions	Coding Entries (Y/N for Italic entries below)
6. Group Targeted	Which groups were targeted for these crimes	*Ethnicity; Religion; Political opposition; Economic/resources;* OR *Other*
7. SGBV Count	How many crimes are reported	*Report(s) 10 or less; Reports 100 or less; Reports 1000 or more*
8. SGBV Victim(s) Gender	Who was targeted	*Male; Female; Unknown*
9. SGBV Victim(s) Age	What was age of those targeted	*Adult* (18 or above); *Children* (17 or below); *Unknown*
10. Timing	When are these crimes reported	*Reported in the same calendar year as the crime committed; Reported year after the crime committed; Reported two years or more after the crime*

reported as the target of the violence, and to notice the gaps and absences. We analyzed at the same time the relationship between coded dimensions of the SGBV reports and major contextual factors, such as the conflict phase and toll of battle deaths, key crisis events including natural disasters, the degree of gender discrimination and inequality, and the presence of international humanitarian actors and media attention in the country. The content of the reports was analyzed and correlated with these macro patterns, then supplemented by in-country interviews with key actors responsible for reporting and recording SGBV; this approach enabled us to probe further the SGBV reporting trends and silences. In particular, we were able to highlight conflicting information between the aggregate reporting trends on the public record and the firsthand accounts through confidential interviews with those working in the country and in conflict-affected communities.

Patterns and typologies of conflict-related SGBV have bias and exclusion problems. Datasets on SGBV may have this problem where the source material itself has been affected by bias in what to report—whether due to politics, the stability of the location, poor or no funding, and degree of public interest. Reports and data collection based on this data are also beset with the very real problem of what to include and exclude. The repertoire of SGBV is complex, large, and unwieldy. Choices have to be made, but these choices affect our knowledge of SGBV patterns, typologies, and locations. We wanted to know whether "unofficial"[6] and media reports could provide an alternative "real-time" source of knowledge about the patterns of SGBV that might overcome bias and inclusion/exclusion limitations. To maximize the information that we can include about SGBV patterns we studied official (government) reports and unofficial media reports, which adhered to a standardized contextual coding analysis protocol. We then compared the reports we identified with existing narratives about the types and practice of SGBV available in the literature for each conflict.

Our approach does have limitations. In contrast to other studies, the database informing this study does not record the intensity or scale of SGBV (Cohen and Nordås 2014). Rather, it compiles information on SGBV reported, where and when it takes place, and in what context. It does reveal that a pattern exists for the nonreports and their locations and to the nonreported actors during specific phases of conflict. The impact of significant events, including but not necessarily conflict events, can be discerned. For instance, we find that the presence of INGOs and NGOs in the country increases SGBV documentation that is unrelated to the conflict. As researchers in this field have long known, increased opportunities to report and record SGBV may not mean increased violence. But researchers have a crucial role in documenting silences and the lack of opportunities to report SGBV as a first step in breaking these silences. The lack of research on SGBV in contexts where we do not think it is happening maintains cultures of silence and impunity.

Conclusion

Conflict-related SGBV is a social and political phenomenon, as are the knowledge, sources, and data about it. Gender discrimination and inequality affect our knowledge of where this violence is taking place, and of who the perpetrators, the targets, and the victims-survivors are. Mixed-method research can improve data collection and interpretation of this data, suggesting new strategies for estimating SGBV occurrence where accurate data collection is not possible. This research approach not only reveals patterns and anomalies but highlights the limitations of existing analysis because of the exclusion of some communities from the production of institutional knowledge. Feminist reflexivity encourages us to understand the limits of all methods of data collection and to use multiple methods where possible in order to promote inclusionary inquiry that recognizes the political concerns of marginalized groups and the political power of those gathering the data.

In the following chapters (three, four, and five), we examine SGBV reporting between 1998 and 2016 in three Asian countries: Burma, Sri Lanka, and the Philippines. Each of these countries has a history of protracted armed conflict before and during the time in which the reports were collected. All three chapters adopt a similar structure in order to build towards comparative analysis of the patterns of SGBV in Chapter Six. Each chapter presents the conflict background including the extent and type of human rights abuses, gendered impacts of the conflict, and ongoing peace processes (Burma and the Philippines) or cessation of hostilities (Sri Lanka). Then, each chapter turns to existing narratives on SGBV incidences and patterns relevant to the country's conflict and presents how SGBV has been understood to date. Set against this state of the existing knowledge, we present our dataset on the events reported in each conflict over the 1998–2016 time frame, and the insights from examining the pattern of SGBV reports in conjunction with the patterns of each conflict. Last, in the case study chapters we present our analysis of how the coded reports complement but also contrast with the narratives of the existing conflicts. Each chapter reveals significant differences in the reporting patterns and the knowledge ascertained from the reports that is meaningful for understanding how SGBV reporting might inform prevention (including early warning) and protection responses. We probe these differences, their significance, and our interpretation of reporting silences in Chapter Six.

3
Interrogating Rumors

Beyond the "Rape as a Weapon of War" Narrative in Burma

Burma (also referred to as Myanmar)[1] has experienced multiple protracted conflicts before and after independence from British rule in 1948. A military coup in 1962 was followed by diplomatic isolation, sanctions, successive failed ceasefires, and failed attempts at democratization. During the period of study in this chapter, 1998 to 2016, Burma was undergoing significant political reform and attempting to broker the largest national ceasefire agreement worldwide with numerous combatant groups. We examine the case of Burma to illustrate the pattern of sexual and gender-based violence (SGBV) reports in a situation where multiple armed conflicts collide with significant gendered inequalities and targeted state discrimination against ethnic and religious minority groups (Ma and Kusakabe 2015). The conditions of systemic gender inequality in that society coupled with the highly politicized nature of this protracted conflict in a militarized state severely constrain the extent and type of SGBV reported in Burma. Our research is concerned with understanding the incidences of SGBV that are not reported, and not counted, and about which there is a generalized silence in Burma.

Conflict Background, 1998–2016

Thant Myint-U describes Burma as a "place of many isolated communities, each with its own dialect and way of life, as well as grand civilizations with connections in every direction" (2019: 8). Dynasties reigned, and kingdoms fought back invasions and conquered new lands. The British arrived in the early 1800s and successfully attacked Burmese forces. In 1824, lands once part of Burma's territory became part of "British Burma." A series of conflicts continued against the British as the Burmese king tried to hold on to Upper Burma and recognition as an independent state. The third war began in 1885 and was decisive. The thousand-year-old Burmese monarchy ended: "The modern state of Burma was born as a military occupation" (Myint-U 2019: 16).

Land, rice, oil, and timber were extracted, and labor was exploited under colonial rule. Demand for representation within the British Empire led to the creation of a Parliament in 1922 and separation from India in 1937. Tensions between Burmese and Indians were high during these decades. The independence movement wanted to re-create a "Burmese" nation led by a Burma National Army. During the Second World War, the Japanese invaded and trained the National Army (Burmese nationalists). Half a million Indians fled Burma, the British withdrew, and bombing devastated the country and economy. The British returned in 1945 but soon left, and Burma was declared independent on 4 January 1948. Communists, ethnic nationalists, democratic socialists, and militia groups fought for control. Within months the country was experiencing civil war. The Karen ethnic group and the Communist Party of Burma were amongst the first nonstate armed groups to revolt against the central government, followed by the Arakanese, the Kachin, and the Mon (Charney 2009). The government imposed martial law to end the uprisings. Democracy held until 1962, when the military took power in a coup. Seven decades of civil conflict followed. As a result, Burma has experienced the most protracted civil conflict in Southeast Asia. Conflict has mainly played out in rural ethnic areas, with the military junta often engaged in brutal crackdowns on protestors and political opponents. The economy suffered as the military regime closed off the country, and international sanctions intensified after the military brutally suppressed protestors in 1988—and then again in 1990 after the military refused to acknowledge the results of a parliamentary election.

The Uppsala Conflict Data Program (UCPD) puts the total battle-related deaths in Burma for reports of SGBV (1998–2016) in the period we examine at almost 4900.[2] Due to the civil war, there are large, displaced populations in the country and refugee populations on the Thai-Burma border, as well as the China-Burma, India-Burma, and Bangladesh-Burma borders. By the end of 2016, over half a million people (644,000) from Burma's total population remained displaced inside Burma due to conflict.[3] Numerous NGOs and rights groups have documented indiscriminate attacks, imprisonment, and unlawful killing of civilians (IHRC 2014; AI 2016; UNHRC 2022a). In 2006 the UN General Assembly Special Rapporteur on the situation of human rights in Burma stated, "Among the most tragic features of the military campaign in ethnic areas is the disproportionate effect on civilian populations.... The killing, terrorizing, or displacement of civilians is often part of a deliberate strategy" (UNGA 2006: para. 47).

Between 1995 and 2008, an intensified effort by the Tatmadaw (Burmese military) battalions led to the "doubling" of force deployment across the country to end the civil conflict. Heightened eviction, relocation, and displacement with attacks in villages took place in the Karen, Mon, Shan, and Karenni states as well as in Arakan in the west (UNGA 2007). Between 1996 and 2006 the UN Special Rapporteur documented an estimated 3077 separate incidents of targeting villages in eastern Burma alone, displacing over a million people (UNGA 2007). Some nonstate militia groups, on orders from the Burmese military would commit atrocities or "one-sided violent" attacks against populations, and the Burmese military itself committed a number of one-sided attacks (see Graph 3.1).

In 2007, protests in Yangon again took place against the military junta, followed by further brutal suppression. In May 2008 the worst recorded natural disaster, Cyclone Nargis, completely devastated the country: 84,000 were confirmed dead, and 53,000 remain missing. Over two million people were displaced in a country of fifty-three million, approximately 5 per cent of the whole population (HRW 2010; IFRC 2011).

Originally, the Burmese government refused international assistance, but the extent of the disaster and suffering led to a direct appeal for humanitarian

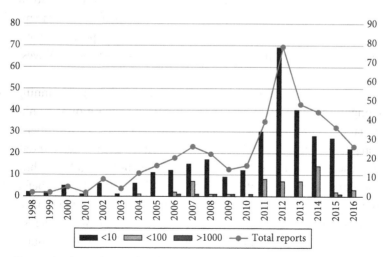

Graph 3.1 Total Conflict-Related SGBV Reports in Burma, 1998–2016

access by the Association of South East Asian Nations (ASEAN) secretary-general Surin Pitsuwan and United Nations (UN) Secretary-General Ban Ki-moon, which eventually led to relaxation of the flow of international aid and humanitarian workers (Haacke 2009).

In the same month, the State Peace and Development Council (SPDC) continued with its constitutional reform. The 2008 Constitution was the foundation of Burma's democratic and peace processes, but it was also one of the main obstacles to any peaceful resolution of the civil war: the Constitution was deliberately drafted to preserve the Tatmadaw's supremacy in national politics (Wansai 2017). The Constitution reserved 25 per cent of seats in Parliament for the military and granted the military veto power over any constitutional amendments (Myoe 2016: 139n8). At the November 2010 parliamentary elections, the government party, the Union Solidarity Development Party (USDP), won 75 per cent of the seats available. However, different ethnic and political parties still ran for seats, and the introduction of regional assemblies in addition to the 650-seat Federal Parliament meant that the push for reform was growing stronger (Wilson 2010; ICG 2011a). In 2012 a by-election in a number of federal Parliament seats was held, and the opposition party led by Aung Sun Suu Kyi, the National League of Democracy (NLD), contested and won the majority of those seats. The promise of a 2015 national election was kept, and in November 2015 the NLD won the majority of federal Parliament seats. Prior to the November 2015 election, constitutional and parliamentary reforms had led to an easing of international trade sanctions by the United States and the European Union (Brunnstrom and Schectman 2015),[4] with Burma predicted to transition from a low to middle-income country by the next decade (ADB 2012). The peaceful November 2015 election led to further easing of sanctions, and foreign investment proliferated across the country.

The elections generated optimism that the world's longest-running civil war might end with eight ethnic and political armed groups signing the National Ceasefire Agreement (NCA) in October 2015, a government-and-military-led process that had begun in 2013. At the point when our data collection ends, 2016, the ceasefire had fallen short of the eighteen ethnic and political armed groups that the government hoped would sign before the November 2015 elections, but there was optimism that more ethnic armed groups would sign with the election of the NLD led by Aung Sang Suu Kyi (who was to become state counsellor). It was hoped that the NLD could bring together a coalition with ethnic parties in the Parliament to overpower the military bloc and achieve reforms that would reduce the military's hold over government institutions and ministries (Thant 2015).

By 2017 and 2018 Burma's peace process had come under threat after experiencing one of the worst cases of ethnic cleansing and genocide carried out against the Rohingya ethnic population, the majority of whom live in the Rakhine state, which has its own secessionist militia group (Arakan Army). Due to these crimes committed by the Tatmadaw and the Arakan Army, over a million people have sought asylum in Bangladesh, and 600,000 remain confined in camps within Burma. A fact-finding human rights mission under the UN OHCHR found that the Tatmadaw between 2017 and 2018 had committed acts of ethnic cleansing, genocide, and war crimes in Rakhine, Shan, and Kachin states against minority ethnic populations. Marzuki Darusman, chair of the fact-finding mission, stated that the Tatmadaw had "systematically targeted civilians, including women and children, committed sexual violence, voiced and promoted exclusionary and discriminatory rhetoric against minorities, and established a climate of impunity for its soldiers" (OHCHR 2018a). The mission also found that, while not on the same scale as the Tatmadaw, the Arakan Rohingya Salvation Army (ARSA) and the ethnic armed organizations (EAOs)[5] operating in Kachin, Shan, and Rakhine states had also committed serious human rights crimes, including extrajudicial killings, failure to protect civilians during attacks, destruction of property, forcible recruitment of civilians, and acts of sexual violence (OHCHR 2018b).

Burma's Nationwide Ceasefire Agreement sought to end a fifty-plus-year conflict amongst eighteen recognized combatant groups (ICG 2015), but the agreement failed to garner widespread trust. Violent conflict and mass displacement increased in the Kachin, Shan, Chin, and Rakhine states.[6] The renewed and large-scale ethnic cleansing of the minority Rohingya Muslim population in the Rakhine state—a group denied citizenship since 1982 (OHCHR 2018b)—was suspected to have been conducted to bring the Arakan Army into a bilateral ceasefire with the Tatmadaw. This did not succeed: the Arakan Army resumed intense conflict with the Tatmadaw in late 2017.

Despite the atrocities committed in 2017, State Counsellor Aung San Suu Kyi did not condemn the Tatmadaw. In fact, she presented Burma's defence in Gambia's case against the country at the International Court of Justice (ICJ) for alleged violations of the Genocide Convention against the ethnic Rohingya population in Northern Rakhine State. There was suspicion at the time that she did this to stall a military coup, but others suggest that the State Counsellor supported the expulsion of a population not considered "Burmese" (Selth 2019). Three peaceful federal elections were held in Burma in 2012, 2016, and 2020, in addition to state-level elections. Yet, by 2020 the nationwide peace process had not progressed beyond ten signatories; 80 per cent of Burma's ethnic combatants had not signed, and Tatmadaw's clearance operation of Rohingya from Rakhine had escalated into heavy fighting across Kachin and Shan states (Lintner 2020). Then, on 1 February 2021, the Tatmadaw disputed the November 2020 election result, which had again heavily favored the National League of Democracy and threatened the military's parliamentary block of seats. Burma senior general Min Aung Hlaing staged a successful military coup (Yamahata 2022). The 2015 Nationwide Ceasefire Agreement has remained in place, although the ceasefire is now in a stalemate with one of the largest ethnic armed group signatories—the Karen National Union / Karen Liberation Army—declaring the NCA to be nullified due to the coup (Loong 2022). Moreover, there was never any prospect of ceasefire with the largest armed rebel group, the Kachin Independence Organization / Kachin Independence Army (Tun 2019). Despite strong demand from signatory and nonsignatory ethnic armed groups for constitutional reform, including the creation of a formal federation system of government and an end to the Tatmadaw's domination and occupation of key ministries, such reform was never on the table (South 2018; Swe 2019). By 2021 all optimism ended. Since the military coup on 1 February 2021, the peace process has effectively stalled, and there has been a rise in conflict between armed political and ethnic groups against the military-installed government.

Civil Conflict–Related Abuses

Burma remains one of the poorest countries in Southeast Asia, with half the population living in extreme poverty (less than US$1 a day) (UNDP 2021). During the period examined in this chapter, poverty rates had started to decline, but the country was still one of the poorest in the region. Poverty levels have started to rise since 2017 due to the return of partial sanctions after the Rohingya genocide, the impact of the Covid-19 pandemic in 2020, and the return of complete sanctions after the February 2021 coup. Rural areas, where the majority of conflicts take place, have remained disproportionately economically vulnerable and poor (Schmitt-Degenhardt 2013; UNDP 2021). High maternal mortality rates and widely uneven access to health services among states and regions negatively impact women. For instance, 76 per cent of all maternal deaths have occurred in rural areas, compared to 23 per cent in urban areas (Lwin and Punpuing 2022). Women and children are particularly vulnerable to poverty, violence, and displacement, in the context of natural disasters and conflicts.

The UN Office of the High Commissioner for Human Rights (OHCHR) has had a Special Rapporteur on the situation of human rights in Burma since 1992; the UN Secretary-General has had a special envoy, now special advisor, on Burma since 1997. Both the OHCHR and UN Secretariat have produced multiple reports for the Human Rights Council, General Assembly, and the UN Security Council, which have led to annual briefings and meetings on the content of the received reports, which document egregious human rights abuses.[7] In 2006 the UN Department of Political Affairs formally briefed the UN Security Council on the situation in Burma, which has continued to the present day (informal briefings had been held prior). The Special Representative on Children and Armed Conflict has made representations to the Security Council about the recruitment of children by both the military and nonstate armed groups (since 2006)[8] and the Special Representative on Sexual Violence in Armed Conflict has documented widespread conflict-related sexual violence in Burma in every annual report (2012–2023) to the Security Council from 2012 to 2013.[9]

In such a highly militarized environment, sexual violence and abuse are common within the country and on the borders. During the doubling of force deployments between 1996 and 2008, one of the first comprehensive reports exposing widespread SGBV was published by a local women's rights group, the Women's League of Burma (WLB). WLB founding members played a vital role in documenting and reporting the various forms of SGBV that (primarily) women experienced. The Shan Human Rights Foundation, a founding member of the WLB, supported ethnic women groups' documentation of conflict-related SGBV events. In June 2002 Shan Women's Action Network (SWAN), also a founding member of WLB, and the Shan Human Rights Foundation (SHRF) Women's Desk released a report, *Licence to Rape*, which documented 173 rape incidents involving 625 women and girls in Central Shan state from 1996 to 2002. This report presented a pattern of SGBV committed by the (then) Burmese armed forces, Tatmadaw, where "rape[s] of Shan women as part of their anti-insurgency activities" were used as a "weapon of war" (SHRF and SWAN 2002: 7).

In 2004 the Karen Women's Organization (KWO)—with the collaboration of the Committee for Internally Displaced Karen People (CIDKP), the Karen Information Center (KIC), and the Karen Human Rights Group (KHRG)—published a report documenting acts of SGBV (rape) committed against Karen women by the Burmese armed forces between 2002 and 2004. Similar to the *Licence to Rape* report, the KWO documented a pattern of girls and women being targeted for rape in military-controlled areas, and during displacement when the armed forces were carrying out military offensives. The report's name, *Shattering Silences*, refers to the plural silences that women were enduring:

> It is very unusual for women who have suffered from rape and other sexual violations to reveal what they have been through because according to the customs and traditions among ethnic groups in Burma rape is a shameful thing to have gone through. Women are afraid of being looked down on or being belittled by the men in their communities if they talk about their experience. (KWO et al. 2004: 11)

These early reports were conducted and led by feminist organizations that were determined to bring the conflict to the attention of international actors. These groups were vital in initiating and influencing SGBV reporting, as we discuss in the section on SGBV narratives later in this chapter.

Women's Role in Burma's Fragmented Peace Process, 1998–2016

The 2008 Constitution guaranteed all persons' equal rights before the law (Section 347) and that the government shall not discriminate against any citizen based on sex (Section 348). However, many constitutional provisions limit women's political and economic rights. For example, the Constitution specifically permits the "appointment of men to the positions [in the civil service] that are suitable for men only," despite provisions preventing the government from discriminating based on gender (Section 352). The Constitution requires those who assume top-level leadership positions in the government and judiciary to be "well acquainted" with defense matters (Section 59(d)); the vast majority of Burma's armed forces are men, who occupy senior roles.[10] This constitutional stipulation hinders women's participation in the highest levels of government (AGIPP 2017: 7). The 1982 Citizenship Law remains in place and restricts full citizenship to those who can prove to have had resident ancestors before the first British annexation in 1824. This clause disproportionately discriminates against women: 54 per cent of Burma's stateless (those who do not hold citizenship cards) are women (Arraiza and Davies 2020). Women face higher obstacles and discrimination in seeking citizenship: unlike men, their citizenships rights are affected by marriage, and unlike men, they cannot confer their citizenship status to their children (UN Women and UNHCR 2018: iii).

Women's groups were quick to organize during the post-2008 period to improve female representation in Burma's political, economic, and social institutions, even if the military and legal institutions remained mostly exclusively male zones (Shwe et al. 2017). Under the authoritarian regime, many women's civil society networks had formed on the borders of Thailand, India, and China. From 2008 they started to return to seek establishment within Burma's incipient democracy (Pepper 2018). The WLB, the Women's Organizations Network of Burma, and, since 2014, the Alliance for Gender Inclusion in Peace Processes (AGIPP) are powerful organizations that unite women's groups across the country and transnationally (Peace Support Fund 2016: 10). After the 2016 national elections, The Asia Foundation (Minoletti 2016) attributed some of the 10 per cent increase in women's representation in the federal Parliament to AGIPP-led public campaigns on gender inclusion. . At the local level, ethnic chapters of these women's networks in Mon, Kachin, Karen, Mandalay, and Shan states run citizenship workshops, and shelter women and children from domestic violence (UNDP 2016). In the early years of the ceasefire agreement, there was unity among them to agitate for women's equal right to be at the peace table.

After the 2015 election, women's political representation increased from 4 to 14 per cent, and the result was attributed to the strong alliance within gender-equality-focused civil society (Minoletti 2016). Also significant was that, for the first time, civil society was contributing to decisions and processes within Burma's bureaucracy, including participation in discussion on the federal draft bill on violence against women (VAW) and a draft National Action Plan (NAP) on VAW. However, while the number of women politically participating was increasing, they were not altering the structural conditions through policy and legal changes: men, particularly the military, continued to determine the terms, conditions, and venues where women could speak (Salween Institute and WLB 2018: 9).

Burma's federal gains on women's inclusion in the political sphere did not filter into local politics at the village tract–ward administrator position level. Village administration remains the key interface between the central government and representation in large rural, often conflict-affected, populations. Here, women are grossly underrepresented. In one national survey, 42 women were elected to the position of village tract or ward administrator among a total of 16,785 positions (UNDP 2015: 18). The military or ethnic armed groups have greater control in rural areas, and gender stereotypes are more entrenched. Men tend to dominate the local political networks and voter education campaigns (Latt et al. 2017). There are also, of course, lower numbers of citizens in rural locations, especially amongst women, which leads to their exclusion from the political process (UN Women and UNHCR 2018: 12–13). At the state/region parliamentary level, women make up less than 10 per cent of state/region MPs, and all the township administrators are men. Generally, the highly influential EAOs have poor female representation within their senior decision-making and political structures, with few women being involved in central executive committees or the supreme councils of these organizations (Minoletti 2016: 9–11).

Finally, there were few opportunities to address grievances related to previous and continued human rights violations during the 1998–2016 period (ICTJ 2014). The 2015 peace process did not include any provisions to address past crimes. The political rhetoric in the peace process urged people to "leave the past behind," and the 2015 elected government seemed to agree. The peace process had little to offer concerning reconciliation or reparation processes to address previous and ongoing victims-survivors of conflict-related sexual assault. The lack of transitional justice was repeatedly identified as a significant gap in discussions on Burma's postconflict society (Faxon, Furlong, and Phyu 2015; Salween Institute and WLB 2018). It has also been suggested that not only the Tatmadaw were reluctant to address conflict-related SGBV crimes but also EAOs whose SGBV acts communities rarely discuss (Hedström and Olivius 2021: 388). Thus, not only did the NCA have no transitional justice mechanism: it effectively also provided immunity for signatories to the process.

As discussed next, progress on gender equality and women's representation in Burma's peace and security institutions was minimal during this period. The gains from women's representation in Parliament and the peace process were difficult to secure and build on with major obstacles placed on when and how politically active women could engage and pursue reform.

Women's Role in Peace and Security

Women's presence in key political, bureaucratic, and security institutions is minimal in the Burmese state as a result of entrenched male dominance and military control (OECD Development Centre 2019; TNI 2020). Traditional gender norms and stereotypes are deeply rooted and especially strong in rural areas and amongst displaced populations (approximately 450,000 to 800,000 people in Burma) (UN Women and UNHCR 2018).[11] The country's first anti-VAW legislation was drafted in the 2012–2015 Parliament but never put to vote. High rates of domestic violence persist across all states and regions (note: the only prevalence survey was conducted by the government in 2016 on "ever-married" women) (Larsen, Aye, and Bjertness 2021).

In 2013 a former Tatmadaw general, President Thein Sein negotiated the Nationwide Ceasefire Agreement (NCA) to commit the military, political, and ethnic armed organizations (EAOs) to a ceasefire. The first Panglong Conference, held in August 2016, created two tiers of representation and engagement for NCA signatories and nonsignatories: the EAO Peace Process Steering Team for signatories and the Delegation for Political Negotiation for nonsignatories (Dolan 2016). Men dominated both, and formal inclusion criteria did not encompass civil society organizations (CSOs). Likewise, the first list of members to the state-level and union-level Joint Monitoring Committees for the Ceasefire was male-dominated (AGIPP 2018).

The terms of the Burma peace process included organized informal representation with the creation of a civil society forum. However, there was no participatory civil democracy process to participate in the formal procedures. The framework for Burma's peace negotiations was laid out in the Framework for Political Dialogue, which recommended the creation of five working groups or committees: political, economic, security, social, and land and environment. The agenda of each committee and the final accord decisions are made by the Union Peace Dialogue Joint Committee (UPDJC). The Burma peace process structure, if viewed as a hierarchy, places the UPDJC above the five working committees and the state-level Joint Monitoring Ceasefires. The UPDJC can block membership to committees, veto committee recommendations, and determine the content of the Panglong Conference. A minimum of fifteen members are allowed on the UPDJC, with two representatives from the upper and lower houses of Parliament, the government, the Tatmadaw, EAOs, and registered political parties related to the peace process. The UPDJC meets every second month and must have 50 per cent consensus to move forward on a decision. It decides the procedures, the announcements, the dialogues, and the political framework (Myanmar Peace Monitor 2019).

Amongst the five working committees, only one—the social group—achieved female representation that equaled the aspirational goal in the agreement of 30 per cent women. Amongst the five-state level and one-union level Joint Monitoring Ceasefire committees, only two states—Mon and Taninthayri—had female representation (AGIPP 2018: 7). In the two primary NCA documents—the Nationwide Ceasefire Agreement and the Framework for Political Dialogue—there were seven references to gender and women ("gender" used when referring to discrimination; "women" when referring to terms of the agreement) (University of Edinburgh 2015). These references were repeated (with similar language) in the four documents. The references fell under three main themes:

1. Prohibition of conflict-related sexual attacks on women: sexual harassment, sexual violence, and rape or sexual slavery of women by the Tatmadaw and EAOs (yet the NCA also had an inclusion of immunity for all past crimes committed by Tatmadaw and EAOs).
2. Representation of women in the process where the agreement would "strive" to include a "reasonable number/ratio" of women representatives in the political dialogue.
3. Gender equality: no discrimination on the basis of gender, race, ethnicity (despite the 1982 citizenship laws upheld by the 2008 Constitution and the 2015 marriage, race, and religion laws permitting such discrimination) (AGIPP 2018).

The peace process documents also include references to women as refugees and having the right to own land (AGIPP 2017).

The language in the documents was noncommittal in terms of mechanisms and quotas to address gender equality and gender-inclusive provisions. The language implies minimal obligation to meet the suggested quota for women's representation: "a reasonable number," "where possible," "where desirable." There are no references to international women's rights instruments or agendas concerning SGBV, no specific references to relief and resettlement for women refugees, and no mechanisms for providing citizenship or gender-responsive programming in healthcare, education, and shelter for displaced populations (AGIPP 2018). In terms of women's representation, the state-level Joint Ceasefire Monitoring Committees should "do their best" to include participation of women. The Military Code of Conduct between the Government of Burma and EAOs includes prohibitions against sexual attacks on women and children—but no language is included on how to create gender-sensitive reporting processes and how to ensure that committees are represented with individuals responsible for responding to, documenting, and investigating these crimes (University of Edinburgh 2015).

Low- to medium-size conflicts continued in the Rakhine, Shan, and Kachin states (OHCHR 2018c). In 2017 an ethnic cleansing of six hundred thousand Rohingyas by the Tatmadaw light infantry brigade and associated paramilitaries took place in the Rakhine state. Tatmadaw jet and helicopter missile attacks continue across non-government-controlled territory. Humanitarian access to these territories was blocked by the Tatmadaw, and communities continued to rely on illegal and quasilegal systems of trade to survive. Some of the women's gender equality networks included groups that opposed the events that occurred in Rakhine, but other groups were silent (Kamler 2019). Managing ethnic tensions and distrust within women's groups took up as much time as gender equality and anti-VAW advocacy: "The ongoing challenge of inclusion in women's CSOs hinders the development of a coherent feminist agenda among rights defenders in Burma and threatens to further cement divisions and hinder progress around women's rights" (Kamler 2019, online).

The Joint Monitoring Ceasefire Committees were set up in locations where the peace process had begun—Bago, Tanintharyi, Kayin, Mon, and Shan. The task of the fourteen- to sixteen-member committees (government, EAO, and civilian) was to monitor the ceasefire and assess complaints that the government or military needed to resolve. Meanwhile, the standard operating procedures for assisting internally displaced persons (IDPs), most of whom were women, were still pending government approval (South and Joll 2016; Ye Mon 2017). The process for disarmament and demobilization did not progress during the short life of the NCA nor did any discussion on complaints procedures for populations subjected to war crimes, including SGBV by the Tatmadaw or EAOs (UNDP 2016: 166, 185–186; TNI 2017).

Existing Explanations for SGBV in Burma

Burma's culture of impunity represented in the peace process applies to all forms of VAW perpetrated by nonmilitary, armed, and nonarmed perpetrators. Despite great agitation from women's civil society networks, the Burmese Parliament has never adopted a law to prevent VAW. No law in Burma defines VAW in the public and private sphere (UNFPA 2015). One of the reasons such a bill continuously failed to progress to a vote in Parliament was the military block on it. In 2020, to present the bill to Parliament, all references to conflict-related SGBV were removed from the draft (Progressive Voice 2020). As it stands, Burma's Constitution already exempts military personnel from any legal process in civilian courts, and Burma's military code has no charge for sexual violence: all adding to a culture of impunity for Burma's military (Global Justice Center 2020; Patrick 2015). The struggle to address impunity speaks to broader concerns about the gendered roots of violence in Burma's conflict, with the prospect of immunity for past and present crimes of conflict-related SGBV by Tatmadaw and nonstate armed groups being a negotiated outcome of the National Ceasefire Agreement (Faxon et al. 2015; Hedström 2015).

To date, victims-survivors of VAW (including intimate partner violence, domestic violence, sexual violence, and sexual harassment with diverse victims-survivors and perpetrators) receive few government services, policing protection, or legal redress (Oo and Davies 2021). The population control and marriage bills passed by Parliament in 2015 further set back the rights of women as equals: the laws permit regional authorities to enforce control on birth spacing (directed in particular against Muslims and ethnic Rohingya population in the Rakhine state). In addition, laws require women to seek the permission of regional authorities to marry non-Buddhist men to ensure that women marry Buddhist men to have Buddhist children (Win 2015).

These new laws exacerbate ethnic divisions and dramatically highlight how women and women's bodies are viewed in Burma. The ethnic divisions within the country, fueled by the prevalence of poverty—especially in Chin and Rakhine states—have perpetuated the identity of women as birthing vessels for the reproduction of ethnic groups. Women are either enemies of the state because they give birth to unwanted populations or they are allies because they may continue the line of "Burma" children—or, in some cases, they further the population for nonstate armed groups' struggles. In Burma, this "politics of the womb" explains why decades of SGBV have been part of the pattern of political violence: the ethnic, religious, or political affiliations of minority-group women are exacerbated by their subordinate gender status (Win and Kean 2017). Laws that perpetuate this status are a danger not only for addressing the long-term structural inequality of women but also because they place women at high risk of ongoing SGBV in conflicts, as has already been seen in Burma.

Research and reports on widespread and systematic SGBV acts—attributed to the conflict in Burma—have sought to explain their prevalence and occurrence. Unlike the Philippines and Sri Lanka, the two other protracted conflicts examined in this book, there has been consistent association of sexual violence in particular as a tactic or practice in the Burma conflict. Consistent reporting of this violence has taken place since the early 2000s. The UN Security Council, the UN General Assembly, and the UN Human Rights Council have received reports for well over a decade of an established pattern of SGBV against civilians, mostly women, in areas where there is combat between ethnic armed groups (the or United Wa State Army [UWSA] and the Kachin Independence Army), political resistance groups (the Restoration Council of Shan State and the Karen National Union), and ethnic minorities (i.e., Rohingya) in Burma. The difference between the sexual crimes regularly committed by Tatmadaw soldiers against Kachin ethnic women, for example, and the sexual crimes committed en masse against Rohingya ethnic women in the 2017 ethnic cleansing of Rohingya from Burma into Bangladesh appears to be tactical. Kachin women have long experienced an individualized risk of sexual violence by Tatmadaw in locations with conflict between the armed groups and the military; these crimes are permitted and overlooked, rather than coordinated and systematic. By contrast, the Rohingya population experienced intense, coordinated waves of violence in 2012 and 2017 perpetrated against entire communities with the intent of expulsion—removing communities from villages. Rape and other acts of SGBV were carried out mostly against women but also men and children, especially in 2017.

There are two concerns with existing explanations for conflict-related sexual violence in Burma. The first is whether the SGBV atrocity crimes committed by Tatmadaw soldiers are coordinated (policy) or tolerated (practice) (Alam and Wood 2022; Ryan 2020; Willis 2021). There are undisputed instances where the Tatmadaw authorized ethnic cleansing that included acts of SGBV to secure the forced removal of populations, such as the clearance operations in the Rakhine state against the Rohingya population, and against the ethnic minority populations in northern Burma (especially Kachin and Shan) (OHCHR 2019). However, as Oatman and Majewski (2020) and Ryan (2020) identify, in a military culture with such high levels of impunity—indeed, an institutional legacy of impunity for over sixty years for all crimes committed by the Tatmadaw—this effort to make the distinction between policy and practice may be redundant. This debate reflects the larger discussion in Chapter One on the significance of the difference between instrumental or coordinated sexual violence versus opportunistic or tolerated sexual violence. Whether the crime was ordered or tolerated is a legal, a security-sector, and political concern, rather than a victim-survivor-centered concern. However, the distinction of order versus tolerance might have implications for reporting, as we examine later.

The second concern is whether the Tatmadaw is the only or the primary armed group perpetrating this kind of widespread violence. A smaller number of reports and research indicates crimes of sexual violence occur within ethnic-controlled areas with armed ethnic groups. Similar to some allegations against Tatmadaw, these crimes are reported as opportunistic acts intended to enforce gendered norms and social hierarchy within the community. The number of reports of ethnic armed organizations committing SGBV crimes is low compared to the number of reports about the Tatmadaw. Given that reports, rather than prosecutions, are the only measure available to trace conflict-related SGBV prevalence in Burma, how should one interpret the state military being more associated with these crimes than other armed groups? In the literature, this is not uncommon. The military is often easier to identify due to the uniform of the perpetrator, and community dynamics might be more disposed to hearing the identification of an "outsider" committing sexual violence than an "insider" (Hoover Green 2018). The importance of the perpetrator's identity in the case of Burma's conflict and reports of sexual violence is twofold: first, to ascertain whether the Tatmadaw are committing more SGBV acts than other militia groups in the same conflict and to understand why; and second, in an environment where any kind of SGBV reporting is difficult, to be sure that there are opportunities to report conflict-related SGBV crimes committed by all groups.

In the research and reports of SGBV associated with Burma's civil conflict, we can identify five common explanations for the patterns of violence observed during this protracted conflict. Two or more of these explanations are often provided in reports. For example, in the annual Special Representative of the Secretary-General (SRSG) reports on conflict-related sexual violence, the explanations provided for this violence in Burma often point to a culture of impunity and opportunity, ethnic targeting, ethnic cleansing, and war tactics.

The first two explanations focus on victims-survivors who are ethnic minorities most often living in conflict areas where they are an ethnic majority (e.g., the Shan in Shan state and Kachin in Kachin state) or an ethnic minority (e.g., Rohingya in Rakhine state). The first explanation is *ethnic targeting*, where the Tatmadaw (primary reported perpetrators) in an ethnic-controlled or ethnic-minority-populated area attack women of ethnic-minority status and commit sexual crimes against them to intimidate populations and to coerce compliance with Burmese authorities. These attacks are sometimes reported as coordinated crimes—that is, attacks on women-populated villages (due to men fleeing or fighting) where the Tatmadaw enter the village and individual soldiers commit sexual violence crimes against women (rape, forced nudity, strip searches), particularly during house raids. The attacks are also reported as opportunistic events, where an individual or a small group of Tatmadaw troops may assault one or two civilian women, for example, in conflict areas, where patrolling soldiers may assault women transiting on foot. The occupation of the Tatmadaw in "enemy territory" coupled with absolute impunity (under the 2008 Constitution) creates a permissive culture where ethnic women have no rights and "deserve" to be attacked.

The second ethnic-based explanation associates ethnicity with women, men, and children being targeted for SGBV, and these crimes are never described as opportunistic. In Burma, *ethnic cleansing* occurs when ethnic-minority populations are targeted for atrocity crimes, which includes SGBV, to intimidate and harm civilians and forcibly remove them from land and villages or isolate them from a majority-ethnic community. These crimes are distinct from opportunity crimes, and while most are often attributed to Tatmadaw, in some instances militia groups have been reported as conducting these crimes in cooperation with Tatmadaw and independently (e.g., allegations against the Arakan Army and UWSA) (OHCHR 2018a; 2018b: 11, 13, 17).

The third explanation is *war tactics*. Rape as a war tactic can be understood in two ways: a practice committed from "below" (by soldiers) or tolerated from "above" (by generals) (Wood 2018), or a coordinated policy that military and political leaders deliberately orchestrate to gain strategic and psychological advantage over the enemy (Benshoof 2014). Ethnicity, gender, and their intersection are the symptoms rather than the cause in this explanation. The underlying trend is the protracted conflict itself and the need for the Tatmadaw to conduct long military operations in enemy territory that require unit cohesion and 'privileges' for service. In the case of Burma, this explanation is attributed to the Tatmadaw more than militias and ethnic armed groups. The ethnic armed groups, living amongst the community, have to exercise control over their units and not permit violations against civilians. The "war tactic" argument—presented inter alia by SWAN (2015), Kamler (2015), Ryan (2020), and the Security Council (UNSC 2020)—has identified the Tatmadaw as using rape as a tactic of war that coincides with military operations. Reports strongly associate the Tatmadaw with gang rape, strip searches, forced nudity, and sexual torture. The Tatmadaw have institutional and cultural impunity because this is how the military has successfully operated for decades. This was what was so concerning about the impunity offered to the military under the 2008 Constitution and the amnesty provided to all armed groups under the 2015 NCA.

The fourth explanation is Burma's socially permissive *culture of opportunity* for SGBV. This perspective refers to the permissive culture of impunity for SGBV not only for Tatmadaw soldiers but also for the wider community. As discussed, no national law prevents VAW. Impunity for all past crimes was included in the 2015 NCA for all armed signatories, and armed groups offered minimal opposition to this amnesty (Karen were the exception). Unusual in the context of Burma, where most reports refer to the Tatmadaw as the primary perpetrators of sexual violence, discussions on Burma's culture of opportunity include additional SGBV perpetrators. It is common knowledge that some armed ethnic groups do commit acts of SGBV that go unreported, that both the majority Bamar and minority ethnic groups have high rates of SGBV within their own communities, and that religious institutions, especially Buddhism, provide protection for monks who target children and women in particular for sexual violence (Davies 2020; Oo and Davies 2021).

The fifth explanation is that conflict-related SGBV in Burma is the product of a culture of gender-based intimidation that arises in a *highly militarized and masculinized state*. The dominance of male representation in the political and security institutions in Burma affirms gender stereotypes such as women "belonging" in the private sphere as mothers and caregivers, and men "belonging" in the public sector as providers and protectors. This culture is reinforced by the threat of SGBV in a militarized state. In this setting, women who comply with gender stereotypes (e.g., stay at home, not engaging in political activism) "deserve" protection, and those who do not (e.g., walking outside of the village, undertaking political and social activism) "deserve" to be attacked. These stereotypes serve to keep women fearful and confined to the private sphere. Rigid gender stereotypes serve the national ethnic project in Burma: to promote the majority-ethnic Bamar amongst some political actors, including the powerful Buddhist organization Ma Ba Tha and the 969 Movement (Walton, McKay, and Kyi 2015). For example, the popularity of one female politician, Aung San Suu Kyi, is often attributed to the legacy of her father—independence leader Aung San—rather than to her own political skills. Her long political campaign is often presented as one of two acceptable gender stereotypes: "daughter" of Burma or "mother" of Burma, with emphasis on her Bamar ethnicity (Ho 2015; Lubina 2021). Prior to her arrest after the military coup in 2021, and despite being the leader of the party that won the majority in the 2016 and 2020 elections, Aung San Suu Kyi could only hold the title of State Counsellor. She has never been able to hold the presidency of Burma due to a constitutional provision that does not permit men and women married to foreigners to hold the presidency (Aung San Suu Kyi was married to a British citizen and had two children born from this marriage).

The extent to which the patriarchal state exercises authority over women's bodies in Burma is evidenced in the 2015 parliamentary laws adopted on the protection of race and religion (Walton et al. 2015). These laws include the Buddhist Women's Special Marriage Law, which requires Buddhist women and men from other religions who wish to marry to register their intention publicly. They may only get married if there are no objections. The Population Control Healthcare Law grants regional officials in charge of civic registration the right to enforce a thirty-six-month birth spacing rule for target ethnic groups. One intended consequence of this law is that ethnic-minority women are hesitant to register children born within the thirty-six-month space rule (OHCHR 2015a). Civic registration is essential for access to welfare services, land ownership, financial rights, and voting. These laws, in addition to discriminatory articles in the 2008 Constitution, reflect an ongoing legitimation of discrimination against women and a strong association of women's legitimate citizenship with ethnicity, religion, marriage, and reproduction. In such an environment, where gender-based discrimination is widespread, women's bodies become a site of political violence (Davies and True 2017a: 10). Women and their bodies are objects of cultural purification, nationalism, and patriotism. In ethnic-held territories, women's social reproduction roles are vital to maintaining conflict readiness, and their bodies are essential to reproducing the fighters necessary to continue the armed ethnic struggle and identity (Hedström 2016). Ethnic identity politics depends upon women fulfilling their "duty" to bear and raise children who will populate the community to continue the fight for recognition and representation.

SGBV, whether targeted, practiced, opportunistic, or tactical, stems from this prior understanding that bodies are part of the political struggle. What may be considered unusual about the Burma context is the paradox of reporting. Rigid gender norms and hierarchies remain, where openly discussing rape, domestic violence, and any type of gender-based violence in the community is unusual (Oo and Davies 2021). The prevalence of local silences contrasts with a strong feminist activism tradition of documenting sexual violence, reporting sexual violence, and demanding international engagement with the sexual and reproductive violence crimes occurring within Burma (Hedström and Olivius 2021).

Over the past twenty-five years, reporting SGBV occurring in Burma's conflicts to the international community has become an incredibly important part of political and ethnic opposition resisting the Tatmadaw. Who reports sexual violence to international communities creates the dominant narrative about the type of violence, victims-survivors of this violence, and the perpetrators. Reporting sexual violence has become a political act and possibly even a war tactic in the case of Burma.

Many of the reports rely on witness-based testimony and narrative accounts provided by interviews with those recording these crimes in the field. In the next section, we present a detailed analysis of all the reports published on SGBV in Burma territory between 1998 and 2016. As discussed, in Burma, dominant explanations already exist for the conflict-related SGBV typologies: mostly ethnic-minority women are the victims-survivors, Tatmadaw are the perpetrators, ethnic-held territory is the site of this violence, and rape is the dominant form of violence committed. We present the reporting data (see Chapter Two for methodology) with the intention of establishing, first, whether the trends we identify reflect the dominant crimes, perpetrators, and relationships as established in the literature to date; and second, does the pattern of reporting serve the political project—is the primary focus on armed/military issues—or does it also include reports that attempt to situate conflict-related SGBV within larger patterns of SGBV?

Our Data—Trends

The first thing to note about Burma from 1998 to 2016 is the reporting gap that grows between reports on sexual violence and reports on gender-based violence between 2010 and 2016. The rise of sexual violence reporting seems to be related to the country becoming more politically open but is also due to events. For example, the 2012 reporting peak is related to a series of retaliatory or revenge attacks that occurred against the Rohingya population in Rakhine state after a local report that local Rohingya Muslim men had gang raped a Rakhine woman (see Graph 3.1). This led to ethnic riots, which included a rise in sexual violence attacks (primarily documented as being attacks on Rohingya women during the mass exodus from villages). During this period of political opening, reports of sexual violence were double those of gender-based violence over the same (nearly) twenty-year period.

Conflict, Violence, and Perpetrators

If we look at the total fatalities due to conflict type that occurred within Burma over this period and compare these conflict types with the total SGBV reports we coded, we see that state-based violence fatalities have a stronger correlation with SGBV events (Graph 3.2). The occurrence of one-sided conflicts and nonstate violence does not seem to affect peaks in SGBV at the same volume as state-based violence.

The total counts of SGBV per report over this nearly twenty-year period document attacks against individuals that number fewer than 10 (see Graph 3.3). Reports of "widespread" attacks against populations that range between ten and one hundred appear at particular intervals over this period of time (2001, 2004, 2006, 2007, 2008) with a substantive rise in 2011, 2012, 2013, and 2014—then a decrease in 2015 and 2016. Reports of over one thousand people being subjected to rape only appear between 2006 and 2010, and then once more in 2015. What is consistent about the perpetrators identified in all of these is that the violence was associated with armed attacks. Between 1998 and 2016 the vast majority of perpetrators reported were armed individuals (see Graph 3.4). This high association of sexual violence with armed perpetrators is unique in the Burma case compared to the Philippines and Sri Lanka cases (except between 2011 and 2015). Burma presents a sustained and remarkably high number of reports of armed individuals and groups being identified as perpetrating SGBV compared to the identification of civilian perpetrators.

Gender-based violence is poorly defined in Burma: there is no national VAW law, and civilian courts are not permitted to investigate alleged crimes

76 HIDDEN WARS

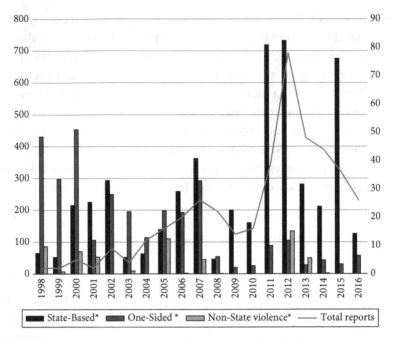

Graph 3.2 Total Fatalities by Conflict Type vs. Total SGBV Reports in Burma, 1998–2016

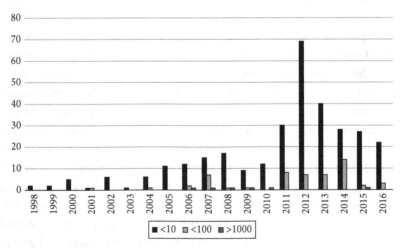

Graph 3.3 Total Victims-Survivors per SGBV Report in Burma, 1998–2016

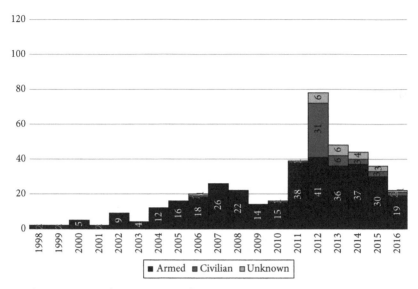

Graph 3.4 Reported Perpetrators of SGBV in Burma, 1998–2016

by the Tatmadaw. There are few reports of criminal investigation procedures for sexual violence crimes amongst armed ethnic groups (WLB and AJAR 2017). There are also few reports of armed perpetrators *not* identified as Tatmadaw as committing acts of conflict-related SGBV (see Graph 3.5). In interviews conducted in the field in 2015 and 2018, we were told about incidences of SGBV—including forced marriages, strip searches, sexual assault, and limited access to sexual and reproductive health care—occurring within conflict communities (Davies and True 2017a; Davies 2019). These same communities are often in remote locations, with little access to humanitarian and social welfare services. There is heavy dependence on ethnic armed groups for safety and resources, and these depend on the community. The Burma case reveals that reporting all types and events of SGBV can be a selective process. The decision to report depends upon a clear definition on what is to be reported, but also for first-responders' certainty about the consequence of reporting. Local actors may be unwilling to provide this detail if they cannot guarantee the safety and confidentiality of victims-survivors (Davies and Oo 2021).

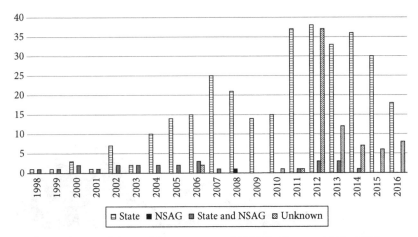

Graph 3.5 Reported Armed Perpetrators of SGBV in Burma, 1998–2016

Reporting Sources

What is also different about the Burma case is the high number of unofficial reports of SGBV (see Graph 3.6). Burma has a higher number of unofficial actors who are reporting this violence compared to official

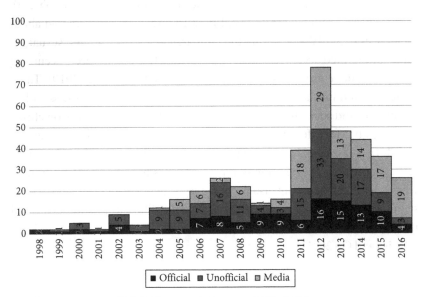

Graph 3.6 Sources of SGBV Reports in Burma, 1998–2016

INTERROGATING RUMORS IN BURMA 79

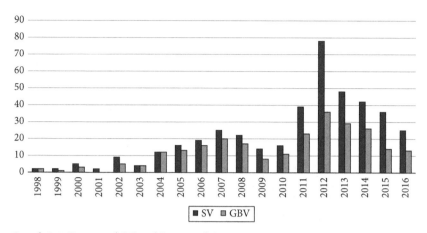

Graph 3.7 Reported SV and Reported GBV in Burma, 1998–2016

(government) reports and media reports. This again is different from the Philippines and Sri Lanka. The Philippines, as Chapter Four discusses, has a much higher volume of media reports, whereas Sri Lanka has a high number of formal and media reports (see Chapter Five). Burma is the only case where the majority of reports on all forms of SGBV are sourced from unofficial reports.

Reporting of gender-based violence may indicate, as we established in fieldwork interviews, local taboos about what gender-based violence is acceptable to be reported as occurring *within* the community. This is upheld in the reporting data: the majority of sexual violence is reported as conflict-related and linked to Tatmadaw perpetrators, whereas the perpetrators of gender-based violence have a more mixed profile of civilian and armed groups, and these reports are less numerous (see Graphs 3.7 and 3.8). Community-level violence may not be perceived as related to the conflict and therefore is not reported by those who are doing the majority of reporting: unofficial actors.

Location

In Burma, the majority of locations where SGBV is reported are in areas that are "unknown," followed by village locations (see Graph 3.9). In the 2011–2013 peak period we see a high occurrence of attacks in villages.

80 HIDDEN WARS

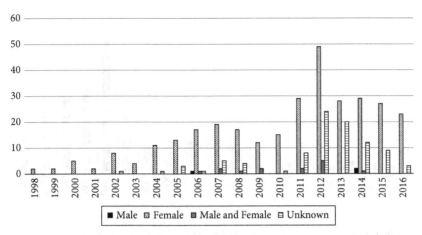

Graph 3.8 Reported Victims-Survivors by Gender in Burma, 1998–2016

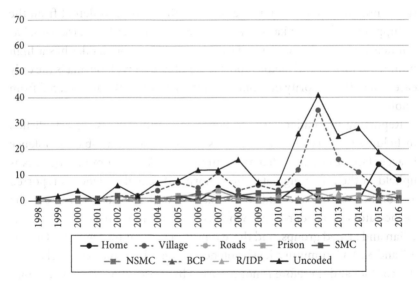

Graph 3.9 Reported Locations of SGBV Crimes in Burma, 1998–2016

This is followed by a number of attacks that occur in the home, followed by a steady number of reports of violent attacks taking place in state military compounds. The reports indicate that danger of and exposure to violence are highest at the village level followed by the home level—but there is also a sizeable risk of experiencing SGBV violence at state military compounds and in prison locations. There is no report of violence occurring in a nonstate military compound, and the number of attacks in internally displaced persons (IDP) camps is reported as low.

Location data clearly reveal reporting limitations. Providing the details of location may be dangerous for victims-survivors' families. Unofficial reporters are able to gain access to communities, which may explain why reports identify villages followed by homes as the highest sites of violence. These locations may indeed be where the majority of violence occurs, which correlates with the trend identified: contested territories with high ethnic group representation (i.e., villages/wards) are the sites where SGBV occurs in Burma's conflict. There may be difficulty with being able to access camps or report the type of sexual violence that occurs there. There may be reluctance amongst unofficial groups, who do the majority of SGBV reporting, to expose the violence that may be occurring within communities due to the political project of reporting: to focus on the violations of international law by state military conducting SGBV. It is unusual for so few reports of SGBV to be coming from displacement camps (cf. the Sri Lanka and Philippines chapters), but in Burma these camps are often controlled by a particular armed group (usually ethnic) and are populated mostly by women and children.

Burma has no shortage of reports on especially sexual violence occurring in conflict locations. Reports are primarily sourced from unofficial sources—local and national NGOs that conduct their own investigations. The presence of international humanitarian actors in the conflict-affected areas within Burma, especially the displacement camps, is modest compared with other conflict situations like South Sudan or the DRC.

Analysis: Localized Conflicts, National Politics, and Gender Discrimination

In the case of Burma, reporting on the SGBV situation has been consistent since 1998. The majority of reports refer to mostly sexual crimes being perpetrated against women and girls. The extent of reported violence is countrywide but focuses particularly on the conflict locations in East, North, and South-East Burma (i.e., Kachin, Rakhine, Chin, and Shan states). A smaller number of gender-based reports relate to the forced marriage of women and girls and cross-border trafficking for the purpose of sexual exploitation. Few of the reports refer to conflict-related SGBV being committed by armed actors who are not the military.

Investigating and reporting SGBV are not impartial acts. In the case of Burma, the pattern of reporting SGBV reveals some truth in all of the explanations provided in the literature to date: an association between this sexualized violence and ethnic targeting, ethnic cleansing, practice, opportunity, tactical reasons, impunity, and culture. The reports reveal the importance of both political reform and international actors' arrival to create safe conditions for the local actors who are investigating and reporting. Local actors were risking their lives to compile reports prior to the political reform that began in 2008. It is arguably no coincidence that the growth of reports in the 2010s coincides with Burma's most democratic decade since its independence. It might also be noted that a broader array of international humanitarian actors was formally permitted access into Burma after Cyclone Nargis in May 2008. The presence of these international actors may have contributed to improved economic and political conditions for more reporting. Even then, their access to areas and populations remained conditional on memorandums of understanding, or cooperative relationships with the central government, nonstate armed groups, and regional- and state-level administrations. International organizations located in Burma have reported SGBV, but it is a highly fractious political exercise. The country has no formal domestic violence reporting database, so knowledge is reliant on unofficial reporting sources.

Our findings from SGBV reports in Burma between 1998 and 2016 are threefold. First, it appears that Burma's significant abrogation of women's civil liberties and physical integrity affects reporting of the full range of SGBV. Reports of gender-based violence were surprisingly low compared to the reports of sexual violence (see Graph 3.7). The reports of perpetrators, particularly armed perpetrators, were overwhelmingly documented as the Tatmadaw (see Graph 3.5), despite evidence of nonstate armed groups committing SGBV. Reports tended to focus on rape and the ethnic targeting of women and girls.

Second, we observed that in a situation where impunity for SGBV crimes is widespread, as it is in Burma, there is greater reliance on media and unofficial reports of SGBV (see Graph 3.6). These unofficial and media reports are often not verified or corroborated by official sources (government and international organizations). Often these reports come from political and ethnic sources opposed to the government which, arguably, compromises the extent to which scholars and international organizations such as the UN can depend on these sources as verified and credible. The consequence is that legitimate grievances cannot be validated due to the government's insistence on impunity for crimes committed by military forces, but also the pervasive culture of restricted civil liberties and physical integrity for women and girls has limited the institutional redress for the designation of gender and sexual crimes as "low-order" crimes. This is apparent in the amnesty for SGBV crimes in the National Ceasefire Agreement (NCA), the VAW legislation, and the marriage and population control bills passed by Parliament.

Third, and finally, we noticed major gaps in the pattern of SGBV reporting in Burma. For example, reports were heavily influenced by first-time access to zones, such as the peak in the 2012 SGBV reports after international humanitarian actors were given access to the Rohingya population in the Rakhine state following a bloody confrontation between the ethnic Rakhine population and minority Rohingya Muslim population, most of whom are in displacement camps (see Graph 3.1). In general, reports on SGBV amongst displaced populations tended to be low—despite international acceptance that this type of violence in these communities is pervasive across Burma (see Graph 3.9). Last, we see the country opening up in association with the democratic transition from 2011, appear to facilitate more diversity in reporting the types of perpetrators committing these crimes (see Graph 3.5). Nevertheless, the number of reports of civilian and nonstate armed groups is still comparatively minimal compared to its counterpart against state actors.

Conclusion

Sexual and gender-based violence is a political project, as is its reporting. The Burma case illustrates three practical research difficulties of using SGBV reports to identify and prevent SGBV risk: reporting silences, reporting bias, and the culture of impunity for SGBV. These practical difficulties place knowledge constraints on scholarly explanations for conflict-related SGBV. The Burma case demonstrates the importance of not ruling out a variety of explanations for SGBV existing in the same theatre of conflict. Indeed, different motivations may be occurring—even for the same perpetrator such as the Tatmadaw—depending on location, group targeted, and conflict intensity. The case reveals the importance of contextualized knowledge, especially about the dominance of gender stereotypes within a society that establish how it is possible to inquire about the silences amongst some communities. This contextualized knowledge should also inform how we analyze and interpret reports of SGBV in low-intensity conflict situations.

4
Probing Silences

Sexual and Gender-Based Violence in Conflict and Peace in the Philippines

The Philippines has experienced prolonged Muslim separatist and communist insurgencies for the past fifty years, with the most recent being an Islamic State (IS)–inspired Islamist jihadist insurgency—the 2017 Marawi siege—where returning IS foreign fighters, originally from the country's second-largest island Mindanao, sought to impose an Islamic caliphate. Fifty years of conflict have severely affected development and security on Mindanao and beyond. These insurgencies must be understood in a broader context of violent histories of Spanish and American colonization, the dispossession of land from Indigenous communities, and the recent history of political authoritarianism. Political violence has spawned a host of other types of clan-based and organized violence that operate with impunity, especially in Mindanao. Despite ongoing protracted violence, over the last two decades (1997–2017) the Philippines government and the largest armed group in Mindanao, the Moro Islamic Liberation Front (MILF), agreed on a ceasefire in 1997 and a comprehensive peace process in 2014, ratifying this into law in 2017 to create the Bangsamoro Autonomous Region in Muslim Mindanao (BARMM) (replacing the former Autonomous Region in Muslim Mindanao). The peace process has been regarded as having some of the strongest measures to date concerning the inclusion of women as signatories, and as economic and social beneficiaries of the process (Davies and True 2022).

The 2014 agreement signed between the government and the MILF includes some comparatively strong gender-sensitive provisions. However, no prevention of sexual and gender-based violence (SGBV) provisions appear in the Comprehensive Bangsamoro Agreement (CBA). The lack of attention to conflict-related SGBV in the CBA is in contrast to the recognition of the government of the Philippines that conflict-related sexual violence has occurred during this conflict in its own statements and policy, including the 2010 and 2017 Philippines Women, Peace, and Security National Action Plan (NAP). In addition, there has been minimal discussion or reference to conflict-related sexual violence in the Philippines by the UN Office for the Special Representative on Sexual Violence in Armed Conflict and UN Secretary-General annual reports on CRSV. Moreover, there has been silence on the presence, scales and type of conflict-related SGBV perpetrated against populations in the Philippines' longest protracted conflict since its independence in 1946. This chapter explores the reasons for such overwhelming silence despite significant concessions by the Philippines government acknowledging the past use of conflict-related SGBV.

This chapter explores the 1998–2016 period, the key years in which the government of the Philippines and the MILF, the largest insurgent group in Mindanao, achieved a peace process that included positive commitments and gains for women's equal rights and security. However, efforts to implement substantive gender inclusions in the peace processes has also revealed significant gendered barriers to translating these inclusions into the political and economic empowerment of women in the postconflict BARMM. Collectively, there has been minimal progress in transitional justice mechanisms, security-sector reform, and disarmament, demobilization, and rehabilitation, especially concerning the issue of SGBV. These limited achievements indicate, we argue, a conspiracy of silence by the representatives of potential perpetrators, both the Philippines army and nonstate armed group insurgency forces. We find that while SGBV is acknowledged, it is rarely appreciated reported as "conflict-related." Instead, this violence is dissociated from conflict and attributed to the personalized culture of violence, impunity, clan wars, economic disenfranchisement, and displacement that primarily affect women, particularly Indigenous women, in the Mindanao region. There is minimal SGBV reporting in this region, and victims-survivors are reluctant to come forward to report their experiences of SGBV.

Conflict Background, 1998–2016

The Philippines is an archipelago made up of three major island groups: Luzon, forming the bulk of the northern islands and the location of the capital (Manila); the Visayas group, situated in the central part of the country; and Mindanao, comprising the southern group of islands. Mindanao accounts for approximately 4 per cent of the total Philippine population of nearly 101 million people, and 41 per cent of the country's land area (PSA 2016). The Philippines is a majority-Christian country due to three hundred years of colonial rule by Spain; much of the country's estimated 5 million Muslims are in Mindanao and have maintained a separate identity, calling themselves Moros (adapted from the term Moors referring to the Islamic occupiers of present-day Spain in AD 700). Although the Philippines declared independence in 1898, the United States, which gained colonial administration from Spain, did not grant the country independence until 1946 (AI 2008: 8).

When a Spanish colony was established in Manila in 1571, it was a small Muslim settlement of two thousand people, and in the southern Sulu province, an Islamic sultanate resided that was 120 years old, with a flourishing Islamic system of governance and a social infrastructure of mosques and schools (Stephens 2011: 3). The Spanish colonialists regarded Islam as a religion that needed to be weeded out and they attempted to convert Muslim and non-Muslim Filipinos alike to Catholicism. This began the systematic neglect and discrimination that Muslims in the Philippines would experience over the next several centuries (Stephens 2011: 3). Colonization by the United States following its acquisition of the Philippine colony from Spain in 1898 led to continued policies of discrimination; the United States encouraged huge Christian migration to Muslim-dominated areas and set unequal limits on private land ownership for Christians and non-Christians, which marginalized Muslims from land ownership in Mindanao (Abinales 2016). These colonial policies continued to be pursued by the government of the Philippines after Philippine independence in 1946.

The Jabidah massacre triggered a conflict in 1969, when Muslim soldiers in the Philippine Army were slaughtered after disobeying commands to conduct sabotage within Malaysian territory. The Moro National Liberation Front (MNLF) was founded in 1972, aiming to forcibly establish an independent state of Bangsamoro (Muslim Nation), covering Mindanao, Sulu, and the Palawan islands. In the early 1970s, a full-scale armed conflict erupted between the Philippines government and the MNLF, accompanied by atrocities committed by Christian vigilante groups such as the Ilaga (Jeffery 2018: 441). The Mindanao region descended into civil war. The conflict situation worsened when President Ferdinand Marcos declared martial law in 1972, primarily in response to a violent communist movement (ICG 2016: 2), discussed shortly.

Early peace discussions began with the assistance of foreign intermediaries such as the Libyan revolutionary chairman Muammar Qadhafi. The 1976 Tripoli Agreement was signed between the warring sides, outlining nominal autonomy, a separate Sharia (Islamic law)–compliant judicial system and independent security forces. Legislation followed to create regional autonomous governments in Western and Central Mindanao (ICG 2016: 2). However, the signing of the Tripoli Agreement sparked a rift within the MNLF, which led to the creation of the Moro Islamic Liberation Front (MILF) in 1977.

Following the end of twenty-one years of military rule under Marcos, Corazon Aquino gained the Philippine presidency in 1986. She ushered in a new constitution that, in addition to other democratic reforms, created space for greater and more meaningful regional autonomy, including the removal of constitutional impediments to Moro autonomy in Muslim Mindanao (ICG 2016: 3). With the assistance of the Organization of Islamic Cooperation (OIC), the MNLF signed the Jeddah Accord, a framework agreement, in January 1987. The group agreed to give up its two-decade fight for independence in return for autonomy. However, discussion about the proposed autonomous region collapsed, and the MNLF returned to armed insurrection in February 1988 (ICG 2016: 3).

A new president in 1996, Fidel Ramos, offered to expand the proposed Autonomous Region in Muslim Mindanao (ARMM) to restart the stalled peace process. The ARMM was renamed the Bangsamoro Autonomous Region in Muslim Mindanao (BARMM) in 2017.[1] The MNLF was close to signing the 1997 peace agreement, but the group fractured to produce the breakaway MILF, which returned to hostilities. In 2000 the MILF insurgency took over the town of Kauswagan, Lanao del Norte, and seized hundreds of hostages, which provoked then-president Joseph Estrada to declare "all-out war" on the group (ICG 2016: 3). The MILF had become the dominant armed group in Mindanao (AI 2009:11) with approximately twelve thousand troops operating in several command posts around the southern Philippines. However, the group claimed to have many more armed combatants—between seventy thousand and one hundred thousand (Hashim 2001; AI 2008: 9).

Peace talks between the Philippine government and the MILF have been going on since the group's formation. In 1997 the first ceasefire agreement was signed, but progress was slow and breaches of ceasefire were common. By 2006, MILF negotiators warned that the peace process was at serious risk of failure. Indeed, by June 2008, localized armed encounters between government security forces and MILF fighters began in several villages in North Cotabato. The fighting quickly escalated in several provinces in Mindanao, after the Supreme Court issued a temporary restraining order on the signing of the Memorandum of Agreement on Ancestral Domain (MOA-AD). The MOA-AD was to give broader political and economic powers to the Muslim leadership and widen the territories of the existing ARMM, but by October 2008 the Supreme Court ruled that the agreement was unconstitutional (AI 2009: 9).

The collapse in peace talks in 2008 caused disaffected MILF fighters to break away and form the Bangsamoro Islamic Freedom Fighters (BIFF). BIFF attacks have become more frequent in Maguindanao communities, and military operations against the group resulted in over twenty thousand displaced people in Maguindanao in 2016 alone (ICG 2016: 13). Other violent and more radical groups have subsequently utilized Islamic extremist ideology as a post hoc justification of criminal enterprises, such as Abu Sayyaf and the Maute group (ICG 2016: 14). Following the Bangsamoro Agreement, the election of President Rodrigo Duterte in June 2016 led to immediate nationwide implementation of his war on drugs policy; in turn, this caused a dramatic escalation in state-led violence. The police, agents of the police, and assailants have been associated since 2016 with thousands of deaths due to antidrug raids. The policy and deaths have led to rising tensions in Mindanao with some people supportive of President Duterte's 'war on drugs' while others remain opposed (Lozada 2021). Finally, outside of the time period examined in this chapter but relevant to continued conflict is the rise of the IS-inspired Maute group, which led the Marawi siege in 2017. For five months, these militants—led by matriarch Farhana Maute and her strong familial and clan associations with the Abu Sayaff Group—took over a city, Marawi, in the Province of Lanao del Sur in Mindanao (Santos 2020). This led to a battle with more deaths per incident of violence than any time over the previous seven years and with the highest level of internal displacement since 2013 (ICG 2019). Finally, most clan violence in the Philippines is located in Mindanao, with approximately 60 per cent of the territory affected.

The 2014 peace process, to date, has not been affected by these events. Following the adoption of the Bangsamoro Organic Law in 2018 and the establishment of the BARMM in 2019, elections for the first Bangsamoro Parliament are scheduled for 2025. However, serious threats to the peace process include "a corrupt, inefficient local bureaucracy, clan conflict and ongoing violence by pro-ISIS groups" (ICG 2019) in a socioeconomic context where welfare needs are high and unmet. Furthermore, the MNLF is divided on the peace process, which secured the MILF as the lead negotiator.

Communities in the Mindanao region, relative to other parts of the country, bear the brunt of the direct and indirect consequences of conflict. The protracted conflict in Mindanao has entrenched socioeconomic inequalities that severely restrict the life chances of many communities in the region. Nationally, the ARMM/BARMM is the poorest region—with the highest representation of people on the poverty line. In 2015 Lanao del Sur was the poorest province in the Philippines (PSA 2017).

Finally, gender inequality in the BARMM is high and at odds with the Philippines' reputation for progressive gender equality performance compared to its neighbors in the region. In 2016 the Committee on the Convention on the Elimination of all Forms of Discrimination Against Women (CEDAW) noted an association between conflict, poverty, and gender-based violence in the Philippines:

(a) The high prevalence of gender-based violence against women and girls and the low reporting of incidents of violence, in particular domestic violence and sexual violence, due to stigmatization of and discrimination against victims.

(b) The limited scope of the Anti-Violence against Women and Their Children Act of 2004 (Republic Act No. 9262), which is focused mainly on domestic violence by intimate partners.

(c) The fact that statutory rape under the Anti-Rape Law of 1997 is limited to cases in which the victim is under 12 years of age.

(d) The increasing incidence of online sexual exploitation and abuse of children.

(e) *Intensified gender-based violence against women, including by members of the armed forces, such as killings and sexual violence and abuse in conflict-affected areas and in areas of large-scale development projects.* (CEDAW 2016: 6, emphasis added)

The report went on to note that no disaggregated data were available from the Philippines on SGBV against women in the context of displacement, armed conflict, disaster, migration, and trafficking situations, as well as on SGBV against women with disabilities (CEDAW 2016: 6–7).

Civil Conflict–Related Abuses

In the Philippine national Parliament, women held 28 per cent of the available seats in 2021.[2] The Philippines is ranked sixteenth on the Global Gender Gap report in terms of political empowerment, with 25 per cent of women holding ministerial positions and approximately sixteen years with a female head of state since 1967 (WEF 2017). However, despite these positive statistics, women's full and equal political participation is constrained by the disproportionate effect that continued insecurity and conflict have had on them throughout the country. In Mindanao, women experience the highest rates of poverty and displacement in the country, as well as being subjected to the highest prevalence of violence and discrimination in public and private spheres (Davies, True, and Tanyag 2016).

Abduction for marriage and underage marriage are common in isolated regions such as Basilan, Sulu, and Tawi-Tawi. The Code of Muslim Personal Laws permits marriage for females below fifteen years, at the onset of puberty, but not below twelve years—in contrast with the legal age of marriage for non-Muslim Filipinos, which is eighteen years (Solamo-Antonio 2015). Reports suggest that armed men are exerting physical force and intimidation to compel marriage in particular (DFAT 2017). Forced marriage has been tied to the practice of *rido* (Davies, True, and Tanyag 2016: 463), which is clan- and family-based violence that may occur over insults to honor or dignity, and may result in extremely violent reprisals such as burning down houses or abductions (AI 2009: 22). Sexual violence is a common yet hidden aspect of *rido* that is targeted at girls and women, which affects their ability to meaningfully participate in public life (Davies, True, and Tanyag 2016: 466). As discussed later in this chapter, the culture of impunity that is endemic in Philippine society means that many of these attacks go unpunished (TJRC 2016).

In the BARMM, women's meaningful participation in the governance of the autonomous Muslim region was constrained until recently. The recent representation of Mindanao's current female leaders is similar to male representation, with most from elite clans and families (Kubota and Takashi 2016: 42). Access to justice appears to be influenced by political processes. Muslim, Indigenous, and Christian people in Mindanao generally prefer informal, family, and clan-based types of dispute resolution over any other form (DFAT 2017; Mollica et al. 2022). A multilayered Sharia and traditional legal system is also available. At the grassroots level, the Barangay

Justice System is an alternative, community-based mechanism for dispute resolution, with other members of the community acting as intermediaries. However, many women experience discrimination at this local level, where barangay officials lack gender sensitivity and awareness, and they and other local state actors discourage women from reporting to or engaging in the legal process in the first place. This perpetuates the view that violence against women is a private issue that the parties involved or their families should resolve (WLHRB 2015).

In addition to the civil abuses particularly affecting women victims-survivors in the justice system, the broader political economy of the BARMM, which is characterized by high rates of poverty and local government corruption, creates vulnerability to SGBV in shadow economies, often supported by local military and political elites (International Alert 2014; 2021). Violence associated with these economies contributed to more than one-quarter (27 per cent) of the total recorded violent conflicts between 2011 and 2014 (International Alert 2014: 23), which includes kidnapping, murder, and human trafficking—where most victims-survivors are women (DFAT 2017).

Women's Role in the CAB Peace Process

The adoption of the CAB in 2014 was internationally recognized for its relatively high level of meaningful participation by women on the government side in the formal negotiations and in parallel peacebuilding efforts (Conciliation Resources 2015: 6; Davies and True 2022). Miriam Coronel Ferrer, head of the government negotiating panel, was the first Philippine woman to be a signatory to a major peace agreement, and three of the twelve signatories were women (Santiago 2015: 3). However, the MILF has not had a woman on its panel or in any of its other structures related to the negotiations since 1997. Indeed, a MILF representative at the Mindanao Women's Peace Summit in 2006 told the participants gathered there that women had no role in public decision-making, reflecting the dominating patriarchal attitudes in Muslim Mindanao that have looked to take power away from women. However, in recognition of the high representation of women in the government of the Philippines peace committee, the chairman of the MILF peace negotiating panel appointed Ms. Raissa Jajurie, a human rights lawyer and a member of its Board of Consultants. The chairman argued that there was no injunction in the Qur'an against women taking leadership positions (Santiago 2015: 10).

Jajurie became a regular member of the delegation to the peace talks and was frequently called on by the MILF chairman to give her legal opinion on behalf of MILF (Santiago 2015: 11). Her position was officially informal, but her power over the MILF during the peace process was acknowledged to be influential. Following the signing of the Comprehensive Peace Agreement, Jajurie was appointed as a member of the commission on the MILF side and as the chair of the Committee on Fiscal Autonomy, covering issues of wealth sharing and, later, gender and development (Santiago 2015: 11). Women also led the legal team, the secretariat, and two important technical working groups that drafted the details of the normalization (demobilization and decommissioning) and wealth sharing annexes (Santiago 2015: 13). However, as mentioned, marginalized women from diverse groups, such as displaced and Indigenous populations, had limited representation in the peace process, which affects the sustainability of any agreement (Davies, True, and Tanyag 2016: 469).

Despite the meaningful women's participation in the peace process, there is no reference to SGBV in the 2014 agreement, no acknowledgment of past or ongoing acts of SGBV, and no reference to reparations, treatment or justice for those who experienced this violence. There remains, as we discuss later, a culture of violence in the community with security-sector reform and disarmament all but stalled. Civic participation continues but in a dangerous and lawless environment, which further compromises the safety of women, especially Indigenous women.

Existing Explanations for SGBV

Violence against women in the Philippines is normalized in the media, political institutions, the economy (sex tourism), and the security sector. This culture of impunity contradicts a very strong tradition of women-led civil society campaigns against gendered violence in the Philippines (Enriquez 2020; Tripon and Garcia 2020). The country has some of the most progressive legislation to address gender equality, gender equity, and gender discrimination, including the Magna Carta of Women (MCW) (Republic Act No. 9710), adopted in 2009, which requires every government department to produce a gender and development plan and budget. The Philippine Commission on

Women was set up to ensure the implementation of the MCW, which covers a large range of social, economic, cultural, religious, education, health, and political rights. Concerning violence against women, the MCW clearly states every woman's right to

> Protection from all forms of violence, including those committed by the State. This includes the incremental increase in the recruitment and training of women in government services that cater to women victims of gender-related offenses. It also ensures mandatory training on human rights and gender sensitivity to all government personnel involved in the protection and defense of women against gender-based violence, and mandates local government units to establish a Violence Against Women Desk in every barangay to address violence against women cases; and
>
> Protection and security in times of disaster, calamities and other crisis situations, especially in all phases of relief, recovery, rehabilitation and construction efforts, including protection from sexual exploitation and other sexual and gender-based violence.[3]

In 2009 the Philippines was the first country in Asia to adopt a National Action Plan on Women, Peace and Security, covering the 2010–2016 period. It adopted a second plan in 2016 for the 2017–2022 period. The 2010–2016 plan outlined the government's response to implement UN Security Council Resolutions 1325 and 1820 (focused on widespread or systematic sexual violence in armed conflict). There is reference in the plan to women, especially Indigenous and Moro women, experiencing conflict and postconflict-related rape and other forms of sexualized violence (GoP 2009: 4, 9). The measures to be adopted include "revision" of laws, policies, and practices that "impinge" on the security of women and an effort to "stop" or "repeal" these practices (GoP 2009: 9). There is also reference to the provision of rapid needs assessments for women and girls in armed conflict (GoP 2009: 11) and the need to prioritize the collection of baseline data to "monitor the impacts of the conflict on women and girls" (GoP 2009: 15). The 2017–2022 NAP is outside of the scope of the reporting time frame that we analyze in this chapter. However, the 2017–2022 NAP noted gaps in implementation and fulfillment of the 2010–2016 NAP, particularly with regard to the impact of trafficking and vulnerabilities to SGBV and women's participation in governance. The new plan states that "individual implementing partner agencies should strive for further institutionalization of the NAP within their respective institutions through policy formulation and creation of NAP specific programs and services that address the gender dimensions of armed conflict and peace." It proposed that "agency practice on data collection should be guided by differential contexts of conflict and non-armed/post-conflict situations (e.g., VAW/SGBV) and basic sex-disaggregation of data," and that "monitoring and evaluation of the NAP WPD should likewise be further systematized" (GoP 2016: 6).

The narrative in the conflict-related SGBV literature echoes the uneven agency described above: strong agency in some contexts to counter SGBV and pervasive silence and lack of agency in other contexts such as in Mindanao. Women living in the conflict are presented as resilient actors with strong agency who determine—by their actions and consent—whether their community is at peace, experiencing violence, or opposing organized crime (Diesta and Distor 2019; Duriesmith 2020; Nario-Galace 2021). However, many studies also discuss the lack of agency held by women in Mindanao with particular profiles on the disempowerment of Moro (Philippine Muslim) women and Lumad (Indigenous) women, and the violence committed against them by community, police, soldiers, and nonstate armed groups (Kubota and Takashi 2016; Veloso 2017; Pasimio 2020). Furthermore, analysis of the implementation of the MCW has found that the realization of these rights and protections are not formally implemented and that implementation is rarely budgeted for (Francisco 2021). Sifris and Tanyag (2019) suggest that the Philippines' uneven agency reveals the intersectional complexity present in most conflicts—where women can be victims-survivors of sexual violence and other forms of gendered violence, but also powerful agents who protect their family and community.

One explanation for the prevalence of SGBV in the Mindanao conflict is the opportunity for this violence, which is associated with gendered norms and practices within the community. This is particularly the case in the context of forced displacement as a result of conflict, which is common in Mindanao. Anecdotal evidence suggests that displacement, in particular, puts women at risk of conflict-related sexual violence (Tanyag 2018). In an interview, Jasmin Nario-Galace, a Professor of International Studies and a key player in coordinating the Civil Society Organization (CSO) Group of the Preparatory Committee for the formulation of the UN Security Council Resolution 1325 National Action Plan (NAP) in the Philippines, explains,

> Unfortunately, armed conflicts have brought sexual abuse. For example, civil society organizations, such as Kalinaw Mindanao, reported that Muslim women had been sexually violated in evacuation centres by men who, allegedly searching for grenades, had been groping their breasts. What makes it even worse, women and their communities are reluctant to report rape and the cases of sexual violence, whether out of fear or "because of their culture" (there is a strong prohibition for women to "dishonor" the family). Evacuation centres across the country lack facilities for women. When in these centres, women often do not have access to social and health services they require. (cited in Trojanowksa 2019: 318)

During the period examined in this chapter, the Philippines had one of the highest internally displaced populations due to the combination of conflict and natural disasters, and the majority of this displacement is located in Mindanao (IDMC 2022). It takes a long time for populations to return home, if they ever do. For example, as of December 2021, of the 65,918 families (267,278 individuals) recorded as displaced in Mindanao, approximately 34 per cent have been displaced for more than 180 days (Fernandez, Baraguir, and Bryant 2022). The Zamboanga siege of 9–23 September 2013 serves as an illustration. In September the MNLF, protesting their exclusion from the Bangsamoro peace process, took siege of the city, which led to the Philippines Army entering to end the siege. During the monthlong violence, sixteen barangays were affected, houses were burned, civilians were held captive by the MNLF, and over 100,000 people, mostly Muslim families, were displaced (UNHCR 2019). During the Marawi City siege, between May and October 2017, over 300,000 people were displaced; a year later, 95 per cent had not been able to return to their homes (Fernandez et al. 2022).

In the context of prolonged displacement conditions, gender inequality, gendered abuse, and sexual violence become widespread, even normalized (Sifris and Tanyag 2019). This does not mean such violence is not strategic or used for an instrumental political or economic purpose. Secure employment and wages are disrupted by the violence, and as such, girls become currency in a situation where they may be abducted, trafficked, or abused. For example, in the Moro and Lumad communities, family preference is for the raped girl to be married to the perpetrator, which is "convenient" for the perpetrator if they cannot afford the bride price. In the Marawi siege there were reports that girls were marrying the individuals who perpetrated SGBV against them to uphold their honor and protect their families (CP/GBV Working

Group 2017: 26). Rival clans are also known to abduct and rape girls in retaliation for honor, or business, land, or drug feuds (Davies, True, and Tanyag 2016). Conflict, combined with the seasonal events creating displacement and *rido* feuds, may not—under UN conditions—be considered "conflict enough" to deliver humanitarian assistance to the populations displaced due to this violence (Fernandez et al. 2022). Nonetheless, SGBV still takes place within these "horizontal" conflicts and may indeed be an instrumental tactic amongst feuding families or clans (Davies, True, and Tanyag 2016; CP/GBV Working Group 2017: 26–27). One study, for example, found that men are more likely to be killed in *rido* conflicts, but women are more likely to be the targets of sexual violence (Dwyer and Cagoco-Guiam 2012: 10, 18). A pattern of both opportunistic and strategic use of SGBV in Mindanao is strongly associated with gendered norms involving culture, political economy, and social reproduction.

The government of the Philippines in both its NAPs on WPS (GoP 2009; GoP 2016) acknowledged the occurrence of conflict-related sexual violence and its association with "fragility" in the region. Specific numbers of those affected, the locations of the violence, and the perpetrators are difficult to obtain in the literature from the government and even in interviews in the field. Much of the advocacy and information provided is generalized. SGBV reports, usually provided by humanitarian and health actors, involve the case of Mindanao. Available clinical health data is low. Health services in general are minimal in these locations, with heavy dependence on the one or two clinics set up to serve thousands. There is a high risk of stigma when seeking medical assistance for sexual violence in displaced communities, both Muslim and Indigenous. It is very difficult in close-knit communities to access services, especially when the health clinic may be available only once a month.

SGBV occurrence in the Philippines conflict is a story of what is not recorded and who is not prosecuted. There is heavy dependence on women civil society groups to provide referral support services and document the violence they witness. Due to the cultural, religious, race, and security environment in Mindanao, it is both stigmatizing and dangerous for victims-survivors (especially women) to come forward with their experience of sexual violence (*rido* or political) (Veloso 2017).

In advocating for the full implementation of the Magna Carta of Women, women's civil society organizations have to rely on informal networks. Even outside of conflict-related SGBV, these organizations make strategic calculations and choices about what information to reveal as part of their advocacy. This practice of local women's groups selectively reporting conflict-related SGBV was also found in the case of Burma (Oo and Davies 2021). Two examples of this practice in the Philippines are provided later in this chapter.

Connected to this, local responders' reluctance to report is high. For example, nearly a year after the Zamboanga siege a child protection rapid assessment reported that "only 7 per cent of the 15 sites would turn to their respective barangay councils for assistance if they came across a survivor of sexual violence" (CPWG 2014: 31). The report goes on to note that "sexual violence is taking place, but is not reported" (CPWG 2014: 36). In an assessment of conflict-affected sites in Marawi after the end of the siege in 2017, only 9 per cent of affected sites reported sexual abuse and exploitation, with 36 per cent of sites reporting "consequences" for reporting such violence (CP/GBV Working Group 2017: 26).

A year after our collection of event data, the Philippines Demographic and Health Survey (DHS) of 2017 surveyed experience of sexual violence (SV) over the previous twelve months (among the fifteen- to forty-nine-year-old age group) (PSA 2018). The BARMM recorded the lowest prevalence in the DHS, but the region also recorded the lowest likelihood of reporting such violence. The 2017 DHS recorded that most experiences of sexual violence for unmarried women are by a partner, boyfriend, acquaintance, or relative. Experience of rape by "strangers" and "other" is very low (below 1 per cent) for married women but third (strangers) and fifth (other) highest for unmarried women (16.8 per cent and 10.9 per cent, respectively) (PSA 2018). The fact that the BARMM recorded the lowest prevalence as well as the lowest likelihood of reporting such violence is not lost on those who advocate for the rights of Moro and Indigenous women caught up in the political conflict and associated horizontal conflicts (*rido, maratabat* [family honor, land claims], and since 2016, war-on-drugs-associated violence) (de Dios et al. 2020: 136; Pasimio 2020; Tripon and Garcia 2020). The risk of stigma and retaliation for those who report SGBV, especially within gender-conservative communities where virginity and purity signify the financial (bride price) value of girls and women (de Dios et al. 2020: 138). There can be life consequences for girls and women who report SGBV.

As one of the poorest regions in the country, there are practical difficulties in documenting SGBV and recording baseline data in Mindanao. The Department of Interior and Local Government (DILG) issued Memorandum

Circular No. 2017-114: Guidelines on Monitoring the Functionality of Violence against Women (VAW) Desk in every barangay. Across the country, including Mindanao, a large number of barangays remain without "functional barangay" or village-level VAW desks (Pasimio 2020; Calleja et al. 2020). Many of those with physical desks have appointed officers who have not undergone comprehensive training (Enriquez 2020: 125).

In such a situation where VAW desks are not adequately staffed, trained, or represented across all barangays, it is not surprising that the government of the Philippines noted in its 2017–2022 WPS NAP that there is a persistent failure to collect baseline data on conflict-related SGBV (GoP 2016). Without significant changes in gendered norms and in the societal value accorded to women's virginity and purity, detailed reporting will remain low with marriage to the perpetrators viewed as the most acceptable form of "protection" (Arcala Hall and Hoare 2015; Veloso 2017; de Dios et al. 2020). The result is that while evidence in the literature indicates that this violence is occurring in conjunction with associated patterns of displacement, sieges, *rido* violence, and emergency measures, precise patterns are rarely documented and understood.

The silence surrounding who conducts this SGBV is pervasive, which limits our precise understanding of SGBV relationship to conflict in Mindanao. Revealing the perpetrators in an environment of conflict, political instability, and rival clans is dangerous for those in the humanitarian, health, and human rights sectors. This danger was heightened in the years of our study with the political changes within the Philippines following the CAB.

The culture of impunity promoted by the Philippines' political leadership through its embrace of hard-line, securitized responses to social problems is a frequent explanation for endemic SGBV in the country. As discussed earlier in this chapter, the election of President Duterte in 2016 led to the nationwide introduction of the war on drugs policy, which had been previously implemented in Mindanao when Duterte was mayor in Davao City. This policy permits police to conduct arbitrary arrests and carry out extrajudicial killings. In 2020 the ICC announced investigations into allegations of crimes against humanity committed by the Philippines government between 2011 and 2019, when Duterte was president and vice-mayor and mayor of Davao prior to that (Englebrecht 2021).

The growth in war on drug-related violence across the region—including Mindanao—where there is a high prevalence of drug production, sales, and use, has also been indirectly connected to escalated reports of SGBV (de Dios et al. 2020: 136). The number of female-headed households has risen as a result of the war-on-drugs policy, under which extrajudicial killings have been officially recorded as six thousand deaths—but many estimate the figure is double (Englebrecht 2021). Prostitution, especially in low socioeconomic areas where drug addiction is high, has become the only viable option for women who need income and to stay home with family (Enriquez 2020). Prostitutes, when interviewed by civil society organizations, have referred to experiencing increased sexual violence and intimidation from police (Enriquez 2020: 125). There has also been a rise in SGBV directly associated with the war on drugs policy. Women report being raped by police in exchange for their relatives' release. The practice is so common that it has a term, "sex for freedom," and is directly associated with police impunity in the war on drugs (Enriquez 2020: 128). Finally, a popular culture of sexualised violence has been associated with President Duterte's presidency. He pushed for the liberalization of sex tourism laws, has been documented as groping and kissing women on and off stage, and has made numerous rape jokes in public with reference to events including the gang rape of an Australian nun, the rape and sexual torture of combatant women in Mindanao, and the promotion of military officers who rape (Tripon and Garcia 2020).

Our Data—Trends

Conflict, Violence, and Perpetrators

We coded SGBV reports for the Philippines between 1998 and 2016, with a focus on those from or connected to the Mindanao region. The total reports of sexual violence peak twice—in 2010 and then again in 2014 (see Graph 4.1). Per reported event, the total population targeted for this violence was ten persons or less. The total population targeted rises (over one hundred and even over one thousand) between 2010 and 2014. This was a politically significant period in Mindanao: the government of the Philippines was negotiating the peace process with the MILF (2009–2014 negotiations that led to the CAB), the MNLF conducted the Zamboanga siege in 2013, and Mayor Duterte introduced his war on drugs policy in Davao in 2011. During this period reports of SGBV rose noticeably (see Graph 4.2). The connection of SGBV to political violence is further discussed later.

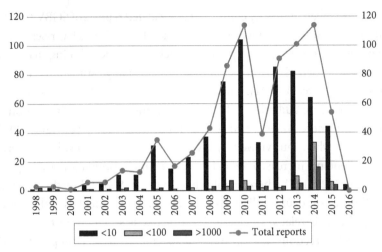

Graph 4.1 Total Conflict-Related SGBV Reports in Philippines, 1998–2016

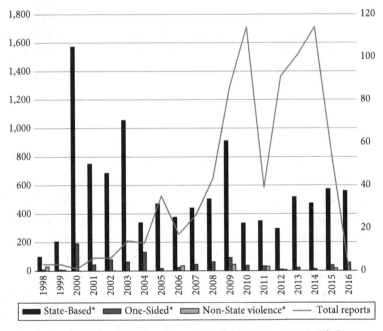

Graph 4.2 Total Fatalities by Conflict vs. Total SGBV Reports in Philippines, 1998–2016

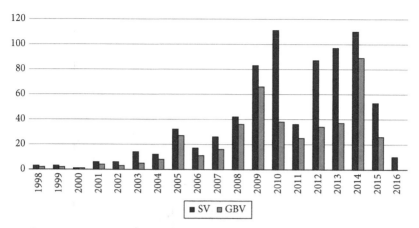

Graph 4.3 Reported SV and Reported GBV in Philippines, 1998–2016

We found overall a higher number of reports of sexual violence than gender-based violence (Graph 4.3). In some years, sexual violence reports were much higher than reports of gender-based violence. Specifically, between 1998 and 2009, reports of sexual violence were just slightly ahead (10 to 20 more events) of reports of gender-based violence; then from 2010—with the exception of 2011 and 2014—a significant difference starts to emerge where reports of sexual violence outnumber gender-based violence reports. For the remaining years coded, gender-based violence only reaches the same number of events as sexual violence in 2014 (110 sexual violence and 89 gender-based violence events). In 2016 there were no reports of gendered violence but 10 reports of sexual violence events. Given the events that transpired in 2017 (the Marawi siege), the pattern of reports is clearly not an early warning of imminent violence in the case of the Philippines. The peak of SGBV reports was in 2014—one year after the Zamboanga siege, rather than before it.

The volume of "unknown" perpetrators during the peak period of conflict-related violence (2009–2014) was between five and ten times higher than the next known category of "state" perpetrators (see Graph 4.4). There are a small number of reports of nonstate armed groups committing violence between 2008 and 2011 but reports on these groups stop after that date (see Graph 4.5). The Transitional Justice and Reconciliation Commission (TJRC) heard testimony that girls and women were victims-survivors of trafficking violence involving police, military, and local government elements (TJRC

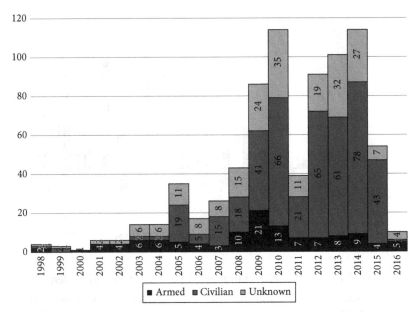

Graph 4.4 Reported Perpetrators of SGBV in Philippines, 1998–2016

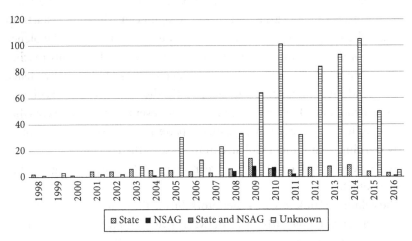

Graph 4.5 Reported Armed Perpetrators of SGBV in Philippines, 1998–2016

2016: 37). There also reports of Indigenous women in particular being targeted for sexual violence by the military (TJRC 2016: 54). The lack of consistent trends on who are reported as the perpetrators is markedly different from the other countries that we examine in this volume.

Only in 2009 do a higher number of reports identify perpetrators as armed, which is still half that of the civilian perpetrators identified in the same year. The reports in this year are mostly attributed to the mass atrocity committed on the roadside of Ampatuan town, Maguindanao province, where fifty-eight men and women, including thirty-two journalists, were killed with automatic weapons—and the majority of murdered women were raped before being shot. Over two hundred defendants, including sixty members of the National Police Force, Armed Forces, and government subsidized militia groups, were eventually identified as being associated with this massacre. Of the sixty suspected armed forces personnel, nineteen have been prosecuted. The defendants were associated with a powerful local political Muslim clan led by Maguindanao governor Andal Ampatuan Sr., whose son Andal Ampatuan Jr. was running for mayor (Mcdonald 2020). Mayor Ampatuan was running against then–vice mayor of Buluan, Esmael Mangudadatu, who sent his family, supporters, and journalists to process his candidacy papers for the mayoral election. He thought his pregnant wife and female family members would not be attacked, especially with a large group of journalists following them. The multivehicle convoy was stopped on its way to Ampatuan and by the road a massacre was committed. It took ten years for prosecution to proceed; there have been at least four witnesses murdered, and to this day journalists are intimidated and face threats of violence if they report too closely on events in Mindanao (Høiby 2020).

As this 2009 event demonstrates, the report of civilian perpetrator(s) does not mean that the crimes are unconnected to conflict. Between 2010 and 2014, the highest years of reported SGBV events, are the years when the highest reports of unknown perpetrators are coupled with the highest reports of civilians committing these crimes. As noted earlier, Mindanao was experiencing a high number of *rido*, *maratabat*, and drug-related crimes during this period. This was in addition to, at the same time, a formal ceasefire agreement taking place between the government and the MILF. We know that the Zombanga siege was triggered by the MNLF's exclusion from the ceasefire agreement. Groups were competing for advantage in this period of instability. In other words, the possibility exists that those involved in *rido* violence and other insurgent groups represent the unknown and civilian perpetrators. For media and local civil society, reporting on the violence committed by these groups can be dangerous, so classifying the violence as "unknown" may be a safe(r) practice.

104 HIDDEN WARS

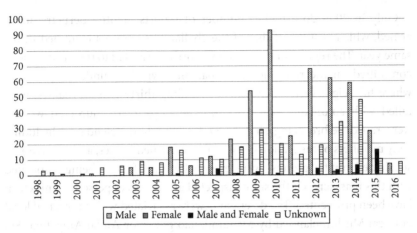

Graph 4.6 Reported Gender of Perpetrators in Philippines, 1998–2016

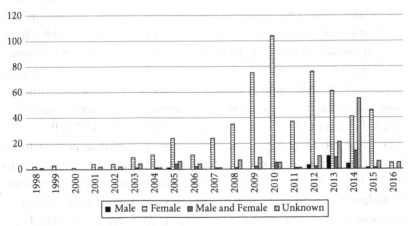

Graph 4.7 Reported Victims-Survivors by Gender in Philippines, 1998–2016

Finally, there is one unusual feature in the Philippines' perpetrator trend—increased reporting of both women and men as perpetrators of sexual violence that begins in 2012 and continues to increase until the end of 2015 (see Graph 4.6). The numbers are low, but they do coincide with the fact that over this same period the reported gender of victims-survivors was changing, with more men being listed as victims-survivors of sexual violence and more children being reported as victims-survivors of sexual violence (see Graphs 4.7 and 4.8).

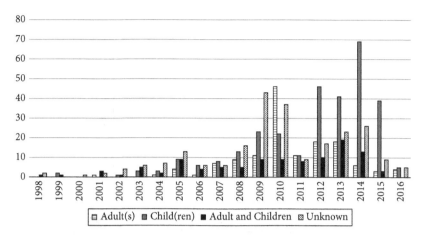

Graph 4.8 Reported Victims-Survivors by Age in Philippines, 1998–2016

Reporting Sources

In the Philippines an overwhelming number of reports come from the media. The highest number of recorded reports of SGBV (199) was in 2014, with 104 of those reports from the media, 4 from unofficial sources, and 6 from official sources (see Graph 4.9). The Philippines is quite unusual in comparison to the other countries examined in this volume in that it has a very low number of official and unofficial reports and a very high volume of media reports. The absence of baseline data on SGBV in conflict and fragile situations in the Philippines has been noted in the Philippines' two NAPs on WPS, but there is no evidence to date that an effort has been made to improve state-level documentation. The lack of specificity in the media reports could be attributed to the fact that these reports are not designed to inform early warning of sexual violence (CEDAW 2016: 6; see also Tripon and Garcia 2020). The absence of "official" reports suggests not only minimal government presence but also, unlike Burma and Sri Lanka, minimal reports on this violence from international organizations and international nongovernment organizations (INGOs). This highlights a theme that we return to in Chapter Six—the importance of (diverse) humanitarian actors' presence and their association with the quality and scale of reporting available on conflict-related sexual violence.

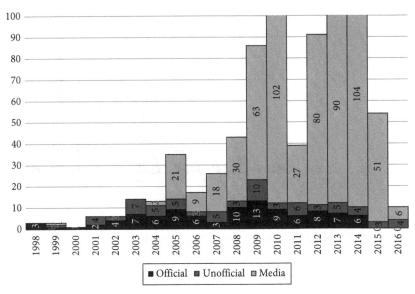

Graph 4.9 Reporting Sources of SGBV in Philippines, 1998–2016

Location

On the question of where sexual violence events reportedly occur, in the case of the Philippines we see a very strong pattern of unknown locations being reported. If we pay attention to the 2010 and 2014 peak periods, we see that in 2010 the vast majority of violence was reported as taking place in an unknown location (sixty-seven events) followed by violence recorded as taking place in a village location (thirty events), followed by violence occurring at home (fourteen events) (see Graph 4.10). In the case of 2014, there was again a very high number of unknown reports of location (sixty-five events) followed this time by more reports of SGBV occurring at home (twenty-nine events) and violent events occurring in a village (twenty-four events). Violence in village locations—not homes—is consistently high across the years. There is also a high point in 2014 for sexual violence being reported from IDP camps—which corresponds with the fact that 2013 and 2014 had highly displaced populations due to the combination of political violence and natural disasters.

In general, the paucity of reports from IDP camps—given the sizeable population and qualitative studies on the scale of SGBV in camps, as mentioned earlier—makes the relative absence of reporting in this location striking.

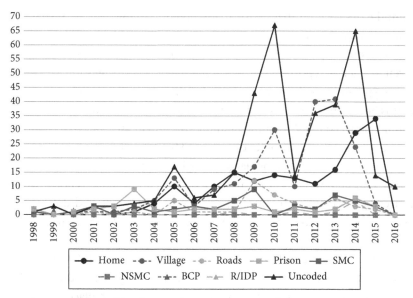

Graph 4.10 Reported Locations of SGBV Crimes in Philippines, 1998–2016

The absence of reports reveals the essential role of humanitarian and health service actors in providing the pathways to report this violence. When SGBV is perpetrated by the state itself or its security sector victims-survivors have literally no one to report to.

In terms of the total SGBV reports compared to the conflict pattern of violence (one-sided violence, state-led violence, and nonstate violence), conflict-related violence (i.e., deaths) tends to *precede* reports of SGBV (see Graph 4.2). In 2010, one of two peak years of SGBV reports, a rise in state-based violence took place the previous year as did a rise in one-sided violence and nonstate violence. The highest peak period of violence recorded in the Philippines (2000) was one of the lowest years for recorded SGBV, but reports of events slowly rose in the following two years. The overarching pattern in the Philippines is that overall political violence tends to drop as SGBV reports increase. We saw this again in 2013 when conflict violence (deaths) started to rise and SGBV reports followed a year later. It is also worth noting that in the presidential and general election years in the Philippines—1998, 2004, 2010, and 2016—no clear pattern of increased conflict-related violence occurred.

From the SGBV reports in the Philippines it is difficult to establish a clear pattern between cycles of conflict violence and incidences of SGBV—apart from the observation that SGBV reports tend to follow battles. Sexual violence seems to be present during and after conflict, with less reports of this type of violence prior to the onset of conflict. However, this is speculation, given the lack of reporting specificity and diverse reporting sources. The reporting patterns are different compared to the other two conflicts we analyze in this book. This could indeed be indicative of the difference in the scale of conflict between the Philippines and the two other cases, but that is not the case, given that the Philippines experienced battles on a scale during this period that were similar to, if not larger than, in Burma.

The Philippines has a heavy reliance on media for SGBV reports, which carries the risk that some of these reports may be unsubstantiated, dramatized, one-sided, and risk-averse—avoiding identification of any armed group committing this violence due to personal safety concerns. However, reports on sexual violence clearly have been rising steadily since 2009—the same year the MCW was adopted—and while there is one significant drop in 2011 and 2016, an overall rise in the volume of reports has taken place. This trend indicates a growing interest in reporting and documenting this violence, but most of the reports are coming from the media. Heavy reliance on media alone to report SGBV is not ideal. Triangulation of media reports without reference to official reports is difficult. However, the fact that we have consistent reports of SGBV occurring outside of the home from 2010 onward—namely in villages, roads, state military compounds, and IDP camps—presents a pattern where SGBV is occurring and is related to political violence during this period. Again, however, the fact that so many reports of SGBV are uncoded in terms of location points to a heavy reliance on the media to provide information that may not always be factual nor designed to identify patterns of this violence to inform and assist with prevention or response.

Conclusion

SGBV reporting in the Philippines has been minimal and inconsistent since 1998. The silence in this conflict, however, is not akin to the silence enforced in Burma and Sri Lanka. In the Philippines, the media provide the majority of reports on this violence, but it is not reliable data. Much detail is missing in these reports, including the perpetrators, the locations, and the victims-survivors. Delving into the case in greater depth, we argue that the reasons for the absence of reliable information are threefold.

First, holes in the reporting are not the result of minimal SGBV or SGBV disassociated from the conflict. Evidence across different sources—civil society, political actors, media, and academics—shows that conflict-related SGBV is taking place in Mindanao. However, there is a reluctance to report due to fear of community reprisals and violence and intimidation against those who report. Girls and women face serious stigma if local actors report their experience of violence. Therefore, most local actors choose not to report. Community preference is for local solutions when this violence occurs, including marriage to the perpetrator, if that is an option. The absence of reporting thus is partly due to the practices communities have devised to "resolve" the violence when it occurs.

Second, the violence taking place in Mindanao is diverse, including violence between clans, violence over land, election violence, violent extremism, and territorial violence. Each type of political violence is associated with acts of SGBV but in unique ways. For example, there may be widespread SGBV when populations are forcibly displaced, but it is not systematic; or there may be systematic violence when girls are targeted for revenge attacks or forced marriage, but it may not be widespread, occurring in multiple locations at the same time. As such, there are only a few instances where it appears that all the violence is happening at once, but SGBV often seems to be reported in the aftermath rather than during episodes of intense political violence. Untangling when sexual violence is sex-for-freedom or clan-associated violence can be difficult when clans are involved with police in the same environment where territorial civil-conflict violence is also occurring.

Finally, connected with the second point, the usual reporting actors present in other conflict situations—that is, international and national humanitarian actors—are largely absent in Mindanao. These actors, it appears, play a crucial role in creating reporting pathways for conflict-related SGBV, especially in locations where this violence is prevalent: in the Philippines case, IDP camps and villages. Numerous reports align the lack of reporting with the lack of services available for victims-survivors. There are calls for GBV desks at each barangay, but no one is adequately trained to staff them and no one is trained to collect baseline data. Moreover, is little incentive to improve the reporting conditions exists when knowledge of SGBV may result in significant stigma for the victims-survivors and the community. The Philippines government is in control of the Mindanao situation and, as such, has rarely sought the assistance or presence of international humanitarian actors. Furthermore, the community wants to retain control, with powerful family dynasties dominating particular territories. Indeed, these powerful local actors use violence and intimidation, as well as strong gendered norms, to (re)inforce authority, including the clans ruled by matriarchs. Practices of forced marriage and bride price value according to girls' purity and virginity give SGBV a currency for influencing political ends. SGBV is further fueled as a weapon in the context of low-intensity conflict where there is widespread impunity for all forms of violence.

5

Deconstructing Victory

Narratives of Absence of Conflict-Related Sexual and Gender-Based Violence in Sri Lanka

This chapter examines the case of Sri Lanka and the patterns of conflict-related sexual and gender-based violence (SGBV) during the civil war from 1983 to 2009 between the government and the Liberation Tigers of Tamil Eelam (LTTE). Official reports on sexual violence are rare in Sri Lanka; "gender-based violence" is the preferred lexicon in Sri Lanka Government reports for SGBV (UNFPA 2016a). In Sri Lanka, the conflict in the North and North-Eastern Provinces against the separatist Tamil Tigers was at times as bloody and intense as the conflict in Burma. Conflict-related SGBV, however, only began to be consistently reported during the final stages of the Sri Lankan civil war, with substantially increased postconflict reporting. We trace SGBV reporting patterns between 1998 and 2016, including the brokered ceasefire between the Sri Lanka Government and Tamil rebels in 2002, the ceasefire breakdown in 2006, and the significant battles that took place in the North and North-East Provinces until the end of the twenty-seven-year conflict in 2009, when the Sri Lanka Government declared victory. We continue to analyze SGBV reports subsequent to the end of this conflict, when the country was subject to a UN Human Rights inquiry.

Dissimilar to the two prior cases in this volume, the conflict has come to a complete end since 2009. Similar to Burma, we find that despite postconflict status, the reporting conditions for SGBV are still influenced by the political context and prevailing narratives of the conflict. In Sri Lanka, the ethnonationalist struggle for a unified national identity marginalizes Tamil and Muslim minorities. Women are often presented as the victims-survivors in these narratives, and rarely as the heroes or warriors, with the possible exception of the women who joined the LTTE as combatants. Unlike Burma, there was a clear Sinhalese victory over the Tamil minority in Sri Lanka and an end to battles in the North since 2009. However, victor's justice did not end the violence. Indeed, SGBV reporting itself has faced intense politicization during the postwar years. In the immediate period after the war, reporting sexual violence in particular was seen as a divisive and highly dangerous activity. As one informant told us, "The moment you say 'sexual violence'... then you are talking about the conflict."[1] More recently, reporting SGBV experiences during the war and within war-affected communities has become more accepted and less dangerous—but the narrative has largely adhered to the victors' justice terms and conditions.

We explore this argument in three parts. First, we provide a background on the Sri Lanka war highlighting the gendered nature of the conflict and how SGBV was part of its dynamic and aftermath. Second, we examine the political, economic, and military dimensions of the postconflict era, examining how the government's postconflict victory has perpetuated impunity for SGBV. We consider the current narrative about conflict-related SGBV in Sri Lanka that views the use of this violence within the context of high-intensity conflict rather than its aftermath and as largely one-sided, involving government armed forces. Our findings suggest, by contrast, that both parties to the conflict employed SGBV, and much of this violence was not reported or able to be reported. We explore the conditions that have led to increased SGBV reporting in the postconflict period. Third, we consider how ethnonationalist political tensions and pervasive gender discrimination affect the power to report in local conflict-affected areas. We argue that patterns of increased reporting can be attributed to the significant advocacy efforts of women's movements for gender justice in the absence of transitional justice mechanisms. The options to address the structural gender and ethnic inequalities at the root of SGBV crimes during and after the civil war are explored further in the final chapter.

Background to the Sri Lanka Civil War, 1983–2009

Sri Lanka's protracted civil war between 1983 and 2009 had a major impact on civilians. The Uppsala Conflict Data Program (2014) estimates the loss of life at over sixty thousand people, while the 2015 UN Office of the High Commissioner for Human Rights (OHCHR) Investigation on Sri Lanka suggests that "likely tens of thousands lost their lives" (OHCHR 2015b). The primary actors in the three-decade-long internal conflict were the LTTE, from the North and East Provinces of Sri Lanka, and the government of Sri Lanka. The LTTE's objective was to create an independent Tamil Eelam state, which involved the removal of the Muslim population (Sri Lanka's second-largest minority group) and Sinhalese from the North and East Provinces (De Alwis 2004: 217). Known as the "Tamil Tigers," the LTTE was a "ruthless and formidable military organization" (OHCHR 2015b: 12) that targeted anyone, including ethnic Tamils, who opposed its sole objective to create an independent Tamil state. The armed group had forcibly recruited children to be combatants, including girls; used abduction and extortion practices; and committed suicide attacks, political assassinations, and arbitrary executions. The LTTE regularly located military units and training grounds within civilian territory, using women and children as human shields to prevent the targeting of their military facilities (OHCHR 2015b: 12–15). This is not the only civil conflict waged in Sri Lanka since its 1948 independence, but it was the longest and most violent, with both parties committing human rights violations throughout it (OHCHR 2015b: 13; Salter 2015: chapter 1).

The conflict ended in May 2009 after an intense period of fighting. The Sri Lanka Government mobilized 300,000 troops to enter the North Province (an LTTE stronghold territory) to wipe out the LTTE and end the civil war. An estimated 40,000 civilians were killed due to shelling and direct fire between the parties. Some of the worst casualties and displacement during the entire thirty-year war were inflicted on the North and East Provinces (OHCHR 2015b: 219). When the Sri Lankan army advanced from the south and the east, 300,000 civilians were herded into a three-kilometer stretch of land, which came under attack from both sides. Between 2008 and 2009, 300,000 people were displaced in addition to the 520,000 previously displaced during earlier battles in the 2000s (OHCHR 2015b: 18).

Conflict-Related Abuses

Amongst the casualties and displacement during this time were alleged atrocities that included rape and other sexual violence against both combatants and civilians. In relation to patterns of SGBV (Office of the ICC Prosecutor 2014: 5; OHCHR 2015b: 223), most documented events concern allegations against the Sri Lanka Government security forces (military and police) (HRW 2013: 26; Sooka, the Bar Human Rights Committee of England and Wales (BHRC), and the International Truth & Justice Project 2014: 78, 80; Sooka and the International Truth & Justice Project 2015: 15–18, 25–26). However, the LTTE were well known for abducting girls for forced marriage and combat, and forcibly detaining women and children as human shields. Families were threatened and beaten if they refused to hand over their children to the LTTE, and there was a pattern in the North of the forced marriage of children to avoid LTTE conscription (OHCHR 2015b: 128–129). According to UN investigations, grave acts of war crimes and crimes against humanity, including SGBV, were committed by both the Sri Lankan armed forces and the Tamil Tigers (OHCHR 2015b; UNSG 2012b; UNSC 2011).

During the intense months of battle in 2008 and 2009, humanitarian actors (OHCHR 2015b: 19) reported sexual violence, torture, enforced disappearances, and extrajudicial killings against LTTE cadres and suspected LTTE combatants being held by the Sri Lankan security forces (UNSC 2011: 21). While in government-controlled camps, civilians were subjected to rigorous screening procedures with women being forced to remove their clothing to partial or complete nudity, often in front of men. Females were reportedly humiliated by male soldiers who would watch them undress, poke their breasts with rifle barrels, and at times record videos or take photos of the naked women on their mobile phones.

Patterns of Conflict-Related SGBV

Rape became a common tactic that the Sri Lankan military and police used during and after the final stages of the war to gather intelligence on the LTTE network, intimidate LTTE members and sympathizers, and secure bribes from family members to release whoever was in custody (HRW 2013: 4). A Human Rights Watch report notes that Tamil men and women as well as Sinhalese and Muslim detainees were subjected to sexual violence in prison for their apparent sympathies to the LTTE or antigovernment sentiment (HRW 2013: 7). Allegations of SGBV inside the internally displaced camps—especially the largest camp, Manik Farm—were also reported immediately after the war (OHCHR 2015b: 124–126). Numerous corroborated reports alleged the rape of women and young girls at night while going to the bathroom or collecting firewood. Sexual favors were allegedly demanded by soldiers and the police in return for access to food rations, dry quarters, quarters closer to the toilet, and early release.

Sri Lankan security forces deliberately used sexual violence against men and boys to torture, obtain information, and intimidate (All Survivors Project 2020). The majority of SGBV victims-survivors are ethnic Tamils with actual or believed links to the LTTE (All Survivors Project 2020: 45–46). A 2015 report, *Tainted Peace: Torture in Sri Lanka since May 2009*, reported that 66 per cent of males interviewed had experienced sexual torture and 30 per cent were victims-survivors of rape (Freedom from Torture 2015: 45). While men and women were subjected to similar forms of sexual violence, men were more likely to experience violence to genitalia (All Survivors Project 2020: 55). Victims-survivors were also subject to humiliation and distress. For instance, forced nakedness would cause victims-survivors to fear imminent sexual violence (All Survivors Project 2020: 47). Most victims-survivors knew little about the perpetrators, although some reported that they were uniformed and intoxicated during interrogation and torture (Freedom from Torture 2019: 10).

In addition to the torture and rape of detained men and women, the Sri Lankan security sector has been accused of committing SGBV crimes postconflict, including rape and sexual harassment of women returning from displacement camps in the North and East provinces. The few available existing reports of sexual violence suggest that women in those provinces experienced the highest levels of personal insecurity, violation of bodily integrity, and sexual violence (FOKUS Women 2016; Guruge et al. 2017). The 2016 UN Secretary-General report on conflict-related sexual violence stated, "The ever-present threat of sexual assault compels women to lead highly circumscribed lives in militarized zones, as seen in eastern Afghanistan or northern Sri Lanka" (UNSG 2016: para. 13). Postconflict economic marginalization and inequality coupled with widespread impunity for war crimes and human rights violations prompted the Oakland Institute (2016) to describe Sri Lanka as experiencing a second "silent war." In 2019, the latest inclusion of Sri Lanka in the UN Secretary-General's report on conflict-related sexual violence, it was noted that Sri Lanka's most recent update on the annual Grave Crimes Abstract of the Sri Lankan Police (2017) recorded 1732 complaints of rape but no convictions for rape cases (UNSG 2019: para. 112). A 2021 report of the UN Secretary-General to the Security Council states,

> More than a decade since the end of the conflict between the Government and the Liberation Tigers of Tamil Eelam in Sri Lanka, a meaningful transitional justice process that would address crimes committed during three decades of civil war, including crimes of sexual violence, is yet to be established. . . . Survivors of conflict-related sexual violence, particularly those who came forward to engage with the transitional justice process, are

experiencing increased barriers to attaining justice in the current context. War widows and other marginalized groups are at heightened risk of sexual violence, in particular in heavily militarized areas such as the Northern Province, owing to an entrenched post-conflict culture of violence. (UNSG 2021: 23–24)

Intimidation, surveillance, and harassment by intelligence services, the military, and police are also mentioned in the latest Human Rights Council report (UNHRC 2022b: para. 30).

The first UN Secretary-General High-Level Panel commissioned to report on violence committed by both the Sri Lankan armed forces and LTTE noted that crimes of sexual violence were "greatly under-reported" due to "cultural sensitivities and associated stigma [which] often prevented victims from reporting such crimes, even to their relatives" (UNSC 2011: 44). The Office of the High Commissioner for Human Rights (OHCHR) Commission of Inquiry into Sri Lanka report (released in 2015) found that the Sri Lanka Government had continually failed to investigate, pursue, or prosecute these gross violations of human rights committed by the LTTE and the government's own security personnel (police and armed forces). In the case of SGBV crimes, the OHCHR report found that Sri Lankan armed forces deliberately targeted female civilians and LTTE combatants (male and female) for sexual violence in the final stages of the conflict (OHCHR 2015b: 117). In the immediate postconflict period, returning displaced women, former LTTE combatants (men and women), and human rights advocates were subjected to sexual violence and harassment in their homes, in administrative buildings, and in prisons and military compounds (OHCHR 2015b: 221–222; Sooka and the International Truth & Justice Project 2015: 5–6).

Sexual torture and rape produce specific psychological responses, which are exacerbated by inadequate legal protections, stigma, and homophobia. Victims-survivors have reported intense shame, intrusive memories, nightmares and flashbacks, social withdrawal, sexual dysfunction, and suicide attempts and ideation (Freedom from Torture 2015: 62–63). Victims-survivors commonly would avoid anything associated with the trauma, including being unable to remember anything or any details of the event, or being unable to disclose or fully disclose what happened (Freedom from Torture 2015: 62). These effects contributed to a reluctance to report sexual torture to government or nongovernment institutions.

Since the end of the civil war in Sri Lanka, pervasive fear of retribution, community stigma, and calls for national unity created strong incentives not to report experiences of violence. At the provincial level in the conflict zones, women-headed households—defined in a classic patriarchal way as households where there is no male "breadwinner"—reported that they were commonly approached for sexual favors in exchange for assistance or protection from the government and police sectors (FOKUS Women 2016: 8; 2017). Early marriage of girls in minority communities, a practice during the war to prevent LTTE recruitment, has continued in the East and North Provinces, visible in the high rates of teenage pregnancy (particularly in the Eastern province) (FOKUS Women 2015a: 21–22). Sexual torture of men and women in prisons was also commonplace during the period examined (CPA 2016: 7–8; OHCHR 2015b: 112, 117; Sooka and the International Truth & Justice Project 2015: 15–18, 25–26). This conflict-related abuse takes place along a continuum with widespread, everyday patterns of domestic violence and community-level discrimination against women across all ethnic communities.

During and after the war there was little capacity or support for state and nonstate institutions to respond to allegations of SGBV. The war disrupted Sri Lanka's tradition of GBV desks located in or near hospitals to provide first-response care for victims-survivors (Guruge, Jayasuriya-Illesinghe, and Gunawardena 2015: 8). Even outside of conflict locations, these desks rely on NGO staffing, which means that funding is informal and data collection is minimal (Guruge et al. 2015). There was no formal systematic data collection on SGBV during the period studied in this chapter (Wijayatilaka 2004). One national report on violence against women in Sri Lanka was completed by the government in cooperation with the World Health Organization (WHO) in 2008, but the report itself noted, "It is difficult to obtain information related to violence from any single organization in Sri Lanka. . . . Detailed information regarding certain types of violence is available with non-governmental organizations involved in violence prevention activities. However, such information does not cover the entire country and is often limited to certain identified geographical locations" (WHO 2008: 5). In 2016 the first Demographic and Health Survey collected national data on GBV, but data collection was limited to "ever married women" ages fifteen to forty-nine (Senanayake 2021: 5). Very little national-level data are available on GBV within Sri Lanka, and very little data on the effectiveness of the Prevention of Domestic Violence Act (PDVA) adopted in 2005 (Senanayake 2021: 49).[2]

Domestic violence is reportedly higher in conflict-affected areas, and women are afraid to leave for fear of stigma and inciting further communal violence against them (Sivenasen 2011; Guruge et al. 2017).

Evidentiary barriers for reporting SGBV are high in conflict and nonconflict situations across Sri Lanka. No law defines conflict-related SGBV, the state provides no witness protection, and no language in the existing penal code recognizes that boys and men can be raped (Medawatte et al. 2022: 5–6). During the conflict it was dangerous and difficult to disclose or fully disclose what happened (Freedom from Torture 2015: 62). In addition to social barriers to reporting, inadequate institutional mechanisms make it difficult for men and boys in particular to formally report SGBV. As we discuss shortly, our study shows that SGBV reporting by male victims-survivors in Sri Lanka has been rising since the end of the war (see Graph 5.9).

We expect that these documents vastly under-report the actual violence, given the specific harm to male victims-survivors who disclose their SGBV experience: their families and communities are likely to perceive them as weak or homosexual (CPA 2016: 11). Legislative provisions are mostly restricted to female victims-survivors, with male victims-survivors assuming the risk of being punished for homosexual acts (All Survivors Project 2020: 3). Comprehensive investigations, due process, and evidence collection are affected by lack of sensitivity and training on sexual violence (All Survivors Project 2020). The overturning of sexual violence convictions and stalled attempts to enact judicial reform indicate that most victims-survivors are unlikely to receive justice for conflict-related SGBV, which undermines the purpose of reporting. One rare case where two Tamil women testified to experiencing gang rape by four soldiers in Northern Sri Lanka in June 2010 reveals the difficulties. The 2010 magistrate's conviction was appealed by the soldiers, but the conviction was upheld by the Jaffna High Court in 2015. The soldiers then appealed to the Court of Appeal in 2019, and this time the conviction was overturned. During this period the two women were under immense pressure to withdraw their allegations against the soldiers by local people in their community. One woman upheld her allegations against the soldiers during this nine-year ordeal. The only protection available to her was through local women's rights groups, which gave her and her family safe shelter, counseling, financial assistance, and eventually assistance to seek refugee status and relocate overseas (Medawatte et al. 2022: 9).

In the next section we examine existing narratives on the military, social, and legal dimensions of the conflict and postconflict period.

Existing Explanations for (Post)Conflict-Related SGBV

Militarization, structural gender inequalities, and impunity are the major explanations regarding the patterns of persistent gendered political violence in Sri Lanka. Opportunism and strategy are rarely discussed in the Sri Lanka case (for exceptions, see Wood 2009). More noted in the white and grey literature on this violence is the climate of social and institutional impunity for SGBV. There have been fewer barriers to reporting than during the war contributing to the increased reported violence. While gender inequality has a long history in Sri Lanka that predates the war and is present among the Sinhalese majority and Muslim and Tamil minority groups (Wickramasinghe and Kodikara 2012: 783; Jayawardena 2016), the discrimination and violence experienced by women in the North and East is particularly endemic.

Militarization

The continued militarization of the Northern and Eastern provinces has altered but not reduced minority women's vulnerability to SGBV. "Api anaarakshithay" (We lack security) is a constant refrain by war widows (Wickremesinghe 2014). Women and girls have been subject to abuse as embodiments of minority-group identity and because gendered cultures of stigma and shame generalize their oppression and punishment across their families and communities. Some estimates put the ratio of military to civilians in the North at one soldier to five to eight civilians (ICG 2014). The military occupies large portions of land with control over agriculture, tourism and other development projects in the Northern and Eastern provinces (Verite Research 2018: 7). The Lessons Learned and Reconciliation Commission (LLRC) was much criticized for its lack of independence from the executive, but even this report stressed that the "immediate needs of women [especially economic livelihood assistance], especially widows who most often have become heads of their households, must be met ... to reduce the immense economic hardships and poverty under which they and their families are living' (Commission of Inquiry 2011: paras. 9.86, 9.87).

Women who live close to military bases or are employed on farms or in hotels or shops owned by the military continue to experience high rates of sexual harassment and abuse (FOKUS Women 2017: 15–18; ICG 2011b). Perpetrators of such violence are not restricted to the government military;

women who work in military-owned or -controlled businesses face retaliation from their local communities for colluding with the military. Some have even been accused of prostituting themselves to the Sri Lankan Army and experienced isolation and stigma for this collusion.

The opportunity exists for sexual violence to occur, as there was during the mass displacement period in 2008 and 2009, as well as extortion linked to sexual violence and torture. There is no evidence of this being a policy executed by the military or police, but there is a clear pattern of impunity when military and police commit these crimes, with little institutional response to investigate, let alone prosecute. Furthermore, victims/survivors have no one to turn to when the security sector is implicated in these crimes.

In terms of the impact of militarization within Tamil communities, the number of female ex-combatants is estimated to be around three thousand, many of whom were forcibly recruited as child brides in the North and East Provinces. They are particularly subject to abuse and harassment. There were reports of these women being shunned by communities and their own families who consider them a security threat and not marriageable (*New Humanitarian* 2011). War widows of LTTE soldiers and women and girl returnees have been targeted for gendered violence in these heavily militarized zones. Across Sri Lanka, 23 per cent of households are female-headed, and more than 50 per cent of these women are widows (Department of Census and Statistics 2015). In the North and East Provinces, at least 60 per cent of returning women are the only income providers for their households and have not always been able to return to their land or village due to discriminatory inheritance laws and practice. Some women and their children were outcasts in their new location; many had to live under emergency rule on their return, where access to wages, land, housing, and identity cards required the cooperation of military, police, and the local administration (FOKUS Women 2016; ICG 2017). Due to stigma and fear, victims-survivors were found to be reluctant to seek medical care, make a claim to police, or engage with the judicial system (CPA 2016: 7).

Structural Gender Inequalities

An economic boom and crisis since the war's end have done very little to resolve the structural inequalities and grievances based on ethnicity, caste, and gender with respect to land, resources, public employment, education, and skills in the North and East Provinces. The economic gap coupled with the impunity gap for the gender and human rights violations committed in the final stages and after the war continues to fuel the country's climate of impunity for SGBV.

Women face limited income opportunities due to their lack of education and experience, as well as cultural, even village-specific, gendered divisions of labor that restrict the jobs and decent work available to them in male-dominated sectors, such as fishing and agriculture but also in construction and garment factories (CEPA 2016a). Women and girl returnees are also vulnerable to abuse *within* their community—where women without male protection at night or dowries to protect their daughters from forced or unsuitable marriages are considered "easy prey" (Wickremesinghe 2014: 7). Similar to the Philippines case study, the absence of reports does not mean the absence of violence.

Within communities, the threat of girls facing SGBV by the police or military instilled gender order during and after the conflict. There is a tradition of early marriage in Tamil society for young girls—to secure a dowry and avoid LTTE conscription. In Tamil society, female widows are considered unlucky. This status adds to their already economically vulnerable condition, which heightens their risk of coercive and transactional sex to secure essential resources. Muslim women—rarely discussed but also significantly affected by the war—face similar inequalities caused by displacement, early marriage, and discrimination by both the Sinhalese and Tamil populations (Guruge et al. 2017). The postconflict situation has continued, and in some instances exacerbated, the daily insecurity for girls and women in North and East Sri Lanka.

For the thousands of women who lost their husbands and other family members during the armed conflict, the postwar period has brought new breadwinning responsibilities to support their families economically. These circumstances also exposed minority women to new opportunities for violent exploitation. The 2012–2013 Household Income and Expenditure Survey from the Department of Census and Statistics (2022) estimated that 1.2 million or 23.5 per cent of all households across the country are female-headed households (FHH) (either married, never married, separated, divorced, or widowed) (FOKUS Women 2015b). According to the Ministry for Women's Affairs and Child Development, the majority live in war-located provinces—there are more than 40,000 war widows in the Northern Province and 42,565 widows in the Eastern Province, whose husbands were either killed or disappeared during the war (Commission of Inquiry 2011; FOKUS Women 2014: 4). In the aftermath of the war, this social situation has created a number of problems for women already facing local stigma as female heads of households. First, the number of men missing in action is in the thousands, and few women have documentation to prove the death of their husbands or relatives to facilitate access to land or compensation, or even the ability to remarry. Second, many widows have not been able to receive Samurdhi, the targeted social assistance benefit. Despite meeting the poverty-based criteria, they have not had the necessary documentation from the state authority to claim the missing person in the household as dead (CEPA 2016b). Widows have also been vulnerable to land grabs for this same reason. Women are trapped in postconflict situations where they or their children may be vulnerable to SGBV: their status as single is known, and their children may be home alone while the women are out working. These crimes may be described as opportunistic rather than strategic, but they are connected to the impoverished and militarized conditions in North and East Sri Lanka that are the product of conflict.

War widows, female heads of households, female ex-combatants, and employed women and girls have been documented as especially at risk of postconflict SGBV due to their status in society. These women have little agency with no registration papers, no right to claim land, and no freedom to move in public spaces or work for income without risk to their children. Civilian and armed men in these societies know the women's vulnerability. Researchers identify social, ethnic, and religious tensions as associated with the Sri Lankan civil and postconflict SGBV victims-survivors and perpetrators.

Impunity

The Sri Lanka Government has faced little international condemnation for its actions during and after the conflict. UN member states did not raise the situation in Sri Lanka before the Security Council, the General Assembly, or the Human Rights Council. As a result, they were not briefed on the situation of concern for SGBV and human rights violations, nor were they added to the UN's agenda (UNSG 2012b: 46, 96). Within Sri Lanka, journalists, civil society actors, and opposition politicians who attempted to draw attention to the alleged violations were targeted for violence themselves (UNSG

2012b: 89). In 2010 UN Secretary-General Ban Ki-moon, committed to an investigation on the failure of UN officials to protect civilians in the final stages of the conflict (HRW 2012). A Panel of Experts was established to investigate accountability for conduct during the conflict, chaired by Marzuki Darusman (UNSC 2011: 44, 47, 50). The panel's 2011 report found that the Sri Lanka Government was "unable and unwilling" to satisfy the international standards of independence and accountability for investigating the allegations concerning the Sri Lanka Government and the military during the final stages of the conflict (2008–2009) (UNSC 2011). The Darusman Report stressed the gravity of the human rights abuses alleged to have been committed by the Sri Lankan military and police in the North and East Provinces (UNSC 2011: 17).

This report was followed by, inter alia, the Human Rights Watch report (HRW 2013), the International Truth & Justice Project (ITJP) reports (Sooka, the Bar Human Rights Committee of England and Wales [BHRC], and the International Truth & Justice Project 2014; Sooka and the International Truth & Justice Project 2015), and the OHCHR Report (2015b). All of these reports refer to the entrenched impunity for grave acts of torture and sexual violence committed primarily by the Sri Lankan military and police. This culture of impunity has prevailed for those who won the war in 2009.

One year after the war, in 2010, the Rajapaska government introduced a reconciliation process, the Lessons Learned and Reconciliation Commission (LLRC). The LLRC was not set up to be a fact-finding mission, nor was it given powers to act independently of the government to pursue individual accountability or judicial investigation of allegations of human rights abuses by the military and police (UNSG 2012b: 16). In 2015 the new government cosponsored a UN Human Rights Council Resolution on the LLRC (Verite Research 2018: 1). It listed thirty-six measures that the government was to implement to meet international standards of accountability, human rights, justice, and transparency, of which only 20 per cent were met (Verite Research 2018: 39). The fact that the members on the LLRC were president-appointed, increased the reluctance of some victim-survivors to report. They saw the design of the LLRC as an "institutional barrier imposed by the Sri Lankan Government to block effective reporting and investigation of rape cases: (Sooka and the International Truth & Justice Project 2015: 7). Likewise, the OHCHR report stated that a large number of sexual crimes were committed but were not reported due to fear of reprisals, stigma, and trauma (OHCHR 2015b: 223). After the release of the OHCHR report detailing some of these crimes, four soldiers were found guilty and sentenced to twenty-five years each for raping a Tamil woman in a displacement camp in Vishwamadu, Kilinochchi (*BBC News* 2015).

This was the first and last case prosecuted by the Sri Lankan military. Both the former (2005–2015) and subsequent (2015–2019, 2019–2022) government administrations have stated that they would not adopt the OHCHR call for a special hybrid international court to try war crimes by both the LTTE and Sri Lankan armed forces. Impunity for military perpetrators is pervasive. One Sri Lankan expert told us, "The president downward is protecting the military. . . . These are heroes, they did nothing wrong."[3] The most recent former Sri Lankan president, Gotibaya Rajapaksa, who was minister of defense during the last battles of the war and implicated in war crimes, has fled the country, ending his sovereign immunity from prosecution (Ganguly 2022).

The Sri Lanka Government's response to allegations of wartime rape and other acts of sexual violence has fallen far short of international legal standards on due process, investigation, and transitional justice (CPA 2016; OHCHR 2015b: 229). In 2016 the former president (Siresena) acknowledged that women and girls in war-affected regions remain vulnerable to community and state-level violence (Bandara 2016). Yet only one conviction has taken place for at least thirty-nine documented investigations, and no investigation or prosecution of cases of conflict-related SGBV against men and boys (UNSG 2016: 26; OHCHR 2015b: 126; PEARL 2022).

The report of the then leader of the opposition's (Hon. Ranil Wickremesinghe) commission on the Prevention of Violence against Women and the Girl Child (Wickremesinghe 2014), documented the rape of girls by military officers. It acknowledged that few military personnel had been prosecuted, that witnesses had been harassed or forced to leave the country, and that impunity was pervasive, particularly if the offenses were committed by the state security forces (Wickremesinghe 2014: 39). The inquiry also documented coercive and transactional sex as survival strategies for women and girls in the context of militarization in conflict areas. Members of the commission heard complaints from several women's organizations that "women are afraid to take any action in cases of sexual abuse due to fear of reprisals and as they do not get access to any form of support" (Wickremesinghe 2014: 39). In conflict-affected districts, if women wish to claim their right to access land, they must go to the military's headquarters, which for many years was the only functioning governing authority in those areas. There they fear sexual harassment or allegations, given their Tamil identity, and more often than not their status as heads of women-only households (ICG 2014; Verite Research 2018: 14). The commission concluded that impunity "is still extremely pervasive in post-war Sri Lanka" and "prevents women from reporting incidents of violence against them" (Wickremesinghe 2014: 36).

In 2016 the former Sri Lanka Government made efforts to establish transitional justice mechanisms. A Consultation Task Force on Reconciliation Mechanisms (CTF) was appointed by the president "to seek truth, ensure accountability for human rights violations and provide measures for redress" based on public consultations.[4] Its seven-hundred-page report released in January 2017 was met with silence from the Sri Lanka Government (AI 2017). Of the four transitional justice mechanisms recommended, only an Office of Missing Persons was established following a long delay (UNHRC 2017).

In March 2021 the UN Human Rights Council passed a resolution expressing serious concern at the ongoing impunity for crimes and human rights violations in Sri Lanka (UNHRC 2021: para. 7). The investigation was granted US$2.8 million to collect and preserve evidence of alleged war crimes (UNHRC 2021: para. 6). Former president Gotabaya Rajapaksa lobbied foreign governments to block support for the initiative (Ethirajan 2021b), diplomacy that reflects a broader pattern of impunity for violence and discrimination in Sri Lanka.

The persistence of SGBV in conflict and postconflict Sri Lanka is explained as the consequence of impunity that is supported by failures in other institutions. As noted earlier, Sri Lanka had no systematic data collection for SGBV during the conflict years (Colombini et al. 2018: 8). For example, medical examination is essential to a victim-survivor's case, yet these examinations are often inappropriately conducted or not conducted at all due to the medical professionals' fear of testifying or of retaliation by the perpetrators (CPA 2016: 8).

For those victims-survivors who make it to trial, there are even further challenges. Sri Lankan law does not recognize command responsibility (CPA 2016: 10). Therefore, victims-survivors may be denied a trial on the basis that they cannot identify their perpetrator, even if they can identify their uniformed affiliation to military or police (CPA 2016: 10). The judicial system also inadequately protects victims-survivors' anonymity, and many victims-survivors are reluctant to testify due to fear of identification and retaliation (CPA 2016: 8). Identification of female victims-survivors can cause stigmatization not only to the victims-survivors but also to their families, including their children. Identification of male victims-survivors can emasculate them, and they can be viewed as homosexual or weak (CPA 2016: 26). In March 2022 CEDAW found that the country had breached the rights of an LGBTI activist who was subjected to discrimination, threats, and abuse (UNHRC 2022c). The penal code still criminalizes sexual conduct between two people of the same gender. Moreover, a November 2021 ECPAT report found that boys remain particularly vulnerable to sexual exploitation and receive inadequate protection from the courts (ECPAT 2021: 40). The effect of impunity for SGBV war crimes is impunity for acts of SGBV in postconflict situations also.

The Sri Lanka Government's response to gender discrimination and human rights violations such as SGBV has been extremely limited (Colombini et al. 2018: 29). There is heavy reliance on NGOs to document SGBV cases, and at the same a preference exists amongst some NGOs to manage SGBV reporting due to mistrust of the state (Tameshnie 2016: 978). Highlighting GBV incidents has sometimes been part of the strategies of nationalist and, increasingly, religious nationalist movements (e.g., a Muslim woman attacked by Sinhalese men, or a Sinhalese woman attacked by a Tamil man). There is the danger that SGBV reports, especially by the media, serve to incite violence and retaliation. Civil-society and rights-based groups such as FOKUS, the Centre for Policy Alternatives (CPA), and the International Truth and Justice Project (ITJP) have called both for conflict-related SGBV crimes to be investigated by a government-appointed prosecutor and for gender-sensitive transitional justice mechanisms (CPA 2016; FOKUS Women 2017: 12; Sooka and the International Truth & Justice Project 2015: 5–6). To date, however, no prosecutor has been appointed to investigate the war crimes and crimes against humanity committed by the Sri Lankan armed forces and the LTTE (Jayawickrama 2015: 5–6).

Despite pledges of "A New Sri Lanka for Women" and the 2016 National Plan of Action to address GBV, the Sri Lanka Governments have not made progress in the areas that affect these women most: continued low rates of investigation and prosecution for SGBV, economic and physical vulnerability in the garment sector, and economic and employment marginalization (Verite Research 2016; Sundar 2022).

In sum, impunity has been identified as exacerbating women's (and men's, though less reported) risk of conflict-related SGBV in Sri Lanka. The postwar Sri Lanka Governments have consistently denied any systematic use of sexual violence amounting to war crimes by its security forces during and after the conflict. This denial has not been tested in a court or tribunal. What is clear is that impunity has permitted individuals and institutions from both conflict parties to avoid investigation and accountability for war crimes and crimes against humanity (OHCHR 2015b: 25). This lack of accountability has reverberated through postconflict communities and, as we discuss next, driven up reporting by NGOs and media in response, it seems, to state failure.

Our Data—Trends

The prevailing narrative about conflict-related SGBV in Sri Lanka views the use of this violence largely within the context of conflict intensity during the last battles of the war and as primarily perpetrated against Tamil minority women and girls by government armed forces rather than the LTTE (Wood 2008b; ITJP 2015; 2016; Deane 2016; Traunmüller, Kijewski, and Freitag 2019). There is no doubt this was a major pattern of Sri Lanka's conflict-related SGBV, but our study reveals other significant patterns as well.

Conflict, Violence, and Perpetrators

The majority of gender political violence reports between 1998 and 2016 were on conflict-related sexual violence (see Graph 5.1). There was only one year—2013—when the number of GBV reports (54) approached anywhere near the same volume of sexual violence reports (82). In the conflict period, total SGBV reports peaked in 2009, at the end of the war they rose to 136 reports in 2013 and 132 reports in 2015 (see Graphs 5.2 and 5.3). There were no official or unofficial reports of conflict-related sexual or gender-based violence involving one hundred to one thousand victims-survivors until 2007, with just one report recording crimes with more than one hundred victims-survivors in each of the 2007, 2008, and 2009 time frames. However, after the war, in 2011 there were two such reports of one-hundred-plus victims-survivors and four reports in 2012 with postconflict crimes in IDP camps and detention centers and involving returnees (see Graph 5.4). By the end of the war, many LTTE commanders had been killed, and hence the likelihood of documenting or prosecuting LTTE crimes would have been limited.

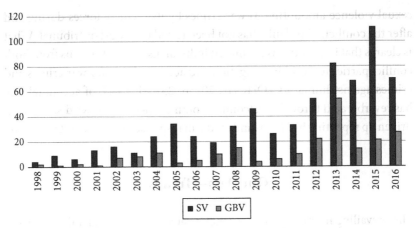

Graph 5.1 Reported SV and Reported GBV in Sri Lanka, 1998–2016

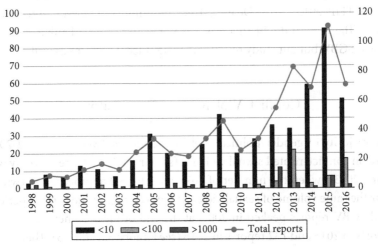

Graph 5.2 Total Conflict-Related SGBV Reports in Sri Lanka, 1998–2016

Our study revealed a similar pattern of increasing reports in the postconflict period with regard to SGBV by armed perpetrators (see Graph 5.5). While there were seventeen reports of SGBV crimes with armed perpetrators in 2009, there were forty-five such reports by 2013. In the postconflict era also, SGBV crimes by civilian perpetrators in former conflict areas increasingly began to be reported. Up to 2013 the majority of perpetrators were reported

DECONSTRUCTING VICTORY IN SRI LANKA 129

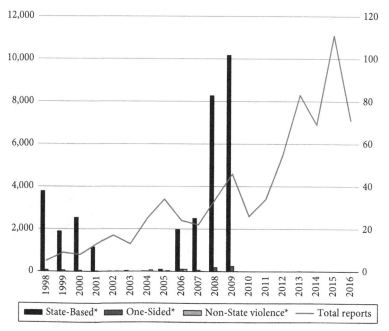

Graph 5.3 Total Fatalities by Conflict vs. Total SGBV Reports in Sri Lanka, 1998–2016

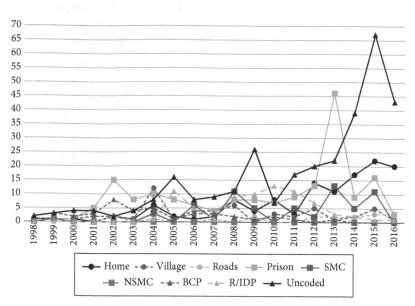

Graph 5.4 Reported Locations of SGBV Crimes in Sri Lanka, 1998–2016

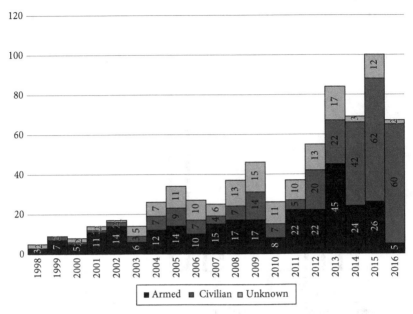

Graph 5.5 Reported Perpetrators of SGBV in Sri Lanka, 1998–2016

to be armed. The majority of perpetrators from 2014 onward were civilian. Reports of unknown perpetrators remained low throughout the period.

The majority of perpetrators were listed as male but reports of female perpetrators emerged in the postconflict period, however small (one or two reports per year; see Graph 5.6). In the case of Sri Lanka, the affiliation of the perpetrator is for the most part unknown in the postconflict years. However, during the period of intense hostilities (2008–2009) the identified perpetrator is primarily the state. Reports on SGBV by nonstate armed groups are rare and tend to appear more often when state perpetrators are also reported (see Graph 5.7). More reports of nonstate armed groups perpetrating this violence emerge postconflict, which may reveal a change in local conditions to report this violence.

Reporting Sources

Interestingly, while most reports during the war were official, in the postwar period NGOs and media have been responsible for most reports—with eighteen and fifty-nine, respectively, in 2013, for example (see Graph 5.8).

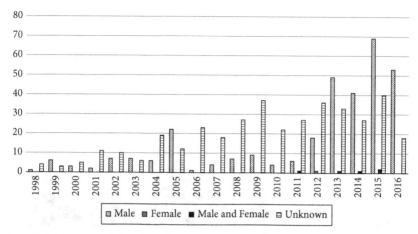

Graph 5.6 Reported Gender of Perpetrators in Sri Lanka, 1998–2016

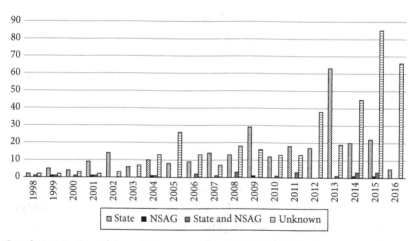

Graph 5.7 Reported Armed Perpetrators of SGBV in Sri Lanka, 1998–2016

A higher volume of reports clearly start to emerge after the end of conflict. The reporting sources change after the conflict also, and we suggest this is crucial. Media started to increasingly report SGBV from 2009 onward: a shift from ten reports in 2009 to eighty-five reports in 2015. State reports and unofficial (civil society organization) reports remain relatively stable—trending around the ten to twenty mark—for the 2008–2016 period. Prior to the end of conflict, the primary source of SGBV reports came from the state (with

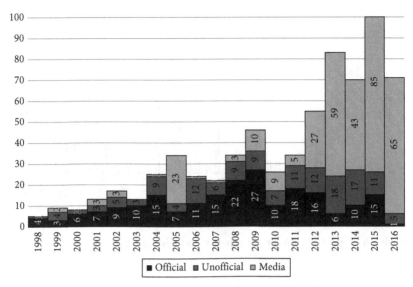

Graph 5.8 Reporting Sources of SGBV in Sri Lanka, 1998–2016

a peak in reports in 2009). Unofficial reports never rise above eighteen (in 2013) for the whole period.

Location

With regard to the location of reports, home, prisons, and IDP camps all trend upward during the postconflict years (see Graph 5.4). The majority of reported acts of SGBV occurred in prison, followed by location unknown. In the 2013 peak period, the highest number of reports record SGBV occurring in prison, followed by the home and state military compounds. In 2008 and 2009, at the height of the conflict, the peak of SGBV was occurring in unknown destinations followed by displacement camps, prisons, and state military compounds. By 2016 a shift begins in location and perpetrator, with more home-based reports and civilian perpetrators.

Finally, reports show a significant variation in the gender and age of victims-survivors (see Graphs 5.9 and 5.10). Adult females represent the highest group of victims-survivors, but male victims-survivors consistently appear across the reporting period as victims-survivors of SGBV. What is also noticeable about Sri Lanka is that it reports a high number of children

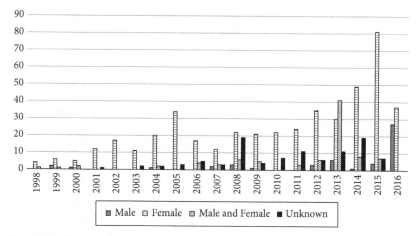

Graph 5.9 Reported Victims-Survivors by Gender in Sri Lanka, 1998–2016

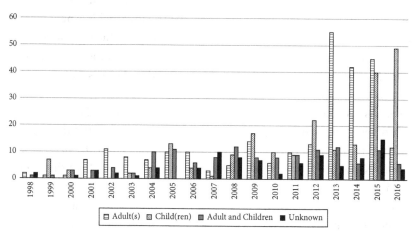

Graph 5.10 Reported Victims-Survivors by Age in Sri Lanka, 1998–2016

being subjected to this violence in the postconflict period. Little narrative is available to explain why children account for a rising number of victims-survivors of conflict-related SGBV in Sri Lanka. This is where Sri Lanka and the Philippines share some similarities, in contrast to Burma, where the majority of the reported victims-survivors remain adults.

Analysis: Militarization, Ethnonationalism, and Gender Injustice

Economic, political, and nationalist struggles are far from over in Sri Lanka, well over a decade since the war.[5] Ethnic-religious tensions are rising in the context of Sinhala Buddhist nationalism, which tends to "other" Tamil and Muslim minorities. These tensions were exacerbated by the so-called Easter Attacks by Islamist extremists (Imtiyaz 2020). Attacks on other religious minority worship places have increased, but most incidents are not reported (Imtiyaz 2020). In April 2022, protests erupted across the country against the serving president Gotabaya Rajapaksa in the context of a heightened economic crisis. In the post–COVID pandemic period, these unprecedented protests in the country have brought together majority and minority communities that have commonly challenged the government's failure to address people's basic economic security with regard to securing fuel, medicine, and food for their families (Marsh 2022). Households where women are the main breadwinners have been most affected by the economic crisis, and women, including GBV victims-survivors, have joined the protests. Some have brought their children to the streets with placards: "We have children too." A woman raising one hand in protest while holding her baby in the other has become an iconic image of the uprising (Sundar 2022).

Women's activism is a continuing thread in Sri Lanka's political history and has been central in holding successive Sri Lanka governments accountable (UNFPA 2016b). It is clear from our study that, for a long time, independent reporting opportunities for civil society on conflict-related SGBV have been narrow and constrained in Sri Lanka. We argue that the absence of safe reporting conditions affects our knowledge of the patterns and incidence of SGBV in Sri Lanka. Immediately after the war, mothers and wives would visit military camps and stand by the roadside with photos of their missing loved ones. Such informal participation has become an essential tool for women to seek truth and justice with regard to SGBV crimes during the war and after (ICG 2017). Notably, women activists have been deliberate in labeling their postwar activism as "political," recognizing the importance of their participation, influence, and voice (Koens and Gunawardana 2021: 479). This contrasts with the women's groups such as the Jaffna Mothers Front, which framed themselves as "nonpolitical" during wartime (Koens and Gunawardana 2021: 469, 479). Women's political activism has become more formalized over time, with women organizing themselves at village and district levels (ICG 2017: 12). In April 2010 a women-only Tamil group contested the local government election as an independent group in the district of Batticaloa on a justice platform (Koens and Gunawardana 2021: 469). The growth in reports from media and civil society during the 2010–2016 period reflects their growing power to report and lead on GBV advocacy.

During and after the civil war, women's grassroots organizations advocated for effective government responses to gender-based violence, including basic health and counseling services to assist victims-survivors, strengthened reporting institutions, and increased access to justice. SGBV victims-survivors in rural locations often lack access to information on how and where to locate justice services, including women's shelters and legal representation (Mollica et al. 2022: 633). Our finding is that women's organizations have quietly supported victims-survivors of conflict-related SGBV, often providing informal trauma-responsive care and healing for individual victims-survivors who would most likely never come forward to a government service due to their fear of retribution and social stigma within their own communities.

These grassroots organizations have also documented women victims-survivors' narratives, but their documentation has been informal to ensure that the experiences of victims-survivors are known and shared confidentially rather than formally, following human rights violation procedures for the preparation of legal prosecutions. Such efforts by nonstate civil society actors include evidence gathering, storytelling by victims-survivors and witnesses about experiences of sexual violence, and the act of documenting this violence itself. Increasingly, these postconflict narratives have become part of a movement for women's empowerment. The recorded narratives have informed the reports of international institutions such as the UN HRC Independent Investigation focusing on transitional justice mechanisms for Sri Lanka, and the UN Committee on the Elimination of Discrimination against Women (CEVAW) focusing on under-reporting and impunity or GBV (CEDAW 2017; UNHRC 2017; UNHRC 2022d; CEDAW 2022).[6] Were these crimes to be investigated, social, racial, and political tensions would doubtlessly be tested. Given this situation, some analysts have suggested that transitional justice mechanisms may deliver accountability but not repair the harm resulting from Sri Lanka's history of conflict-related sexual violence (Kodikara 2016; Manikkalingam 2016). By contrast with the local informal responses of women's organizations to gender-based violence, Vasuki Nesiah (2012: 6) argues that gender advocacy in post–civil war Sri Lanka focused on peace and reconciliation has often not been effective in protecting those most vulnerable. In other words, some acts of SGBV have not been recorded, and reports have deliberately not identified perpetrators or victims-survivors. Agency is held by victims-survivors and civil society actors on what to report and what to conceal.

Unity has been the objective in how SGBV advocates have organized in Sri Lanka; they have sought four forms of gender justice: gender security, reparations, economic justice, and participatory justice (Jordal, Wijewardena, and Olsson 2013; De Alwis 2013: 21). *Gender security* involves bringing security to women and girls living in militarized areas in particular and promoting a culture of gender equality that aims to end patriarchal norms (Saravananthan 2016: 29). *Reparative justice* is needed to redress the unequal compensation awarded to the families of Sri Lankan army members and those of missing, disappeared, or surrendered minorities, and to provide long-term support to these latter families, which are often single and female-headed. *Economic justice* is crucial for the right to nonrecurrence given the conditions of structural violence disproportionately affecting minority women and girls, as already discussed. *Participatory justice* refers to the need to cultivate citizens' trust in the government, to enable male victims-survivors to have a voice in gender justice, and to allow all ethnic and religious communities to voice their security concerns and lived realities (True 2012: 77–94; Jayasundere and Valters 2014).

Given successive governments' reluctance to pursue a judicial transitional justice response, the equal weighting of these forms of justice suggests the need for an alternative approach to addressing the structural and physical violence currently experienced by many female-headed households, former female combatants, rural women, and SGBV victims-survivors. Despite the increased reporting that we observe in our study indicating a high prevalence of SGBV in postconflict areas in Sri Lanka, the likelihood of prosecuting individuals for committing war crimes is low while social stigma and weak institutional conditions for reporting exist. It also remains difficult to measure whether reporting matches the actual prevalence of SGBV due to the lack of consistent and transparent data collection methods in the country, which has been a frequent subject of UN CEDAW reports over the last decade.

Conclusion

In this chapter, we have highlighted the relationship between the dynamics of conflict and postconflict and the persistent patterns of SGBV in Sri Lanka. Silence and impunity persist for the SGBV crimes committed during and immediately after the war as a result of the victory of the government and its continuing militarization. Since the civil war ended, the Sri Lanka Government has consistently denied reports of military perpetration of SGBV and voiced opposition to any form of international oversight of transitional justice processes. As a result, the national process has failed to deliver equitable and transitional justice—let alone transformative justice for SGBV victims-survivors. There remains no justice for the human rights and political opponents of the former Rajapaska regime, the Tamil women and men detained often on nothing more than suspicion of association with LTTE, and returned displaced women, many of whom are now single heads of households.

The continuum of violence is particularly evident with respect to the structural and physical violence against minorities, political opposition, and women. Increased SGBV reporting in the postwar period indicates both the opportunity to report but also a high prevalence situation with multiple reports confirming that these groups since 2009 have been consistently targeted for sexual violence for the purposes of intimidation and extortion. The rise in reports of gender-based violence is associated with postconflict communal disharmony where ethnonationalist dynamics collide with displacement, leading to early and forced marriage of girls. Victims-survivors fear reporting this violence and are stigmatized in all communities, reinforcing the impunity.

The Sri Lanka Government's protracted failure to address conflict-related SGBV is compounded by the inequity of the postconflict economy and the current crisis's negative impact on women and especially households where women are the main providers. Despite improvements in legal justice and institutional reporting processes, impunity and structural gender discrimination in the country remain. The activism and documentation efforts of grassroots women's organizations has supported victims-survivors and has expanded the struggle for postconflict justice with the focus on gender justice, but organizations have had to be selective with their documentation and activism to protect victims-survivors.

Given the endemic nature of SGBV, the resistance in Sri Lanka to formal war crimes and truth and reconciliation mechanisms, and ongoing economic development challenges, a broader gender justice approach could be feasible. Feminist scholars of transitional justice have long argued for an approach that moves beyond retributive justice to address the structural gender inequalities that are root causes of violence against women and girls in particular (Rubio-Martin 2006). Such an approach shifts attention away from the perpetrators towards the victims-survivors of violence and the opportunities through gender-just development interventions to reclaim their lives and capabilities. Any program for gender justice in Sri Lanka must provide access to social and economic resources to ensure political and economic equality to prevent future gendered harms. Implementing a reparative development approach is necessary and may provide greater opportunities for women long disenfranchised and harmed by war.

6
Comparing Regional Patterns and Trends in Conflict-Related Sexual and Gender-Based Violence across Asia

Scholars, states, and international organizations have begun to systematically count, document, and compare the incidence of sexual and gender-based violence (SGBV) in conflict-affected countries. They are beginning to make more visible its scale, extent, and egregious forms because of its historical impunity. In this book, we have argued that the focus on recognized high-intensity conflicts and thresholds for the number of conflict-related SGBV cases in the UN Security Council has limited the attention paid to SGBV in low-intensity conflicts, which includes the violence that occurs in displacement from conflict and continues after conflict. Women's and girls' severe lack of access to social and economic resources in conflict-affected and displacement situations impacts their vulnerability to violence. Highly gendered societies increase the risk of SGBV being used to silence and intimidate women and men, girls and boys.

The three countries from Southeast and South Asia in our book have experienced some of the world's most protracted civil conflicts. Differences as well as common patterns are discernible in SGBV across these countries, based on official and unofficial open-source reports. SGBV in these low-intensity conflicts has not been widely acknowledged or known nor attracted consistent international censure and action. All three countries discussed in this volume have been undergoing uneven transformations towards democracy and peace, although that process abruptly halted in Burma in 2021 and was threatened by economic crisis in Sri Lanka and violence in the Philippines in 2017.

We have argued that the Rome Statute definition of "widespread and systematic" SGBV in the International Criminal Court (ICC) directs us to consider any situation where the use of this violence is systematically linked to a war-fighting objective or where there is a pattern of such violence even if the country in question is not listed in the annual report of the UN Secretary-General on conflict-related sexual violence (Burma and Sri Lanka have been listed in the annual report, but never the Philippines, UNSG 2012a, UNSG 2013, UNSG 2014, UNSG 2015, UNSG 2016, UNSG 2017, UNSG 2018, UNSG 2019, UNSG 2020, UNSG 2021, UNSG 2022, UNSG 2023). There is an assumption in the scholarly literature, however, that high-intensity conflicts based on a high count of battle deaths are also those cases with a high prevalence of conflict-related SGBV, rather than low-intensity conflicts with low death numbers. As a result, low-intensity, often protracted conflict cases have been neglected in SGBV scholarship. Attending to this neglect is essential in contexts where gender discrimination and impunity are pervasive. We appreciate that SGBV reporting may not fully reflect the actual violence perpetrated, but official and unofficial reports do indicate some clear patterns consistent with human rights violations, which makes it salient to interrogate the substantive information contained in the reports themselves as opposed to their mere count of SGBV incidence.

In this chapter we compare our findings across the three cases, interrogating reported and nonreported violence by media, government, and nongovernment organizations between 1998 and 2016 in order to reveal the effects on SGBV of conflict dynamics and patterns of human rights violations before and during the armed conflicts.

We highlight four common trends within and across the sites of our study that are relevant to and should be further examined in other low-intensity or protracted conflicts in Asia and beyond:

1. Escalation of SGBV reports takes place along with increased international access to conflict areas and the politicization of these reports.
2. Consistently low reports may be the result of no state provision of services or institutions for reporting conflict-related SGBV; this is emblematic of state denial of conflict as is common across Asia and low prioritization of gendered political violence, a more general trend.
3. Little reporting of SGBV perpetrated by nonstate armed actors does not mean low nonstate armed actor prevalence.
4. How a conflict ends may sustain conflict-related SGBV and impunity.

Concerning the relationship between systematic or widespread SGBV and the onset or upswing of conflict violence, we found variation across the three cases and no consistent pattern. We suggest that addressing the reporting limitations identified here and throughout this book may assist with identifying the onset and escalation of SGBV in low-intensity conflict environments.

Escalation of Reports with International Access

First, awareness of conflict-related SGBV is growing, but there are either limited or no formal institutions to report to or justice processes to appeal to in low-intensity conflict contexts. At the same time, SGBV is highly politicized and is part of the dynamics of the respective conflicts. Graph 6.1 shows the trend of increasing SGBV reports across all three cases since 1998—including after the end of the civil war in Sri Lanka. We see significant increases in reported SGBV in all three countries, especially in Burma after 2010.

As we discussed in Chapter Three, awareness of SGBV was triggered in Burma by the presence of international actors in the context of regime change—and by reports of sexual violence that captured the attention of the global media (GEN 2015). While the total number of SGBV reports is lower in Burma compared to the Philippines and Sri Lanka, the number of reports since 2012 is not greatly different. Once the country opened to the world during the incipient democratic transition after Cyclone Nargis in 2008, reports began to increase. Similarly, reports in Sri Lanka began to

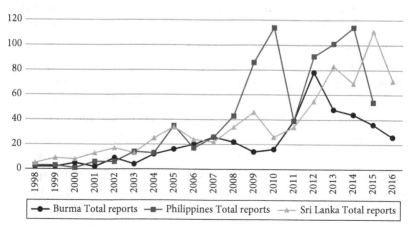

Graph 6.1 Total Conflict-Related SGBV Reports for Three Countries, 1998–2016

increase only after its war ended, with the highest reported incidence from 2012 to 2015.

Awareness of this violence is used to advance particular armed-actor struggles. SGBV perpetrated against civilian women by uniformed men is highly controversial and socially more contested than incidents of intimate-partner or domestic violence, which are often seen as normal or acceptable and therefore are not reported (Sepali et al. 2017). We observe that reports of conflict-related SGBV, including gender-based and domestic violence perpetrated by civilians in conflict areas, began to escalate at the same time as the international opening of Burma after Cyclone Nargis in 2008 (see Davies and True 2017a; Faxon, Furlong, and Phyu 2015).

The Philippines case reveals the importance of international actors being present to document and report SGBV in the absence of state institutions collecting reports, compounding the reporting (knowledge) gap on SGBV in this conflict. The peaks in unofficial reports of SGBV coincide with mass displacement events caused by conflict and typhoons in Mindanao, where national and international humanitarian actors were temporarily present in higher numbers. Crucially, in these reports, there are references to widespread (but not systematic) SGBV, with the exception of the Marawi siege in 2017 (identified as systematic). In a low-intensity conflict, the pattern of widespread but not systematic SGBV along with the absence of national and international actors reporting this violence can lead to these sites being ignored.

Further to this argument, there are political conditions for reporting and generating knowledge about SGBV crimes in conflict and postconflict affected areas. Graph 6.2 shows the official, unofficial, and media sources of reporting for all three conflict cases taken together.

The major pattern revealed in the graph is that most SGBV reports are by media organizations, but the Philippines accounts for the vast majority of media reports. This is interesting because when the media pick up on the impunity, it becomes evident that less unofficial and official reporting comes from state and nonstate institutions that can lead to justice or other redress mechanisms. A rise in media reporting to report impunity was apparent in the Philippines after the ceasefire agreement and became apparent in Sri Lanka with a demand for democratic reform leading up to the 2015 elections. An additional pattern of reporting for the Philippines however, is that media sensationalism and rumors are rife: media reports are voluminous and we observe that the government does little to confirm or deny them. In

COMPARING PATTERNS AND TRENDS ACROSS ASIA 143

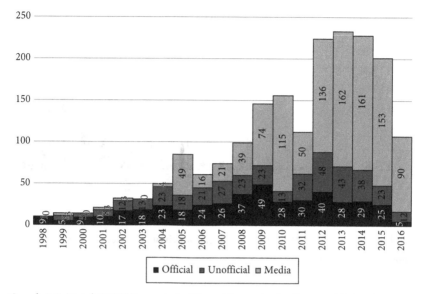

Graph 6.2 Total SGBV Reports for Three Countries by Source, 1998–2016

authoritarian contexts, the official and unofficial reports remain in step, and sometimes the official source outreports the unofficial sources and media. Here reporting may not indicate the incidence of violence per se. However, it may illustrate the freedom to report.

In conflict areas that are difficult to access, SGBV reporting is also difficult. Therefore, we should expect to receive fewer reports from states where the militaries are committing offenses and less reporting from all sources in authoritarian states with tighter control over all institutions, and we expect reporting volume per year to be higher when a conflict has received international attention. Both patterns are clear in the cases of Burma and Sri Lanka in the 1998–2016 period.

With regard to the age and sex of victims-survivors of conflict-related SGBV, while most reports are of female victims-survivors, there is an escalation of reports of child victims-survivors, especially in the Philippines and Sri Lanka, and of male victims-survivors in Sri Lanka since 2012 after the end of the civil conflict in that country (see Graphs 6.3 and 6.4). Women are still three times more likely, according to our reports, to suffer and report SGBV, but children appear to be at as much risk as adults, with 276 reports on children and 275 reports on adults. In the Sri Lankan context, there have been concerted training efforts by the UK Preventing Sexual Violence Initiative

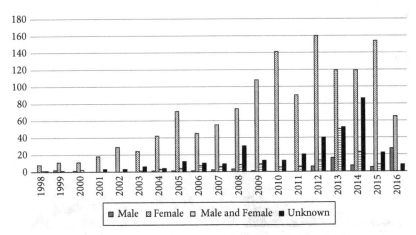

Graph 6.3 Total SGBV Reports by Victims-Survivors Gender for Three Countries, 1998–2016

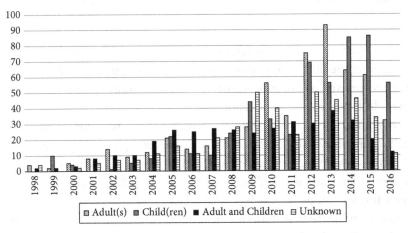

Graph 6.4 Total SGBV Reports by Victims-Survivors Age for Three Countries, 1998–2016

to work with men and boys postconflict (FOKUS Women and British High Commission 2017) and with the distinct gender-based stigma they experience as SGBV victims-survivors (Schulz and Touquet 2020). By contrast, there are few reports of child or male victims-survivors in Burma, although there is some evidence of rape and other sexual violence against men and children in the context of civilian attacks on Rohingya communities in

Rakhine state in 2017 (see Chapter Three, this volume). As that chapter notes, men and boys are harmed by the culture of "entrenched male dominance" that masks their experiences of victimization (Chapter Three). The Philippines' reports of SGBV against men and children, especially by the media, are an increasing trend, although in the context of an overwhelming silence on conflict-related sexual violence (see Chapter Four). In 2016, however, the CEDAW Committee highlighted the link between conflict, poverty, and GBV in the Philippines, noting the increasing occurrence of online sexual exploitation and abuse of children (Chapter Four).

Attention to children as being particularly vulnerable to conflict-related SGBV is a tentative finding (our sample is small) that requires further examination.

Low Reporting Due to Low Awareness, Low Prioritization

When countries deny that they have a conflict or are a conflict- or postconflict-affected state—as is the case with Burma, the Philippines, and Sri Lanka, and across the Asian region to different extents—then they also do not have to acknowledge that they have a problem with conflict-related SGBV. In these cases, providing or strengthening services to enable SGBV in conflict to be reported and redressed is not a priority. In addition, gender social codes and norms are strong in these environments; the harms from reporting—by victims-survivors and by first response services—may outweigh any benefit. Our expectation was that there would be a low number of SGBV reports in sites where there is limited state access and access to services. Our dataset on the location of SGBV incidents enabled us to confirm this hunch.

In Burma, all SGBV crimes are extremely under-reported. Despite successive efforts, there is still no law prohibiting domestic violence in Burma, whereas both Sri Lanka and the Philippines have such laws. During this period, all forms of SGBV against Rohingya in Rakhine state were extremely under-reported, but the paucity of reporting did not reflect the actual levels of violence they were experiencing. Conflict broke out in Rakhine in 2012, 2016, and 2017 between the Burma border police and military, Arakan militia, and the Rohingya minority, with deaths and human rights violations, including SGBV, recorded by the UN.[1] Restricted humanitarian access limited safe SGBV reporting, as did fears of retaliation and mistrust of health services, which (at the time) had to report all cases of SGBV to the police.

There is low reporting of conflict-related SGBV among displaced Rohingya and other populations despite the international consensus that this type of violence is pervasive. As we argue in Chapter Three, it can be dangerous to report trafficking, forced marriage, and abduction perpetrated by civilians and nonstate armed groups. As a result, reporting by international actors with conditional humanitarian access to some areas is highly political (see Chapter Three). Traditional gender norms and stereotypes are also deeply entrenched amongst displaced populations, making it unlikely that SGBV would be reported within communities (Chapter Three). Overall, the likelihood is that the SGBV reports documented as occurring within Burma are a small representation of the extent of the crimes committed.

By contrast, take the case of the Philippines. This country has amongst the highest national levels of reported domestic violence against women in Southeast Asia, reflecting the government's early adoption of an elimination of violence against women law (the Anti-Violence Against Women and Their Children Act) in 2004 and the government's institutional capacity to implement that law (The Asia Foundation 2017). However, despite this national capacity, the conflict-affected Autonomous Region of Muslim Mindanao (ARMM, at the time) recorded the lowest number of SGBV cases of any subnational region in the Philippines in 2014 and 2015, while the neighboring, peaceful region of Davao recorded the highest number of cases, though it has a much smaller population (Davies, True, and Tanyag 2016). This paradox in subnational reporting patterns is a common finding in our study of low-intensity conflict settings in Asia.

Due to strong gender-based codes of honor within families and communities in Mindanao, and the shame associated with rape and other sexual violence, women and girls are expected to keep silent about the violence they have experienced. They may do this to prevent the escalation of clan violence (Hilsdon 2009) in contexts where abduction, rape, and forced marriage are common, and where daughters may be offered for marriage to appease warring clans (Davies et al. 2016: 467). As a high-ranking police official from the autonomous region stated, "Because of culture, people will not report [crimes] to the police. They consult their village chiefs because once they report it to the police, it is tantamount to a declaration of war" (*Manila Times* 2014). Moreover, in a region where group belonging is defined by ethnic, religious, and political identities, trust in the police was rare given its association with colonization and the federal state (Guanzon 2008).

The Sri Lanka case also features under-reporting of SGBV despite the government's institutional capacity to respond. A seven-hundred-page report released by the government-appointed Consultation Task Force on Reconciliation Mechanisms (CTF) in January 2017 was met with silence from the Sri Lanka Government (see Chapter Five, this volume). Former president Gotabaya Rajapaksa lobbied foreign governments to block support for the United Nations Human Rights Council (UNHRC) resolution expressing serious concern at ongoing impunity from crimes (Ethirajan 2021a). Despite an SGBV national plan, there is no systemic data collection, which makes it difficult to offer and tailor services to victims-survivors, such as healthcare services (see Chapter Five, this volume). Moreover, as Chapter Five highlighted, the social stigma associated with being a victim-survivor of SGBV creates a strong incentive not to report the violence—as a result, there is little support for state and nonstate actors to provide services to respond to SGBV.

In sum, SGBV in conflict areas may be largely unreported even when governments have the institutional capacity to respond to this violence. The upshot of this finding is that scholars and international organizations tend to underestimate conflict-related SGBV in Asia's civil conflicts, and states are able to fly under the radar when it comes to introducing institutions that will count, respond to, and redress this violence. Local civil society organizations must carefully balance the need to raise awareness and report this violence with the political and social repercussions of doing so. These combined circumstances may contribute to the lack of political and institutional will to address this violence, and the consequences for victims-survivors and their communities is that the violence remains—paradoxically—known but hidden.

In all three conflict-affected cases, the top five locations of SGBV crimes where it could be identified in reports was, first, the village; next, home; then prison and state military compound; and last, refugee/IDP camp (see Graph 6.5). In Sri Lanka, the most prevalent locations are prison followed by IDP/refugee camp. In the Philippines and Burma, it was the village, with the home the location for the most reports in Burma during 2015–2016, for the first time. It makes sense that reports of these crimes in villages will be high since conflict-related SGBV is targeted against communities, not merely individuals. Report peaks in homes tend to follow—no more than one year after—the peak violence recorded in the village, prison, or IDP camp for each case. Highly political sexual violence or gender-based violence may occur in

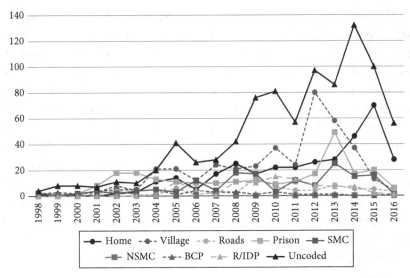

Graph 6.5 Total SGBV Reports by Location for Three Countries, 1998–2016

family homes in acts of retaliation or may be reported when populations return home.

We would expect reports in refugee/IDP camps to be higher than shown, given that they have been targets in the three cases of low-intensity conflicts and, technically there should be available humanitarian institutions to which to report. However, the pattern of nonreporting in IDP camps is very significant in these cases. As Chapter Three discusses with regard to the qualitative research of humanitarian organizations based in Burma's Rakhine state, the in-group barriers and risks to reporting are high, thus explaining the lack of SGBV reports in this conflict situation. In the case of the Philippines, humanitarian actors noted the difficulty with victims-survivors coming forward to report SGBV that they knew was occurring. Finally, in Sri Lanka, reports of SGBV within the displacement camps in 2008 and 2009 primarily came from international humanitarian actors and media. Local civil society groups felt safe to report violence they witnessed or recorded only when the UN call for an investigation commenced in 2012. Displacement camps are not safe sites to report when the state remains in control of security and humanitarian access; these sites need to be prioritized as safe places to implement monitoring, analysis and reporting arrangements (MARA) procedures (Seatzu 2021).[2]

Nonstate Armed Actors Do Perpetrate, But . . .

Overall, more SGBV crimes in our dataset are reportedly committed by civilian perpetrators than armed and uniformed perpetrators (see Graph 6.6). Allegations against armed uniformed perpetrators are higher for state perpetrators than nonstate armed perpetrators (see Graph 6.7). This tends to confirm the prevailing narrative that SGBV is perpetrated by government armed forces. Yet when there is an absence of formal state institutions to report SGBV to in nongovernment areas, crimes perpetrated by nonstate armed actors may go unreported, leading to the false assumption that they do not occur. Also, civilians outnumber armed perpetrators in total reports for our three countries (albeit by a small difference: 762 reports for civilians compared to 745 reports for armed perpetrators). Our qualitative comparison of the three cases reveals that a practice of nondisclosure of SGBV perpetrated by nonstate armed actors may occur when there is no presence of humanitarian institutions to report to and no safe space to retreat to for victims-survivors. Humanitarian institutions may also decide on a nondisclosure practice when these institutions are tasked with responding to SGBV prevention—as well as protection—and need to maintain their access to communities.

Having no SGBV reports, although actors on the ground know about the presence of actual violence, reinforces the political narrative that state militaries are the main or only perpetrators. We observed this phenomenon

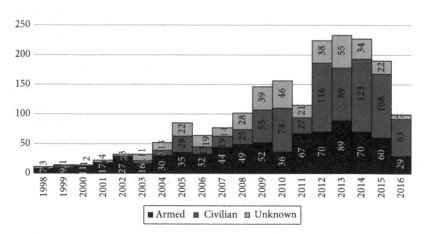

Graph 6.6 Total Reported Perpetrators of SGBV for Three Countries, 1998–2016

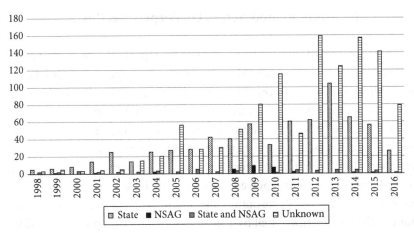

Graph 6.7 Total Reported Armed Perpetrators of SGBV for Three Countries, 1998–2016

in the cases of Burma and Sri Lanka discussed in Chapter Three and Chapter Five. Our analysis of SGBV reports enables us to explore this phenomenon further. In all three cases in our study, the identification of the perpetrator as uniformed state-affiliated military is high and almost always definite. By contrast, the identification of nonstate armed group perpetrators is minimal. In Burma, for example, there were no SGBV crimes reported by an armed nonstate actor in 2015–2016 and just one case was reported in 2014. In Sri Lanka, reports of nonstate armed groups rose after 2013 when there were nineteen reports, but civilians also become the most prevalent perpetrators reported after 2013 in the postconflict period. In the Philippines, there is a very high number of "unknown" armed perpetrators reported each year, but their affiliation with state military or nonstate armed groups is never recorded.

As shown in Graphs 6.8, 6.9, and 6.10, there is variation in armed, civil, and unknown perpetrator types across the three low-intensity conflict cases. In the Philippines and Sri Lanka, civilians overall are the major perpetrators, although in Sri Lanka, armed state perpetrators were the highest number of reported offenders at the end of the war between 2008 and 2009. In Burma, the majority of offenders are armed perpetrators. During the conflict—which for Burma is the entire period of study, 1998–2016—SGBV perpetrators were most likely to be armed.

Nonstate armed actors (including ethnic armed organizations) may rarely be reported as SGBV perpetrators when compared with state armed actors

COMPARING PATTERNS AND TRENDS ACROSS ASIA 151

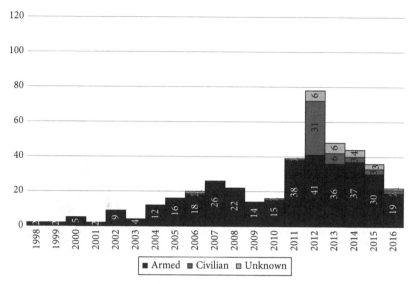

Graph 6.8 Total Reported Perpetrators of SGBV in Burma, 1998–2016

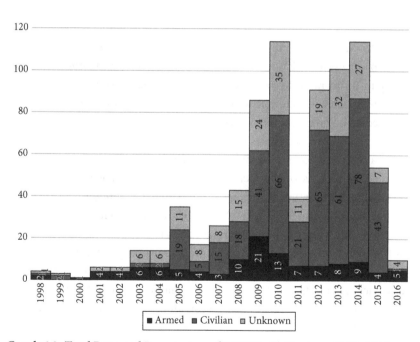

Graph 6.9 Total Reported Perpetrators of SGBV in Philippines, 1998–2016

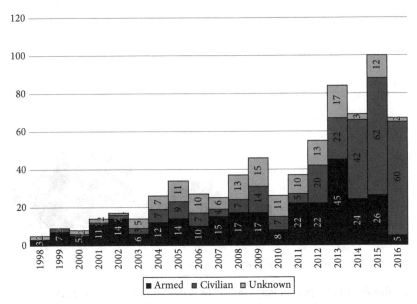

Graph 6.10 Total Reported Perpetrators of SGBV in Sri Lanka, 1998–2016

in these low-intensity conflict situations for two main reasons. First, state actors who engage in SGBV will be primarily the military and police. They are usually in uniform and readily identified by civilians. This is typically not the case for nonstate actors who may or may not be in uniform and readily identified as belonging to an armed group. In the Philippines for instance, the higher number of reports of civilian perpetrators does not mean the perpetrators were not armed, but rather that they likely were not in clearly identifiable uniforms, or connected with clan-based violence on which there is little official reporting (Chapter Four). It may be difficult to investigate nonstate actors' use of SGBV as systematic or widespread in these situations. In Burma, international humanitarian actors must seek permission to access the areas that are controlled by ethnic armed groups. In Sri Lanka, until the loss of the LTTE, their areas were tightly controlled and had provided limited access to outsiders (Chapter Five). Under these conditions of insurgency, there are few agencies to which individuals can safely report if they are experiencing SGBV.

A second reason for the low number of reports of nonstate actors is that in all three low-intensity conflict cases analyzed in this book, civilians have been residents in rebel or nonstate combatant–held territory for long periods

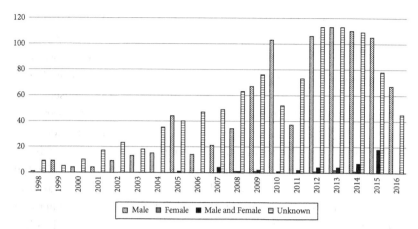

Graph 6.11 Total Reported Gender of Perpetrators for Three Countries, 1998–2016

of time. Under these conditions, insurgency environments are often intensely gendered in terms of the roles and contributions that women and men are expected to make. For instance, women are frequently expected to provision soldiers on the frontline and be mothers to the next combatant generation. This has been the case for Kachin state, for the Bangsamoro Autonomous Region in Muslim Mindanao, and the LTTE held region under their defeat in Sri Lanka (Hedström 2017; Hilsdon 2009). As such, acts like forced marriage may not be considered or framed as conflict-related SGBV, and even when humanitarian actors gain access, there is a reluctance to report these acts for fear of being 'shut out' from these communities. Finally, the recorded sex of most perpetrators is male, but female perpetrators begin to be reported in small numbers in the Philippines and Sri Lanka in the later years of our dataset (see Graph 6.11). The numbers are too small to establish a meaningful pattern but it might reveal that, over time, especially in ceasefire and/or post-conflict situations there may be more opportunity for different experiences of SGBV to be recorded and reported.

How Conflict Ends Matters for SGBV Impunity

How a conflict ends has crucial implications for the reporting and nonreporting of SGBV. Whether there is a ceasefire or peace agreement brokered between conflicting parties or a state victory, the end of the conflict shapes the patterns of SGBV in the postconflict period. We find that SGBV may continue with impunity in postconflict areas. In Sri Lanka, for example, gender-based violence is referenced widely in government reports however, only a few official reports have appeared about conflict-related SGBV (Davies and True 2017b). There remain a high number of accused, a very small number of formal investigations, and no prosecutions for war crimes including SGBV. In Sri Lanka, a civil war victory by the government led to further repression of minority groups and political opposition. Since the civil war ended in 2009 the Sri Lanka Government has consistently voiced opposition to any form of international oversight of local transitional justice processes. Multiple reports confirm that Tamil minorities and former political prisoners have since 2009 been consistently targeted for sexual violence for the purposes of intimidation and extortion. As Chapter Five detailed, international efforts calling for the Sri Lanka Government to investigate allegations against their security sector were repeatedly rejected.

In Burma, a protracted peace process took place between 2012 and 2016 during the period of study under much international attention that encouraged reporting if not justice. However, impunity for all past crimes for all signatories was included in the 2015 nationwide ceasefire agreement. The only mention of SGBV was that armed groups should not commit these crimes. In Burma there has been no prosecution for conflict-related SGBV. Indeed, one of the most cited reasons for the domestic violence legislation failing successive attempts to be introduced in Burma's lower house of Parliament was a dispute over including the term "conflict-related SGBV" in the bill (the term was eventually removed and the bill has still not been adopted; see Chapter Three, this volume). In the case of the Philippines, there was an internationally mediated peace process culminating in a comprehensive agreement but no mention of conflict-related SGBV in the document. In two Women, Peace and Security National Action Plans (GoP 2009, Gop 2016), the Philippines government refers to setting up an early warning monitoring system for conflict-related SGBV but has not yet done so (see Chapter Four, this volume).

The comparative analysis of the three conflict cases examined in this book shows that conflict-related SGBV reporting is deeply politicized across local, regional, and international contexts in Asia. Discussion of situations where reports are either not taking place or being publicly shared is limited. The reasons for this silence may be to protect peace accords, to protect combatants (existing or demobilised) over victims-survivors, or because the reporting of particular crimes is considered too sensitive or risky, affecting the guarantee of safety of victims-survivors. However, only when we have analyzed the particular discriminatory gendered context of a conflict-affected situation can we know how far and in what ways impunity for SGBV crimes affects reporting, by whom, and when. Moreover, the absence of SGBV language in a peace agreement does not mean the crimes were absent from the conflict.

Qualitative studies of conflict situations are vital to explain the variation in reporting of SGBV committed by the military, nonstate armed groups, or civilians, as our study shows. We must disaggregate the data on victims-survivors according to gender and age as well as trace the patterns of SGBV through the phases of each conflict and the location where violence was perpetrated. In low-intensity conflicts such as the cases we examined, it is still difficult to get reliable SGBV data in conflict-affected and post-conflict-affected conditions. Social, political, and institutional barriers thwart the collection of SGBV data that could lead to more effective responses and access to justice.

Implications for Justice

While justice and transitional justice systems are not the focus of this book, a clear cross-cutting theme of the study is the relationship between limited or politicized reporting institutions and curtailed access to justice for victims-survivors of conflict-related SGBV. Justice is highly contextualized—embedded in cultural traditions and social norms including gender norms but also closely associated with universal principles of equity, fairness, and impartiality, which are institutionalized in international and national law (UNSC 2004). In the three low-intensity conflict cases discussed here, the lack of or the weak institutions to report to is associated with and likely a cause of the poor justice response. In none of the cases has there been a transitional justice process for SGBV. The governments in Burma and Sri Lanka have resisted transitional justice processes, and while the 2014 Bangsamoro Comprehensive Peace Agreement in the Philippines provided limited transitional justice provisions, none included redress for SGBV, reinforcing the silence of victims-survivors.

Existing laws against sexual violence or violence against women are another avenue for conflict-related SGBV victims-survivors. In Burma, however, there were no civil or criminal laws against SGBV despite significant advocacy and international pressure on the government to adopt such a law during the period of study. In Sri Lanka and the Philippines, where national laws and action plans exist to eliminate VAW, the gap between the provision and implementation of these protections is demonstrable. In both countries, the conflict- and postconflict-affected areas, in particular, are often rural and remote and historically nongovernment areas during insurgencies. There is no or little proximity to justice institutions or services that enable victims-survivors to report and seek recourse for SGBV. Reporting to state-run institutions when state of emergency provisions are in place, as was the case in the Philippines and Sri Lanka during the years we examined, can be harmful and stigmatizing for women.

In these contexts of impunity for conflict-related SGBV crimes, even when awareness and reporting have increased, especially in postconflict Sri Lanka, this has not been matched by increased access to justice remedies. Moreover, as we find, the presence of international actors rather than greater state capacity and responsiveness promoted the increased reporting. In the cases we examined, states continue to ignore SGBV and adequate justice provision.

Moreover, in authoritarian contexts, when state militaries commit crimes, governments may opt for military rather than civilian formal or informal justice processes. This has been the case in each country we examined. Military compared with civilian courts are neither transparent, independent, nor safe for victims-survivors.

Even when conflict-related SGBV victims-survivors seek justice through existing mechanisms given the absence of transitional justice, they may be denied a trial because they could not identify the perpetrator, as in the rare Sri Lanka case discussed in Chapter Five. Where there is no transitional justice mechanism, as in all three cases, the harms from reporting—especially the social stigma and ongoing presence of the military in postconflict-affected areas—will almost always outweigh the benefits. While the governments in these cases in the Asian region are keen to leave the past behind, victims-survivors suffer ongoing stigma, fear, and economic marginalization if they can't return home. Whether a conflict ends with a winner, a ceasefire, or a negotiated peace settlement, impunity for perpetrators ensures that the violence continues in postconflict areas, setting back the recovery of victims-survivors and communities.

In sum, since limited or politicized reporting institutions for conflict-related SGBV exist in Burma, the Philippines, and Sri Lanka, the understanding of and possibility for justice is also limited and politicized. This phenomenon is not isolated to these cases and is a more general pattern in Asia where social, economic, cultural, and institutional factors perpetuate inequalities and restrict access to reporting and access to justice, especially due to discrimination against women and against ethnic minorities within the pluralist legal structures that dominate the region (see Mollica et al. 2022).

Conclusion

The linkages between conflict-affected SGBV and gender inequality in Asia are still being established. Existing studies in other regions point to a "tip of the iceberg" phenomenon where there is a high prevalence of SGBV but a low level of actual reporting. In our study, we not only highlight this converse relationship with respect to the scale of SGBV but we also analyze how the systematic silences, limitations of reporting, and political bias in reporting impact counting and SGBV knowledge.

Our study of the local contexts of low-intensity conflict-affected situations in Asia leads us to predict that SGBV reporting will most likely continue to be scarce. Reports will be silenced or just difficult to produce where populations have little power. Furthermore, where reports are made, they may become part of the power play of conflict. As we argued in Chapter Two, our knowledge of *where* widespread and systematic SGBV is occurring and *who* is most affected requires careful consideration. It requires us to reflect on the patterns of nonreporting discussed in Chapter Three, Four, and Five as well as official and unofficial reporting when we analyze and interpret SGBV reports.

In the final chapter, we reflect on our findings about the local politics of SGBV knowledge in the three cases in Asia and the implications for how we document and count SGBV at the international level, address the shortcomings of statistical analysis, and include context-specific knowledge.

Conclusion

Exposing Hidden Wars and Interrogating Silences to End Impunity

Hidden Wars is the first published book-length study of sexual and gender-based violence (SGBV) in three contemporary conflict-affected settings in Asia along with a comparison of the findings. Within the field of conflict-related sexual violence, this is the first study to systematically analyze all the dimensions of SGBV reports in conflict-affected Asian contexts as well as qualify and contextualize this data by mapping the social, political, and institutional barriers to reporting, and the prevailing degree of gender discrimination and inequality. Our comparative framework is reliable and consistent. We ask the same questions of each conflict case, based on the study of official, unofficial and media GBV reports between 1998 and 2016 and a close examination of patterns of reporting in field-based qualitative research conducted in each country between 2015 and 2017. Specifically, we interviewed a range of civil-society, national, and international grassroots, nongovernmental, governmental, and international organization representatives within each country to understand the actual processes of reporting and how they may affect the number and types of reports, on which we based our analysis of reporting patterns. This field-based study of the three conflict situations provides new insight into the specific types of SGBV committed by the military, nonstate armed groups, or civilians across these conflict situations. But what are the implications of this research for ending impunity for SGBV in Asia's civil conflicts and for future scholarship on conflict-related SGBV?

In this Conclusion, we reflect on more recent events in each country since our period of data collection—what they likely indicate for the patterns of conflict-related SGBV—and we address the implications of our research. Exposing hidden forms of violent warfare against populations is very significant for ending impunity for this violence, especially in situations of protracted subnational conflicts. Thus, we consider the common findings among the cases we have studied that have relevance for other cases in and for regions beyond Asia. Above all, we suggest the need to prioritize contextual analysis of conflict-related SGBV and to interrogate the silences concerning conflict-related SGBV in each and every situation in order to understand how specific and often pervasive and deeply embedded gender norms influence the motivations for violence and its silences.

The Current Situation in Burma

The military staged a coup against the civilian government in February 2021 following a significant loss by its proxy party, the Union Solidarity and Development Party (USDP), in the 2020 elections. Massive civilian protests erupted across the country, now formally known as the Civil Disobedience Movement (CDM). In response, the military brutally cracked down on dissent, including shooting live ammunition at civilian protestors, destroying entire villages, and massacring civilians and opposition fighters (Maizland 2022). The 2014 Nationwide Peace Agreement has stalled since the coup, and the country is now experiencing greater conflict in urban as well as rural areas (TNI 2023). Massive waves of displacement continue in response to the coup and conflict escalation. Displacement doubled each year between 2021 and 2023, from 430,000 newly displaced to 1.2 million newly displaced persons (UNHCR 2023). As noted in Chapter Four, the UN investigation into the forced displacement of the Rohingya minority population in Rakhine state in August 2017 has been described as an act of ethnic cleansing and genocide. As a result, over one million Rohingya are still living in refugee camps in Bangladesh. Conditions are overcrowded in these camps, with women, men, and children risking a journey with people smugglers to seek asylum in India, Indonesia, Malaysia, and Thailand. The government of Bangladesh has sought to promote "voluntary return" to Burma. However, the UNHCR has stated that the conditions in Rakhine are too dangerous for refugees to return safely (UNHCR 2023). While during the 2011–2016 period, there was a glimmer of hope that justice for SGBV victims-survivors might be possible through the adoption of a new law to end violence against women, or through the military courts, that window has now closed. Since 2021 there has been no prospect that the military intends to investigate alleged crimes against humanity committed by its forces, including crimes of sexual violence, during the Rohingya exodus or other battles in the country. No laws on VAW have been introduced at the national level.

The Current Situation in the Philippines

Between 2016 and 2022, violence against civilians reached an intense period in the Philippines. This rise in violence can be attributed to two events. First is the Philippines-wide war on drugs during the presidential term of Rodrigo Duterte. This campaign resulted in thousands of arrests and the extrajudicial killings of a UN-estimated 8663 individuals (Aljazeera 2023). The number of incarcerated individuals doubled in a decade from 94,000 (2008) to 188,000 (2018) (Walmsley 2017; WPB 2022). The International Criminal Court (ICC) announced in 2023 that it would reopen its investigations into the Philippines government for crimes against humanity during the antidrug campaign. An ICC investigation was first announced in 2018, then postponed in 2021 when the Duterte administration promised to conduct its own review of the allegations. In the statement on reopening the investigation, the ICC claims that the Philippines government has not undertaken relevant investigations to warrant a deferral of the court's investigations.

The second event was the 2017 terrorist siege in Marawi (Province of Lanao del Sur) in the Bangsamoro Autonomous Region in Muslim Mindanao (BARMM). This urban battle (May to October 2017) led to more deaths per incident of violence than during the previous seven years. Once Marawi was "liberated" after the end of the siege, humanitarian actors documented reports of sexual violence, including sexual slavery, forced marriage, rape, and forced strip searches (UNFPA 2018; Action Against Hunger et al. 2017). Research on the gender dimensions of terrorist mobilization in Marawi has also documented how racialized gender norms and identities have been significant factors in recruitment to violent ISIS-affiliated groups, wherein the Arab male fighter is lauded (Johnston et al. 2020; UN Women 2019; True 2020). To date, only one successful prosecution has taken place for sexual crimes committed during this siege. In 2019 the Taguig Regional Trial Court sentenced Junaid Macauyag Awal, alias "Vice/Vice Junaid" and "Junaid Romato," to eight to fourteen years in prison for rebellion and for rape and sexual slavery under the national law that penalizes crimes against international law (in this case, the Rome Statute of the ICC, to which the Philippines is a signatory). The court at the time noted that violation of this law was possibly the first filed in the Philippines. The testimony came from a sixteen-year-old woman who was subjected to rape, intimidation, sexual slavery, and forced marriage (Pangalangan 2022: 470) by Junaid Awal during the siege. Over 350,000 people were displaced during this siege. In 2022 the

Philippines government announced a Marawi Siege Compensation Act that will compensate families for damaged properties and structures and the deaths of family members (Umel and Rosauro 2023). However, to date the act does not include compensation for victims-survivors of sexual violence. Once again silence is promoted while impunity prevails.

The Current Situation in Sri Lanka

In postwar Sri Lanka, ethnoreligious tensions are rising, and Sinhala Buddhist nationalists have treated minorities as outsiders. Recent political and economic crises fuel these tensions. The brother of President Mahinda Rajapaska (2005–2015), Gotabaya Rajapaska, became president in 2019, and in that year Mahinda was appointed as prime minister. Gotabaya had been secretary to the ministry of defence and urban development during the administration of his brother and was defence secretary when the Sri Lankan military led and won a one-sided victory against the Tamil Tigers in 2009. In the aftermath of the civil war, then-president Mahinda Rajapaska sought to fast-track a number of urban developments across the country with financial loans from the Chinese government–owned Export-Import Bank of China (EXIM Bank) to invest in postwar economic recovery. The opposition temporarily held power between 2015 and 2019, and some progress was made during this period. For instance, the government created a civil society–led Consultation Task Force on Reconciliation Mechanisms, which was designed to investigate how it should create a mechanism for truth, reconciliation, and justice. However, progress was slow and difficult in an environment of growing nationalism associated with the Sri Lankan military's success in 2009 (Nundakumar 2022).

In 2019, tensions were heightened after the so-called Easter Attacks by Islamist violent extremists in the capital, Colombo. Islamophobia has increased, including violent actions by Buddhist protectionists who protest against—and attack locations of—various Islamic practices, such as Halal food certifications and places of worship. Attacks on other religious minority worship places have occurred (including non–Theravada Buddhist and Hindu temples, Christian churches. or Muslim mosques), but most are not nationally or internationally reported (Imtiyaz 2020). These attacks against minorities are allegedly organized by Buddhist protectionist groups such as the Bodu Bala Sena (BBS), which are known for inciting violence

(AFP 2018). Within these groups, a clear gender hierarchy exists as within the Buddhist religion and temples.

In the 2019 elections, as stated, Gotabaya came to power as president and Mahinda was appointed as prime minister. A sudden drop in tourism following the Easter Attacks combined with the COVID-19 pandemic and the EXIM Bank's demand for loan repayments led to the 2022 economic crisis. In April 2022, protests erupted across the country against President Gotabaya Rajapaksa due to the ensuing economic crisis and its impacts. Interestingly, the protests bridged ethnic and religious divides, bringing together majority and minority communities. Tamils and Muslims protested together with Buddhist monks for a common goal: criticizing the government and securing fuel, medicine, and food for their families (Marsh 2022).

The prime minister and the president both resigned in July 2022 and fled the country. Since then, President Wickremensinghe has been in charge, with both the parliamentary and presidential elections to be held in 2024. As noted by the UN Human Rights Council in early 2023, the creation of a truth, reconciliation, and justice mechanism to investigate the allegations of war crimes and crimes against humanity during the Sri Lankan civil war have all but stalled (Shivji 2022).

Conflict resolution in the cases of the Philippines and Sri Lanka is fragile—and in Burma nonexistent. Access to justice for victims-survivors of conflict-related SGBV remains rare, and impunity for these crimes is widespread in all three countries. These facts reveal the degree to which gendered violence is normalized. As we revealed in Chapter Six, reporting patterns are inconsistent in each case, with so much that remains unknown about the circumstances that give rise to this violence, especially about its perpetrators. Investigations are infrequent at best and fuel the pattern of impunity. Those who speak out are rare and risk it all. Acts of SGBV carry little chance of harm for their perpetrators. Finally, the confluence of politicized conditions and gendered norms in each situation makes it difficult to accurately document and consistently report this violence. We discuss each of these issues in turn.

The Political Conditions of Conflict-Related SGBV

Reporting patterns have the power to create particular impressions about whether conflict-related SGBV is present or not. Reports can facilitate the documentation and prosecution of SGBV. An absence of reporting can be (mis)interpreted as the absence of SGBV (Traunmüller et al. 2019; Ju 2023). In the case of conflict-related SGBV, serious political and gender-sensitive constraints remain on reporting—such as who can report, who wants to report, and who will take action. This political process starts with whether agreement exists about a situation and whether it should be labeled as "conflict." The "conflict" label is particularly contentious when sovereign countries continue to maintain territorial control. Across Asia, claims of "sovereign\ty" and "noninterference" are almost reflexive responses to wrenching free from over a thousand years of imperialism and colonialism. The nationalist project is strong in each of the cases in this book, and international pressure creates little inducement to change behavior (Staniland 2021: 277). Regional actors, such as the Association of Southeast Asian Nations (ASEAN), are reluctant to characterize a situation as a conflict or even a coup unless the member state consents to this label. The United Nations Security Council rarely addresses situations that are escalating into conflict or even protracted conflict situations with low-intensity levels of violence. Usually the reason is that it is not worth expending political capital on trying to get each situation before the UNSC when raising that situation is going to lead to a veto by a Permanent Five member state, or the government will oppose a political or peacekeeping mission. These considerations of what counts as conflict are political, normative, and consequential to how early and accurately we identify conflict-related SGBV—its patterns, its motivations, and its consequences for victims-survivors and communities.

In conflict and political transitions, women and girls are often marginalized or experience social, economic, and political discrimination. This status places them at high risk for SGBV from all groups, and there may be no safe space for women and girls to report such violence. The case of Burma highlights the severe risks associated with the very act of reporting SGBV. In that country, multiple armed struggles and pervasive gender discrimination over several decades have compounded the challenges of reporting. SGBV has both fueled and been exacerbated by political violence between state and nonstate armed groups, as shown in Chapter Three. This violence has disproportionately affected minority women, whose subordinate gender status within and across groups has deliberately targeted their bodies as markers of ethnic, religious, or political affiliation. The conflict dynamics and status of minority women at the heart of the conflicts have effectively constrained the few possibilities for reporting SGBV. Each conflict examined in this book has revealed how politicized conditions inform our knowledge of SGBV prevalence.

The Gendered Norms of Conflict-Related SGBV

As well as providing a more complete picture of the politics of conflict-related SGBV—including the politics of reporting this violence as conflict-related—this book contributes to the scholarly debate about the appropriate methodologies for SGBV reporting in conflict situations. Feminist analysis guided our study to take seriously the pervasiveness of silence in any context of gendered social and cultural relations and depending on the degree of institutionalized and intersectional discrimination (see Parpart and Parashar 2019; Ackerly, Stern, and True 2006).

The book's attention to what data are collected, who reports this data, and when SGBV crimes are reported in low-intensity conflict environments encourages scholars to consider the presence of reporting silences and gaps. This book also sheds new insight into which SGBV reporting methods should be prioritized and why. In each case, we identified how gender is an organizing principle for the reporting conditions and prioritization of its reporting. Gender is also an organizing principle for the military and nonstate armed groups in each location, and thus we document and analyze the role of gender norms and gender ideology in fueling, justifying, and legitimizing SGBV violence in each context.

Reproduction is vital for the continuation of ethnic and religious groups in each conflict. Control over the reproductive system of women and girls ensures the group's future destiny. In Sri Lanka, members of the government have put forward the message that Sinhala women should reproduce to counteract the "fertile" Muslim-minority population, instrumentalizing women's bodies for their agenda (Kodikara 2014). As discussed in Chapter Four, in Burma in 2015, legislation called "Race and Religion Laws" was passed that "aimed to limit any potential growth of the Muslim population through conversion, interreligious marriage, polygamy, and birth" (Malji 2021). The laws are intended to prohibit Buddhist women from marrying Muslim men, to decrease conversion to Islam, and to prevent Muslim men from marrying more than one wife and from having large families (Zin 2015; Fink 2018). These laws had the support of military and civilian members of Parliament, revealing the social importance attached to an ethnic and religious-majority

Bamaar Buddhist state. In Mindanao, the abduction of young girls as an act of rido has a powerful effect on mobilizing clan violence because a girl's virginity has economic and political value in that context. The Islamic State recruitment prior to the Marawi Siege used gendered language to recruit "mothers/sisters/wives" and "fighter women" to shame inactive men (Ingram 2023). In each case, we studied all combatants—state and nonstate armed groups—referring to cases of rape and sexual violence committed by their opponents and intended to incite violence.

As each chapter discussed, violence against women has low reporting incidence in conflict-affected areas. Attitudes towards violence against women are permissive. The conflicts have created strong ethnic and religious bonds that entrench a traditional gender order to maintain war economies and labor that supports the war effort. Even "progressive" nonstate armed groups that include women as combatants have gender hierarchies where some women can fight but other women must marry (see, for example, Hedström 2017). All are led by strongmen. As a result, in each case, conflict-related SGBV is easily traded away by all groups when peace negotiations are on the table. One thing they can agree on is men's dominance over women.

Scholars can learn from our study in comparatively analyzing silences and hidden wars in other regional contexts. We need to take seriously the presence of silence and voice and reflect on our epistemologies and methodologies to assess how well they can capture these conditions. Feminist methodologies that are sensitive to victims-survivors' voices and experiences should inform the process of conceptualizing, collecting, analyzing, contextualizing, and qualifying data on SGBV in conflict-affected situations (see also Ackerly and True 2018; Oo and Davies 2021).

Implications for Future Studies: Interrogate the Silence

The findings of *Hidden Wars* show that reporting does not reflect actual violence. Therefore, we should be mindful of the lamppost-key metaphor, analyzing data from reports where the lamppost light is shining rather than investigating the contexts where the violence is occurring—where the keys are—but is not getting reported. We need to look for silences and gaps and not interpret them as absence but rather ask those with local knowledge about the political conditions for reporting. As Ackerly and True (2018: 270) argue, feminist research should "prioritise further investigation and highlight the limitations of existing analysis because of the exclusion of some communities from the production of institutional knowledge." Towards that end, we must map gendered discrimination across groups and the practical institutional barriers to reporting in order to assess and qualify the validity of reporting data.

Ending impunity coupled with ongoing hardship and vulnerability from previous SGBV crimes and ongoing gender violence requires a focus on justice, as we argued in Chapter Six. Alternative forms of justice that can address women's human rights and economic insecurity in low-intensity conflict and postconflict situations are most crucial. Foremost, we need research that can identify opportunities to improve the prevention of conflict-related SGBV.

Scholars can use our method to analyze the open-access SGBV reports available for any situation and test our findings to explore what violence is and is not reported. They can adapt our qualitative research approach to examine the material and institutional reporting conditions as well as those actors responsible as an alternative to analyzing quantitative SGBV datasets or searching for victims-survivors' testimonies in order to study conflict-related SGBV. All methodological approaches have limitations, but it is important to understand the contexts in which SGBV occurs, including the contexts of reporting and measurement, just as it is vital to mitigate the risks including the possible retraumatization of victims-survivors and their communities that is a concern in this field of study.

Ethnonationalist-religious extremist groups use SGBV, and what we tentatively term "terrorism-related SGBV," as has been documented in Afghanistan, Iraq, Mali, Marawi, and Northern Nigeria (True 2020). How is extremism conducive to SGBV, and why are these groups often able to commit these crimes with relative impunity? What are the political and gendered conditions enabling this violence, and how do these conditions affect reporting and documentation of these forms of violence? These important research questions follow from our study and the current situations in the three cases.

Protracted or intractable conflicts are on the rise across all regions. The Syrian conflict is entering its second decade, the Democratic Republic of Congo is entering its fourth decade of conflict, and Burma its seventh. Reports on SGBV for the former two situations over time are unexplored to date. Our study of Burma revealed that, in 2012, an escalation in SGBV reports prior to an influx of communal violence within the Rakhine state led to civilian deaths and large internal displacement (approximately two hundred thousand persons). SGBV reports in protracted conflicts may provide crucial early-warning insight into changed political and economic conditions for fighting and indicate whether an armed group is about to gain a tactical advantage. What insights might be gained from a longitudinal study of reports of conflict-related SGBV in civil conflicts? This insight would inform current understandings of the relationship between territorial gains and conflict-related SGBV, the protective role of UN peacekeepers, and the efficacy of prohibitions on sexual violence within armed groups.

International consensus on which situations require the presence of international observers and humanitarian aid is being affected by the return of diplomatic deadlock and divisions at the UN Security Council. The UNSC was divided on political responses to the military coup in Burma in 2021,[1] the civil wars and right to humanitarian access in both Ethiopia and Syria, and the Russian invasion of Ukraine in 2021. Alternative international sources for the collection of conflict-related SGBV need to be located outside of UNSC processes. Additional institutions, such as the UN Human Rights Council and the UN Convention on the Elimination of All Forms of Discrimination Against Women (CEDAW) Committee, may be alternative sites where reports can be received and validated on an annual basis to ensure that a variety of reporting conditions and sources are being heard at the highest political levels.

Finally, there is a need to anticipate how other endogenous and exogenous forces that we do not yet know will affect conflict-related SGBV. Climate-induced disasters will compound and affect patterns of conflict-related SGBV, as we have growing evidence that so-called natural disasters impact gendered violence (True 2013). A longitudinal study of conflict-related SGBV events will serve to inform our understanding of how disasters and crises affect the reporting and documentation of these crimes. The COVID-19 pandemic revealed how quickly a crisis can affect and compound the factors that contribute to violence against women (Mintrom and True 2022; Wenham et al. 2020). Little is known about how this crisis impacted conflict-related SGBV reporting and incidence, however. We do know, for example, that the investigation and documentation of the crimes committed by Da'esh in Iraq were affected by the pandemic. Moreover, the impunity window that the pandemic provided may have led to the proliferation of this violence elsewhere (UN 2022b). Climate-induced disasters in conflict and postconflict regions pose a serious risk to reporting conditions. Considering how reporting conditions can be maintained during such crises will be vital for the prevention and mitigation of SGBV. Crises such as the pandemic and climate-induced disasters require serious attention to the gaps currently identified in the reporting process, which will worsen rather than improve in extreme conditions (Smith et al. 2022). Finally, there is a need to incorporate the reporting of conflict-related SGBV in online spaces. Documentation of SGBV events in public locations is imperfect, as our data showed. This imperfection continues in the online arena, where anonymous posts of threats, rumors, scapegoating, and trolling can target politically active women in the public space, where there is a genuine fear that online violence may fuel offline violence (ACLED 2021).

In this book, we have sought to better understand the obstacles to reporting SGBV in protracted conflict situations. However, there is an urgent need to continually test the silences and improve the collection of data and knowledge to inform and transform policy, prevention, and justice initiatives. As such, future studies must pay critical attention to the anomalies in SGBV data determined by local gender norms and reporting conditions, and what real time interventions can occur to cover the major limitations of that data. Our research suggests that the presence of international humanitarian and development actors seems to improve the conditions for documentation and reporting. Further investigation into this finding is required. Our study of the "hidden wars" in three Asian civil conflicts highlights the systemic failure of the international community to consistently address these situations as conflict-related SGBV cases. This failure has created a culture of impunity for state and nonstate actors that harms the prospect of equitable and inclusive peace in Asia as well as other global regions.

Notes

Introduction

1. Sexual and gender-based violence (SGBV) includes physical, psychological, and sexual violence, including rape, forced prostitution and trafficking, dowry-related violence, and other traditional harmful practices such as female genital mutilation, marital rape, spousal violence, sexual harassment and intimidation at work, and economic abuse and violence (UNGA 1993). Other forms of violence are also considered under the UN's Convention on the Elimination of All Forms of Discrimination against Women (CEDAW), such as "early and forced marriage, and online sexual abuse." SGBV affects women and girls disproportionately, but men and boys also experience SGBV, although in Asia most laws and policy frameworks focus on SGBV against women and girls.
2. In this book we define Asia as including five political regions: South Asia, South East Asia, Central Asia, East Asia, and Western Asia. "Asia" borders Europe in the west, along the Ural Mountains, and across the Caspian Sea—and stretches to the Arctic Ocean in the north, the Pacific Ocean in the east, and the Indian Ocean in the south.
3. There have been studies on SGBV perpetrated by Japanese soldiers in the region during World War II (Totani 2011); committed during the Indonesia coup and ethnic cleansing of ethnic Chinese and alleged communist sympathizers in 1965–1966 (Pohlman 2015); during the India/Pakistan partition in 1948 and the Bangladesh-Pakistan wars of 1971 (Saikia 2011); during the period of Indonesia's occupation of East Timor/Timor Leste (Swaine 2015); and during the Cambodian genocide (Palmer and Williams 2017).
4. We refer to Burma/Myanmar as Burma in this book in recognition that the Tatmadaw launched a coup d'état in February 2021. Given it was the military regime that renamed Burma as Myanmar after it killed thousands of people in the postelection violence in 1988 and 1989, we use "Burma" in solidarity with those fighting against the military regime.
5. Conflict intensity in all three cases range from twenty-five battle deaths per calendar year to fewer than one thousand deaths per calendar year. A conflict with more than one thousand deaths per calendar year is "upgraded" by the UCPD to "war."

Chapter 1

1. According to the Uppsala Conflict Data Program, one of the most widely cited conflict databases, over one thousand deaths per year signifies a high-intensity conflict or war. See Definitions—Department of Peace and Conflict Research—Uppsala University, Sweden (https://www.pcr.uu.se/research/ucdp/definitions).

2. The threshold for a low-intensity conflict is that the conflict must produce a minimum of twenty-five battle deaths per year (Gleditsch et al. 2002). Protracted conflicts do not have a quantitative threshold. One definition of a protracted conflict is episodic, cyclical, "frozen," long-lived insurgencies; long-standing situations of occupation; or wars between states where violence simmers at a relatively lower level than one might traditionally associate with armed conflict. Conflicts may appear to be resolved but later "relapse." Across our period of study (1998–2016), the three cases in this book meet the thresholds of high-intensity and low-intensity conflict at various stages. They all exhibit protracted conflict characteristics.
3. S/Res/1325 (2000), paras. 9, 10 and 11.
4. S/Res/1820 (2008); S/Res/1888 (2009); S/Res/1889 (2009); S/Res/1960 (2010); S/Res/2106 (2013); S/Res/2122 (2013), and S/Res/2467 (2019).
5. See https://www.un.org/sexualviolenceinconflict/digital-library/joint-communiques/.
6. S/2012/33, pp. 2–3.
7. Walter Lotze (2020), for example, notes that UN peace operations, even with the deployment of Women Protection Advisors, often report lower levels of SGBV. Reports were more reliably sourced from UNFPA and UNICEF than the UN peacekeeping mission stationed there.
8. Wood (2006: 325–326) questioned the relationship between gender and sexual violence in conflict in asking why gender inequality would produce sexual violence in one setting yet in another lead to the participation of women in rebel militias. Of course, in many cases, notably Rwanda (Brown 2014), we know that the presence of women in armed roles can co-occur with mass SGBV.
9. We support Baaz and Stern's clarification in that we (too) do not reject "rape as a weapon of war" discourse but call for continued interrogation into how "conflict settings and armed groups differ in their intricate complexities" (2013: 62–63).
10. For example, see Schopper (2014) and Wood (2014).
11. Even in situations where there has been a clear practice of widespread, systemic, and strategic sexual and gender-based violence to expel populations or eliminate that group, recognition and justice do not always follow. In Iraq, for example, the Islamic State, also known as ISIS, adopted a widespread practice of abducting Yezidi women and girls in 2014, raping them, forcibly converting them to Islam, trafficking them, and beating and sexually humiliating them. Those who escaped to tell their story have not received justice for these crimes, as no international investigation or prosecution under the ICC has taken place (HRW 2015; 2020).
12. In this book we define Asia as including five political regions: South Asia, Southeast Asia, Central Asia, East Asia, and Western Asia. "Asia" borders Europe in the west, along the Ural Mountains and across the Caspian Sea; and stretches to the Arctic Ocean in the north, the Pacific Ocean in the east, and the Indian Ocean in the south.
13. There are a growing number of studies on SGBV perpetrated by Australian colonizers against Indigenous women during the frontier wars in Australia (Connors 2017). Additional studies on sexual violence and rape in twentieth-century Asia include Japanese soldiers in the region during World War II (Totani 2011); during the Indonesia coup and ethnic cleansing of ethnic Chinese and alleged communist

NOTES 171

sympathizers in 1965–1966 (Perempuan 2007; Pohlman 2015); during the India/Pakistan partition in 1948 and the 1971 Bangladesh-Pakistan wars (Saikia 2011; Hasanat 2022); during the period of Indonesia's occupation of East Timor / Timor Leste (Swaine 2015; Cohen 2016); and during the Cambodian genocide (Palmer and Williams 2017; Szablewska and Jurasz 2019).

14. Additional conflicts that occurred during this time period include Afghanistan, North Korea (technically in armistice with South Korea), the Kashmir border (India-Pakistan), and Nagorno-Karabakh (Armenia-Azerbaijan). There were also low-intensity conflicts that occurred sporadically in the early and middle years of the 1998–2016 time period in East Timor, Indonesia, and Thailand.

Chapter 2

1. See the Sexual Violence in Armed Conflict Dataset (Cohen and Nordås, 2014; Nordås and Cohen, 2021) from the Sexual Violence in Armed Conflict Dataset website, http://www.sexualviolencedata.org/dataset/, and the UCDP/PRIO Armed Conflict Dataset Codebook Version 4-2014a (UCDP and PRIO 2014), https://ucdp.uu.se/downloads/old/ucdpprio/ucdp-prio-acd-4a-2014.pdf.
2. See Women's Media Center, Women Under Seige, n.d., https://womensmediacenter.com/women-under-siege/conflicts
3. ACLED Political Violence Targeting Women (https://acleddata.com/political-violence-targeting-women/). See https://acleddata.com/acleddatanew/wp-content/uploads/dlm_uploads/2019/01/ACLED_Country-and-Time-Period-coverage_updated Feb2022.pdf
4. A study conducted in 2013 found a high rate of intimate partner violence prevalence from 26 to 80 per cent across nine sites. Women's experience of partner victimization was 25 to 68 per cent with an average prevalence rate of 30–57 per cent (Fulu et al. 2013: 27). Among women respondents, between 10 and 59 per cent reported rape by a nonpartner (Fulu et al. 2013: 39).
5. Interview with INGO official, Yangon, 17 August 2015.
6. We adopt "unofficial" nomenclature to describe media reports. This language is similar to the event-based public health surveillance approach, where media, rumors, blogs, and community member posts are used to compile information on potential disease events. These reports are "unofficial" until an "official" government or agency confirms or denies these events with reports of hospitalization, infections, or deaths. Unofficial may also be termed as unverified or unauthorized. See https://www.cdc.gov/globalhealth/healthprotection/gddopscenter/.

Chapter 3

1. As noted in the Introduction, in this book we use "Burma" to refer to the Southeast Asian state that has been ruled by military junta for most of its postcolonial history

since independence in 1948. The military regime renamed Burma as "Myanmar" after the regime killed thousands of people in postelection violence in 1988 and 1989. The Tatmadaw launched a coup d'etat in February 2021 after democratic elections were held in November 2020. We use "Burma" in solidarity with those fighting against the military regime.
2. UCDP—Uppsala Conflict Data Program, data by conflict country at (https://www.pcr.uu.se/research/ucdp/ucdp-data/).
3. Myanmar | IDMC (internal-displacement.org).
4. An arms embargo remains in place as of November 25, 2023.
5. For the purposes of comparative research with Sri Lanka and the Philippines, ethnic armed organizations (EAOs) in Burma are later discussed in the book as non-state armed groups (NSAGs).
6. See situational analysis of displacement in the context of the ongoing Myanmar conflict and crisis at https://www.icrc.org/en/where-we-work/asia-pacific/myanmar/myanmar-conflict.
7. The full list of reports can be found at the website of the Secretary-General's Good Offices on Burma, https://dppa.un.org/en/myanmar
8. The full chronology of UN Security Council discussions on Burma can be viewed at https://www.securitycouncilreport.org/myanmar/
9. S/2012/33, S/2013/149, S/2014/181, S/2015/203, S/2016/361, S/2017/249, S/2018/250, S/2019/280, S/2020/487, S/2021/312, S/2022/272, S/2023/413. Available at UN Secretary-General Annual Reports, United Nations Office of the Special Representative of the Secretary-General on Sexual Violence in Conflict. https://www.un.org/sexualviolenceinconflict/
10. In 2014, ninety-two female military cadets (nonmedical) graduated from Burma's Army Officer Training School in Yangon, Burma. Between 2014 and 2019, an estimated four hundred female officers and seven hundred noncommissioned female officers and enlisted soldiers have been placed in service within the Burma armed forces: uniformed women represent approximately 0.2 per cent of Burma's armed forces. See https://www.armyupress.army.mil/Journals/Military-Review/English-Edition-Archives/November-December-2019/Byrd-Myanmar-Gender-Armed-Forces/
11. Children are registered for ID cards through their father's name, citizenship is granted according to patriarchal lineage, and the majority of land is registered in men's names. The Federal Parliament passed laws in 2015 on marriage, citizenship, and religion that link both women and their children's right to citizenship to the husband (father).

Chapter 4

1. The Bangsamoro Organic Law, the legal foundational document for the implementation of the 2014 CAB, was adopted in 2018. A Bangsamoro Transitional Authority was

established in 2019 with authority until 2021; this has been extended with elections due to be held for the first Bangsamoro Parliament in 2025.
2. https://genderdata.worldbank.org/indicators/sg-gen-parl-zs/, see Philippines in the Data Table.
3. https://psa.gov.ph/content/q-magna-carta-women-republic-act-no-9710.

Chapter 5

1. Personal interview with the authors, Colombo, Sri Lanka, 14 December 2016.
2. In 2019 the Sri Lanka Department of Census and Statistics conducted the first dedicated national prevalence survey on VAW and the first using the WHO methodology. Known as the Women's Wellbeing Survey (WWS), it covered all twenty-five districts in Sri Lanka and interviewed more than twenty-two hundred women ages fifteen and above. Fieldwork took place between March and September 2019, collecting data through computer-assisted personal interviews.
3. Personal interview with the authors, Colombo, Sri Lanka, 14 December 2016.
4. We no longer have online access to this report, as the CTF has been closed.
5. In 2015, Maithripala Sirisena, a former deputy to President Rajapaksa, led a new opposition party to victory in the national elections on a promise of a one-hundred-day work program of significant governance reform. On assuming power, Sirisena promised new laws to prevent abuse of women, and the introduction of measures "to ensure that women and children can live without fear in Sri Lanka" (Verite Research 2016). The government introduced a national action plan to reduce gender-based violence, which it viewed as a barrier to economic development through women's participation in the labor market. As well, the government aimed to address women's empowerment in the war-affected provinces through targeted development interventions. Governance reforms were carried out to ensure the impartiality of police and justice institutions and to reduce presidential powers in the Constitution (Verite Research 2016). Police and security sectors were devolving, and some progress was made with security-sector reform, rule of law, and freedom of expression (Verite Research 2018: 15). A new multisectoral national framework and action plan on GBV were coordinated through the Ministry of Women and Child Affairs. In addition, a national secretariat for the empowerment of widows and female-headed families was established as a main resource center to provide services mainly for widows and women-headed households in the North and East Provinces. Furthermore, of potential significance for these provinces is a provision in the Local Authorities Act that women make up 25 per cent of representatives in local government, and 15 per cent in the Provincial Council and Parliament (Verite Research 2016: 19).
6. Women's organization leader, personal interview with the authors, Colombo, Sri Lanka, 14 December 2016.

Chapter 6

1. "OHCHR reported in February 2017 that more than 50 of the 100 women and girls interviewed described having been subjected to rape, gang rape, or other forms of sexual violence, apparently employed systematically to humiliate and terrorize their community" (UNSG 2017: para. 51).
2. Such as, for example, when a UN peacekeeping force has a mandate for civilian protection and seeks to understand the practices of SGBV occurring in that conflict (see Olsson et al. 2020; specifically Lotze 2020).

Conclusion

1. The Security Council adopted its first resolution on Burma since 1948 on 21 December 2022. Resolution 2669 (2022) called for all forms of violence to end across the country. The resolution includes no reference to sexual violence or gender-based violence.

References

Abinales, Patricio N. 2016. "The 2016 Philippine Elections: Local Power as National Authority." *Asia Pacific Bulletin* No. 344, East-West Center, Washington DC, May 31.

Ackerly, Brooke and Jacqui True. 2018. "With or Without Feminism? Researching Gender and Politics in the 21st Century." *European Journal of Politics and Gender* 1(1–2): 259–278.

Ackerly, Brooke, Maria Stern and Jacqui True eds. 2006. *Feminist Methodologies for International Relations*. Cambridge: Cambridge University Press.

ACLED (Armed Conflict Location & Event Data Project). 2021. "Violence Targeting Women in Politics: Trends in Targets, Types and Perpetrators of Political Violence. Report, December." Available at: Violence Targeting Women in Politics: Trends in Targets, Types, and Perpetrators of Political Violence (acleddata.com).

Action Against Hunger et al. 2017. *Child Protection Rapid Assessment Report: Marawi Displacement (October 2017)*. Child Protection Rapid Assessment Task Force (CPRA TF), Report, 20 December. Available at: Child Protection Rapid Assessment Report: Marawi Displacement (October 2017)—Philippines | ReliefWeb. https://plan-international.org/uploads/sites/25/2022/03/cpra_marawi_displacement_final_edited.pdf

ADB (Asian Development Bank). 2012. *Myanmar in Transition Opportunities and Challenges*. Report, August. Available at: Myanmar in Transition: Opportunities and Challenges (adb.org). https://www.adb.org/sites/default/files/publication/29942/myanmar-transition.pdf

AFP. 2018. "Rise of Violent Buddhist Rhetoric in Asia Defies Stereotypes." *Bangkok Post*, 12 March. Available at: https://www.bangkokpost.com/world/1426722/rise-of-violent-buddhist-rhetoric-in-asia-defies-stereotypes.

Agerberg, Mattias and Anne-Kathrin Kreft. 2020. "Gendered Conflict, Gendered Outcomes: The Politicization of Sexual Violence and Quota Adoption." *Journal of Conflict Resolution* 64(2–3): 290–317.

AGIPP (Alliance for Gender Inclusion in the Peace Process). 2017. "Analysis of Myanmar's Second Union Peace Conference—21st Century Panglong from a Gender Perspective." Available at: agipp_gender_analysis_paper_eng_version.pdf.

AGIPP (Alliance for Gender Inclusion in the Peace Process). 2018. "If Half the Population Mattered: A Critique of the Myanmar Nationwide Ceasefire Agreement and Joint Monitoring Committee Framework from a Gender Perspective." Policy Brief No. 4, May. Available at: if_half_the_population_mattered_a_critique_of_the_myanmar_nationwide_ceasefire_agreement_and_joint_monitoring_committee_framework_from_a_gender_perspective.pdf (agipp.org).

AI (Amnesty International). 2008. *Shattered Peace in Mindanao—The Human Cost of Conflict in the Philippines*. London, October. Available at: https://www.refworld.org/docid/490971ee2.html.

AI (Amnesty International). 2009. *Shattered Lives—Beyond the 2008-2009 Mindanao Armed Conflict*. London, August. Available at: Yellow (amnesty.org.ph). https://reliefweb.int/report/philippines/philippines-shattered-lives-beyond-2008-2009-mindanao-armed-conflict

AI (Amnesty International). 2016. *Myanmar: "We Are at Breaking Point"— Rohingya: Persecuted in Myanmar, Neglected in Bangladesh*. Report, London, 19 December. Available at: Myanmar: "We Are at Breaking Point"—Rohingya: persecuted in Myanmar, neglected in Bangladesh—Amnesty International. https://www.hlrn.org/img/documents/ASA1653622016ENGLISH.PDF

AI (Amnesty International). 2017. "Sri Lanka: Consultation Task Force Report Must Lead to Justice." Press release, London, 11 January. Available at: https://www.amnesty.org/en/latest/press-release/2017/01/sri-lanka-consultation-task-force-report-must-lead-to-justice/.

Al-Ali, Nadje. 2018. "Sexual Violence in Iraq: Challenges for Transnational Feminist Politics." *European Journal of Women's Studies* 25(1): 10–27.

Alam, Mayesha and Elisabeth Jean Wood. 2022. "Ideology and the Implicit Authorization of Violence as Policy: The Myanmar Military's Conflict-Related Sexual Violence against the Rohingya." *Journal of Global Security Studies* 7(2): 1–18.

Aljazeera. 2023. "ICC to Resume Investigation into Philippines's Deadly Drug War." 27 January. Available at: ICC to resume investigation into Philippines's deadly drug war | ICC News | Al Jazeera. https://www.aljazeera.com/news/2023/1/27/icc-to-resume-investigation-into-philippiness-deadly-drug-war

All Survivors Project. 2020. "Submission to the United Nations Human Rights Committee 128th Session, 2–27 March." 10 January. Available at: https://allsurvivorsproject.org/submission-to-the-un-human-rights-committee-on-sri-lanka-128th-session-2-27-march-2020/.

Allen, Beverly. 1996. *Rape Warfare: The Hidden Genocide in Bosnia-Herzegovina and Croatia*. Minneapolis: University of Minnesota Press.

Altunjan, Tanja. 2021. "The International Criminal Court and Sexual Violence: Between Aspirations and Reality." *German Law Journal* 22(5): 878–893.

Arcala Hall, Rosalie and Joanna Pares Hoare. 2015. In *Women in Conflict and Peace*, edited by Jenny Hedström and Thiyumi Senarathna. Stockholm: International Institute for Democracy and Electoral Assistance (IDEA), 89–122.

Arraiza, José María and Sara E. Davies. 2020. "Enduring Peace: A Case Study of the Opportunities and the Challenges for Engaging in Myanmar's Peace Process." *Global Responsibility to Protect* 12(1): 115–136.

Asal, Victor and Robert U. Nagel. 2021. "Control over Bodies and Territories: Insurgent Territorial Control and Sexual Violence." *Security Studies* 30(1): 136–158.

ASEAN (Association of Southeast Asian Nations). 2022. "ASEAN Regional Plan of Action on Women, Peace and Security." 16 November. Available at: ASEAN Regional Plan of Action on Women, Peace and Security—ASEAN Main Portal. https://asean.org/wp-content/uploads/2022/11/32-ASEAN-Regional-Plan-of-Action-on-Women-Peace-and-Security.pdf

Aspinall, Edward, Robin Jeffrey and Anthony J. Regan, eds. 2013. *Diminishing Conflicts in Asia and the Pacific: Why Some Subside and Others Don't*. Abingdon: Routledge.

Baaz, Maria Eriksson and Maria Stern. 2009. "Why Do Soldiers Rape? Masculinity, Violence, and Sexuality in the Armed Forces in the Congo (DRC)." *International Studies Quarterly* 53(2): 495–518.

Baaz, Maria Eriksson and Maria Stern. 2013. *Sexual Violence as a Weapon of War?: Perceptions, Prescriptions, Problems in the Congo and Beyond*. London: Zed Books.

Baaz, Maria Eriksson and Maria Stern. 2018. "Curious Erasures: The Sexual in Wartime Sexual Violence." *International Feminist Journal of Politics* 20(3): 295–314.

Bandara, Chandrani. 2016. "The Road to Reconciliation: Justice, Hope and Dignity in Sri Lanka." 17 March. Available at: https://www.un.int/srilanka/news/active-participation-sri-lanka-sixtieth-commission-status-women-csw-new-york-14-24-march-2016.

Barbour, Stephanie. 2020. "Supporting Accountability for Sexual Violence in the Syria and Iraq Conflicts: Innovations, Good Practices, and Lessons Learned through Private Criminal Investigations." *Journal of International Criminal Justice* 18(2): 397–423.

Bardall, Gabrielle, Elin Bjarnegård and Jennifer M. Piscopo. 2020. "How Is Political Violence Gendered? Disentangling Motives, Forms, and Impacts." *Political Studies* 68(4): 916–935.

Bastick, Megan, Karin Grimm and Rahel Kunz. 2007. *Sexual Violence in Armed Conflict: Global Overview and Implications for the Security Sector*. Report, Geneva Centre for the Democratic Control of Armed Forces, Geneva.

BBC News. 2015. "Four Sri Lankan Soldiers Convicted of Raping Tamil Women." 7 October. Available at: https://www.bbc.com/news/34470053.

Bellamy, Alex J. 2017. *East Asia's Other Miracle? Explaining the Decline of Mass Atrocities*. New York: Oxford University Press.

Benshoof, Janet. 2014. "The Other Red Line: The Use of Rape as an Unlawful Tactic of Warfare." *Global Policy* 5(2): 146–158.

Bhatia, Sangeeta, Britta Lassmann, Emily Cohn, Angel N. Desai, Malweena Carrion, Kraemer Moritz UG, Mark Herringer, John Brownstein, Larry Madoff, Anne Cori and Pierre Nouvellet. 2021. "Using Digital Surveillance Tools for Near Real-Time Mapping of the Risk of Infectious Disease Spread." *NPJ Digital Medicine* 4(73): 1–10.

Binningsbø, Helga Malmin and Ragnhild Nordås. 2022. "Conflict-Related Sexual Violence and the Perils of Impunity." *Journal of Conflict Resolution* 66(6): 1066–1090.

Boesten, Jelke. 2017. "Of Exceptions and Continuities: Theory and Methodology in Research on Conflict-Related Sexual Violence." *International Feminist Journal of Politics* 19(4): 506–519.

Boesten, Jelke. 2022. "Sexual Violence as a Weapon of War in Ukraine." *BMJ* 377: o1172.

Boesten, Jelke and Marsha Henry. 2018. "Between Fatigue and Silence: The Challenges of Conducting Research on Sexual Violence in Conflict." *Social Politics: International Studies in Gender, State & Society* 25(4): 568–588.

Brown, Sara E. 2014. "Female Perpetrators of the Rwandan Genocide." *International Feminist Journal of Politics* 16(3): 448–469.

Brunnstrom, David and Joel Schectman. 2015. "Myanmar Vote Boosts Hopes of Lifting Sanctions—If Army Accepts Result." Reuters, 10 November. Available at: Myanmar vote boosts hopes of lifting sanctions—if army accepts result | Reuters. https://www.reuters.com/article/uk-myanmar-election-usa-idUKKCN0SY1W420151110/

Buss, Doris. 2014. "Seeing Sexual Violence in Conflict and Post-Conflict Societies: The Limits of Visibility." In *Sexual Violence in Conflict and Post-Conflict Societies: International Agendas and African Contexts*, edited by Doris Buss, Joanne Lebert, Blair Rutherford, Donna Sharkey and Obijiofor Aginam. New York: Routledge, 3–27.

Butalia, Urvashi. 2000. *The Other Side of Silence: Voices from the Partition of India*. London: Penguin Books.

Butler, Christopher K., Tali Gluch, and Neil J. Mitchell. 2007. "Security Forces and Sexual Violence: A Cross-National Analysis of a Principal-Agent Argument." *Journal of Peace Research* 44(6): 669–687.

Calleja, Kristine S., Niza Concepcion, Jhay de Jesus, Maroz Ramos, Naomi Fontanos and Zeena Manglinong. 2020. "Struggling from the Margins to the Intersectionalities of Power: The State of Lesbian, Gay, Bisexual, Transgender, Intersex, Queer (LGBTIQ) Filipinos from 2015 to 2020." In *Philippine NGO Beijing + 25 Report*, edited by Rosalinda Pineda Ofreneo and Jeanne Frances I. Illo. UP Center for Women's and Gender Studies and Oxfam. Quezon City, 15 September, 353–384. Available at: https://www.resea rchgate.net/profile/Naomi-Fontanos/publication/346474713_Struggling_from_ the_Margins_to_the_Intersectionalities_of_Power_The_State_of_Lesbian_Gay_ Bisexual_Transgender_Intersex_Queer_LGBTIQ_Filipinos_from_2015_to_2020/ links/5fc44e91299bf104cf93e625/Struggling-from-the-Margins-to-the-Intersection alities-of-Power-The-State-of-Lesbian-Gay-Bisexual-Transgender-Intersex-Queer-LGBTIQ-Filipinos-from-2015-to-2020.pdf.

Campbell, Kirsten. 2018. "Producing Knowledge in the Field of Sexual Violence in Armed Conflict Research: Objects, Methods, Politics, and Gender Justice Methodology." *Social Politics* 25(4): 469–495.

CEDAW (Committee on the Elimination of Discrimination against Women). 2016. "Concluding Observations on the Combined Seventh and Eighth Periodic Reports of the Philippines. Convention on the Elimination of All Forms of Discrimination Against Women." United Nations, 25 July. Available at: Treaty bodies Download (ohchr.org). https://digitallibrary.un.org/record/841795

CEDAW (Committee on the Elimination of Discrimination against Women). 2017. "Concluding Observations on the 8th Periodic Report of Sri Lanka: Committee on the Elimination of Discrimination against Women." 66th session, 9 March. Available at: https://digitallibrary.un.org/record/1286137?ln=en.

CEDAW (Committee on the Elimination of Discrimination against Women). 2022. "Ninth Periodic Report Submitted by Sri Lanka under Article 18 of the Convention." Convention on the Elimination of All Forms of Discrimination Against Women. United Nations, 10 August. Available at: CEDAW_C_LKA_9-EN.pdf. https://www.ecoi.net/en/file/local/2074202/N2245649.pdf

CEPA (Centre for Poverty Analysis). 2016a. "The Political Economy of Violence: Women's Economic Relations in Post-War Sri Lanka." Working Paper 50, December. Available at: https://securelivelihoods.org/wp-content/uploads/WP50_The-Political-Economy-of-Violence_Womens-economic-relations-in-post-war-Sri-Lanka.pdf.

CEPA (Centre for Poverty Analysis). 2016b. "Samurdhi Unpacked: Selecting Beneficiaries." Development Dialogue. *Financial Review*, 18 May.

Chang, Iris. 2012. *The Rape of Nanking: The Forgotten Holocaust of World War II*. New York: Basic Books.

Chappell, Louise. 2014. "Conflicting Institutions and the Search for Gender Justice at the International Criminal Court." *Political Research Quarterly* 67(1): 183–196.

Charney, Michael W. 2009. *A History of Modern Burma*. Cambridge: Cambridge University Press.

Chi, Primus Che, Patience Bulage, Henrik Urdal and Johanne Sundby. 2015. "A Qualitative Study Exploring the Determinants of Maternal Health Service Uptake in Post-Conflict Burundi and Northern Uganda." *BMC Pregnancy and Childbirth* 15(1): 1–14.

Chinese Human Rights Defenders. 2022. *Zero Tolerance for Human Rights Defenders in the Year of "Zero COVID": Annual Report on the Situation of Human Rights in China (2021)*. Report, 7 March. Available at: https://www.nchrd.org/2022/03/zero-tolerance-for-human-rights-defenders-in-the-year-of-zero-covid-annual-report-on-the-situation-of-human-rights-defenders-in-china-2021/

Cho, MiJin. 2020. "Victim Silencing, Sexual Violence Culture, Social Healing: Inherited Collective Trauma of World War II South Korean Military 'Comfort Women.'" Paper, Virginia Commonwealth University. https://scholarscompass.vcu.edu/cgi/viewcontent.cgi?article=1000&context=pkp

Christie, Nils. 1986. "The Ideal Victim." In *From Crime Policy to Victim Policy: Reorienting the Justice System*, edited by Ezzat A. Fattah. London: Palgrave Macmillan, 17–30.

Chynoweth, Sarah. 2017. *We Keep It in Our Heart: Sexual Violence against Men and Boys in the Syria Crisis*. Report, UNHCR, October. Available at: https://www.refworld.org/docid/5a128e814.html

Clark, Janine Natalya. 2014. "Making Sense of Wartime Rape: A Multi-causal and Multi-level Analysis." *Ethnopolitics* 13(5): 461–482.

Cockburn, Cynthia. 2011. "'Why Are *You* Doing This to Me?' Identity, Power and Sexual Violence in War." In *Sexuality, Gender and Power: Intersectional and Transnational Perspectives*, edited by Anna G. Jónasdóttir, Valerie Bryson and Kathleen B. Jones. New York: Routledge, 189–205.

Cohen, Dara Kay. 2013. "Explaining Rape during Civil War: Cross-National Evidence (1980–2009)." *American Political Science Review* 107(3): 461–477.

Cohen, Dara Kay. 2016. *Rape during Civil War*. Ithaca, NY: Cornell University Press.

Cohen, Dara Kay and Amelia Hoover Green. 2012. "Dueling Incentives: Sexual Violence in Liberia and the Politics of Human Rights Advocacy." *Journal of Peace Research* 49(3): 445–458.

Cohen, Dara Kay, Amelia Hoover Green and Elisabeth Jean Wood. 2013. *Wartime Sexual Violence: Misconceptions, Implications, and Ways Forward*. Special Report, United States Institute of Peace (USIP), Washington DC, February.

Cohen, Dara Kay and Ragnhild Nordås. 2014. "Sexual Violence in Armed Conflict: Introducing the SVAC Dataset, 1989–2009." *Journal of Peace Research* 51(3): 418–428.

Colombini, Manuela, Susannah Mayhew, Ragnhild Lund, Navpreet Singh, Katarina Swahnberg, Jennifer Infanti, Berit Schei, and Kumudu Wijewardene. 2018. "Factors Shaping Political Priorities for Violence Against Women—Mitigation Policies in Sri Lanka." *BMC International Health and Human Rights* 18(1):1–12.

Commission of Inquiry. 2011. *The Report of the Commission of Inquiry on Lessons Learnt and Reconciliation*. Government of Sri Lanka, November. Available at: https://reliefweb.int/report/sri-lanka/report-commission-inquiry-lessons-learnt-and-reconciliation.

Conciliation Resources. 2015. "Women's Participation and Inclusive Peace Processes: Lessons Learned from Mindanao and Beyond." Submission to the Global Study on Women, Peace and Security, March. Available at: Microsoft Word—CR submission_1325 Global Study.doc (peacewomen.org). https://peacewomen.org/system/files/global_study_submissions/47%20%7C%20Women%E2%80%99s%20participation%20and%20inclusive%20peace%20processes%3A%20lessons%20learned%20from%20Mindanao%20and%20beyond%20%7C%20Conciliation%20Resources.pdf

Connors, Libby. 2017. "Uncovering the Shameful: Sexual Violence on an Australian Colonial Frontier." In *Legacies of violence: rendering the unspeakable past in modern Australia*, edited by Robert Mason. New York: Berghahn Books, 33–52.

Coomaraswamy, Radhika. 1996. "Reinventing International Law: Women's Rights as Human Rights in the International Community." *Bulletin of Concerned Asian Scholars* 28(2): 16–26.

Coundouriotis, Eleni. 2013. " 'You Only Have Your Word': Rape and Testimony." *Human Rights Quarterly* 35(2): 365–385.

CP/GBV Working Group. 2017. *Child Protection Rapid Assessment Report: Marawi Displacement (October 2017)*. Report, Joint Regional Child Protection and Gender-Based Violence Working Group, 20 December. Available at: https://plan-international.org/uploads/sites/25/2022/03/cpra_marawi_displacement_final_edited.pdf.

CPA (Centre for Policy Alternatives). 2016. "Accountability and Reparations for Victims of Conflict Related Sexual Violence in Sri Lanka." Discussion Paper, July. Available at: https://www.cpalanka.org/wp-content/uploads/2016/07/CSV-paper-June-2016.pdf.

CPWG (Child Protection Working Group). 2014. *Child Protection Rapid Assessment Report: Central Mindanao*. Report with UNICEF and United Nations Children's Fund, June. Available at: https://resourcecentre.savethechildren.net/document/child-protection-rapid-assessment-report-central-mindanao-june-2014/.

Danielsson, Sarah K. 2019. "Introduction: War and Sexual Violence—New Perspectives in a New Era." In *War and Sexual Violence—New Perspectives in a New Era*, edited by Sarah K. Danielsson. Paderborn: Brill Ferdinand Schoningh, 1–14.

Davies, Sara E. 2019. "Reporting Sexual Violence during Conflict: A Case Study of Humanitarian Workers in Myanmar." *St Antony's International Review* 14(2): 80–101.

Davies, Sara E. 2020. "Atrocity Prevention in Practice: Studying the Role of Southeast Asian Women in Atrocity Prevention." In *Implementing the Responsibility to Protect: A Future Agenda*, edited by Cecilia Jacob and Martin Mennecke. London: Routledge, 156–176.

Davies, Sara E. and Jacquie True. 2015. "Reframing Conflict-Related Sexual and Gender-Based Violence: Bringing Gender Analysis Back In." *Security Dialogue* 46(6): 495–512.

Davies, Sara E. and Jacqui True. 2017a. "The Politics of Counting and Reporting Conflict-Related Sexual and Gender-Based Violence: The Case of Myanmar." *International Feminist Journal of Politics* 19(1): 4–21.

Davies, Sara E. and Jacqui True. 2017b. "When There Is No Justice: Gendered Violence and Harm in Post-Conflict Sri Lanka." *The International Journal of Human Rights* 21(9): 1320–1336.

Davies, Sara E. and Jacqui True. 2017c. "Connecting the Dots: Pre-existing Patterns of Gender Inequality and the Likelihood of Mass Sexual Violence." *Global Responsibility to Protect* 9(1): 65–85.

Davies, Sara E. and Jacqui True. 2022. "Follow the Money: Assessing Women, Peace, and Security through Financing for Gender-Inclusive Peace." *Review of International Studies* 48(4): 668–688.

Davies, Sara E., Jacqui True and Maria Tanyag. 2016. "How Women's Silence Secures the Peace: Analysing Sexual and Gender-Based Violence in a Low-Intensity Conflict." *Gender & Development* 24(3): 459–473.

D'Costa, Bina and Sara Hossain. 2010. "Redress for Sexual Violence before the International Crimes Tribunal in Bangladesh: Lessons from History, and Hopes for the Future." *Criminal Law Forum* 21(2): 331–359.

De Alwis, Malathi. 2004. "The 'Purity' of Displacement and the Reterritorialization of Longing: Muslim IDPs in Northwestern Sri Lanka." In *Sites of Violence: Gender and Conflict Zones*, edited by Wenona Giles and Jennifer Hyndman. Berkeley: University of California Press, 213–231.

De Alwis, Malathi. 2013. "'Housewives of the Public': The Cultural Signation of the Sri Lankan Nation." In *Crossing Borders and Shifting Boundaries: Vol. II: Gender, Identities*, edited by Ilse Lenz, Helma Lutz, Mirjana Morokvasic-Muller, Claudia Schöning-Kalender and Helen Schwenken. Springer: Amsterdam, 19–38.

Deane, Tameshnie. 2016. "Historical and Political Background to the Erosion of the Rule of Law and Human Rights during Sri Lanka's Civil War and the Way Forward." *Small Wars & Insurgencies* 27(6): 971–999.

de Dios, Aurora, Dawn Marie Castro, Beverly Orozco and Karen Tañada. 2020. In *Philippine NGO Beijing + 25 Report*, edited by Rosalinda Pineda Ofreneo and Jeanne Frances I. Illo. UP Center for Women's and Gender Studies and Oxfam. Quezon City, 15 September, 133–156. Available at: https://www.researchgate.net/profile/Naomi-Fontanos/publication/346474713_Struggling_from_the_Margins_to_the_Intersectionalities_of_Power_The_State_of_Lesbian_Gay_Bisexual_Transgender_Intersex_Queer_LGBTIQ_Filipinos_from_2015_to_2020/links/5fc44e91299bf104cf93e625/Struggling-from-the-Margins-to-the-Intersectionalities-of-Power-The-State-of-Lesbian-Gay-Bisexual-Transgender-Intersex-Queer-LGBTIQ-Filipinos-from-2015-to-2020.pdf.

Denov, Myriam, Pok Panhavichetr, Sopheap Suong and Meaghan Shevell. 2022. "'We Vowed by Force, Not by Our Heart': Men's and Women's Perspectives on Forced Marriage during the Cambodian Genocide." *The International Journal of Human Rights* 26(9): 1547–1570.

Department of Census and Statistics (Sri Lanka). 2015. "Household Income and Expenditure Survey 2012/13. Report, Government of Sri Lanka, March. Available at: http://www.statistics.gov.lk/Resource/en/IncomeAndExpenditure/HouseholdIncomeandExpenditureSurvey2012-2013FinalReport.pdf.

Department of Census and Statistics (Sri Lanka). 2022. "Labour Force." Report, Government of Sri Lanka. Available at: http://www.statistics.gov.lk/LabourForce/StaticalInformation/AnnualReports.

DFAT (Department of Foreign Affairs and Trade, Australia). 2017. "Ways for Women to Participate in Peacebuilding." Consolidated Policy and Research Brief. Available at: https://www.dfat.gov.au/sites/default/files/policy-brief-ways-for-women-to-participate-in-peacebuilding-philippines.pdf.

Diesta, Victorena and Charmaine B. Distor. 2019. "Reconstructing Marawi: Gender-Based Approach to Addressing Sexual Violence in Post-Conflict Marawi." Paper presented at the 1st International Conference on Action with Women and Peace. Seoul, 3 July. https://www.researchgate.net/publication/375661198_Exploring_a_gender-based_approach_towards_post-conflict_rehabilitation_The_Case_of_Marawi_Philippines

Dolan, Chris. 2014. "Into the Mainstream: Addressing Sexual Violence against Men and Boys in Conflict." Briefing paper prepared for the workshop held at the Overseas

Development Institute, London, 14 May. https://reliefweb.int/report/world/mainstr eam-addressing-sexual-violence-against-men-and-boys-conflict

Dolan, Richard. 2016. "The Problem with the 21st-Century Panglong Conference." *The Diplomat*, 6 August. Available at: https://thediplomat.com/2016/08/the-problem-with-the-21st-century-panglong-conference/

Duriesmith, David. 2020. "Adaptation of Militarized Masculinity and Violent Extremism in the Southern Philippine." In *Conflicting Identities: The Nexus between Masculinities, Femininities and Violent Extremism in Asia*. Report, edited by Kelly O'Neil. United Nations Development Programme (UNDP) Regional Office for Asia and the Pacific and UN Women Regional Office for Asia and the Pacific, 11–30.

du Toit, Louise and Elisabet le Roux. 2020. "A Feminist Reflection on Male Victims of Conflict-Related Sexual Violence." *European Journal of Women's Studies* 28(2): 115–128.

Dwyer, Leslie Katherine and Rufa Cagoco-Guiam. 2012. *Gender and Conflict in Mindanao*. Report, The Asia Foundation. Available at: Gender and Conflict in Mindanao (ndi.org). https://www.ndi.org/sites/default/files/Gender%20and%20Conflict%20in%20Mindanao.pdf

ECPAT. 2021. *Sri Lanka Report: Sexual Exploitation of Boys*. ECPAT International, November. Available at: https://ecpat.org/wp-content/uploads/2021/11/ECPAT-Global-Boys-Initiative-Sri-Lanka_EN.pdf.

Ekhator-Mobayode, Uche Eseosa, Lucia C. Hanmer, Eliana Rubiano-Matulevich and Diana Jimena Arango. 2022. "The Effect of Armed Conflict on Intimate Partner Violence: Evidence from the Boko Haram Insurgency in Nigeria." *World Development* 153: 1–16.

Ellsberg, Mary, Junior Ovince, Maureen Murphy, Alexandra Blackwell, Dashakti Reddy, Julianne Stennes, Tim Hess and Manuel Contreras. 2020. "No Safe Place: Prevalence and Correlates of Violence against Conflict-Affected Women and Girls in South Sudan." *PLOS ONE* 15(10): e0237965.

Engle, Karen. 2020. *The Grip of Sexual Violence in Conflict: Feminist Interventions in International Law*. Stanford, CA: Stanford University Press.

Englebrecht, Georgi. 2021. "Philippines: The International Criminal Court Goes After Duterte's Drug War." International Crisis Group (ICG), 17 September. Available at: Philippines: The International Criminal Court Goes after Duterte's Drug War | Crisis Group. https://www.crisisgroup.org/asia/south-east-asia/philippines/philippines-international-criminal-court-goes-after-dutertes-drug-war

Enriquez, Jean. 2020. "Violence Against Women." In *Philippine NGO Beijing + 25 Report*, edited by Rosalinda Pineda Ofreneo and Jeanne Frances I. Illo. UP Center for Women's and Gender Studies and Oxfam. Quezon City, 15 September, 105–132. Available at: https://www.researchgate.net/profile/Naomi-Fontanos/publication/346474713_Struggling_from_the_Margins_to_the_Intersectionalities_of_Power_The_State_of_Lesbian_Gay_Bisexual_Transgender_Intersex_Queer_LGBTIQ_Filipinos_from_2015_to_2020/links/5fc44e91299bf104cf93e625/Struggling-from-the-Margins-to-the-Intersectionalities-of-Power-The-State-of-Lesbian-Gay-Bisexual-Transgender-Intersex-Queer-LGBTIQ-Filipinos-from-2015-to-2020.pdf.

Ethirajan, Anbarasan. 2021a. "Sri Lanka Human Rights: UK Seeks New UN Resolution on Abuses." *BBC News*, 23 February. Available at: Sri Lanka Human Rights: UK Seeks New UN Resolution on Abuses—BBC News.

Ethirajan, Anbarasan. 2021b. "UN to Collect Evidence of Alleged Sri Lanka War Crimes." *BBC News*, 23 March. Available at: https://www.bbc.com/news/world-asia-56502221.

REFERENCES 183

Farr, Kathryn. 2009. "Extreme War Rape in Today's Civil-War-Torn States: A Contextual and Comparative Analysis." *Gender Issues* 26(1): 1–41.

Faxon, Hilary, Roisin Furlong and May Sabe Phyu. 2015. "Reinvigorating Resilience: Violence Against Women, Land Rights, and the Women's Peace Movement in Myanmar." *Gender & Development* 23(3): 463–479.

Fernandez, Maria Carmen and Bai Shaima Baraguir with John Bryant. 2022. "Inclusion and Exclusion in Displacement and Peacebuilding Responses in Mindanao, Philippines: Falling through the Cracks." Humanitarian Policy Group Working Paper. ODI, London, July. Available at: HPG report (odi.org). https://cdn.odi.org/media/documents/Inclusion_exclusion_Mindanao.pdf

Ferrara, Anita. 2014. *Assessing the Long-Term Impact of Truth Commissions: The Chilean Truth and Reconciliation Commission in Historical Perspective*. London: Routledge.

Fink, Christina. 2018. "Myanmar: Religious Minorities and Constitutional Questions." *Asian Affairs* 49(2): 259–277.

FOKUS Women. 2014. *Shadow Report to the United Nations Human Rights Committee*. 112th Session, 7–31 October.

FOKUS Women. 2015a. *Post-War Trends in Child Marriage in Sri Lanka*. Report, January. Available at: https://www.girlsnotbrides.org/learning-resources/resource-centre/post-war-trends-in-child-marriage-sri-lanka/#resource-downloads.

FOKUS Women. 2015b. *A Report on the Status of Female Heads of Households and Their Access to Economic, Social and Cultural Rights*. May. Available at: https://d3jkvgmi357tqm.cloudfront.net/1516008978/escr-in-anuradhapura.pdf.

FOKUS Women. 2016. *Whither Justice? The Language Barrier in Accessing the Criminal Justice System*. Report, Colombo (hardcopy on file with authors).

FOKUS Women. 2017. *Shadow Report to the United Nations Committee on the Elimination of Discrimination Against Women*. 66th session, 8th Periodic Review of Sri Lanka, February–March. Available at: https://www.ecoi.net/en/file/local/1328665/1930_1463657465_int-cedaw-ngo-lka-23894-e.pdf.

FOKUS Women and British High Commission. 2017. *Tackling Stigma of Conflict-Related Sexual Violence in the Sri Lanka National Action Plan on Sexual and Gender-Based Violence*. Report, Jetwing, Colombo, 29 August. Available at: https://assets.publishing.service.gov.uk/government/uploads/system/uploads/attachment_data/file/645640/SV_Workshop_Report_-_Sri_Lanka.pdf.

Francisco, Gay Marie Manalo. 2021. "Utilizing Informal Modes of Engagement: Civil Society, Substantive Representation of Women, and the Philippine Women's Rights Law." *Journal of Civil Society* 17(2): 119–135.

Freedom from Torture. 2015. *Tainted Peace: Torture in Sri Lanka since May 2009*. Report, August. Available at: https://www.freedomfromtorture.org/sites/default/files/2019-04/sl_report_a4_-_final-f-b-web.pdf.

Freedom from Torture. 2019. *Too Little Change: Ongoing Torture in Security Operations in Sri Lanka*. Report, August. Available at: https://www.freedomfromtorture.org/sites/default/files/2019-02/fft_sri_lanka_report_v5_lr.pdf.

Fulu, Emma, Xian Warner, Stephanie Miedema, Rachel Jewkes, Tim Roselli and James Lang. 2013. *Why Do Some Men Use Violence against Women and How Can We Prevent It? Quantitative Findings from the United Nations Multi-Country Study on Men and Violence in Asia and the Pacific*. Report, P4P (Partners for Prevention): UNDP, UNFPA, UN Women, UNV. Bangkok, September. Available at: https://www.undp.org/asia-paci

fic/publications/why-do-some-men-use-violence-against-women-and-how-can-we-prevent-it.

Ganguly, Meenakshi. 2022. "Sri Lanka's Former President Must Be Investigated for War Crimes." *Washington Post*, 22 July. Available at: https://www.hrw.org/news/2022/07/22/sri-lankas-former-president-must-be-investigated-war-crimes.

GEN (Gender Equality Network). 2015. "Behind the Silence: Violence Against Women and Their Resilience." Briefing Paper, Yangon. October.

George, Alexander L., and Andrew Bennett. 2005. *Case Studies and Theory Development I the Social Sciences*. Cambridge, MA: MIT Press.

Ghatak, Antara. 2022. "Negotiating Gender and Disability in the Bangladesh Liberation War, 1971." In *The Routledge Companion to Gender, Sexuality and Culture*, edited by Emma Rees. London: Routledge, 99–108.

Gleditsch, Nils Petter, Peter Wallensteen, Mikael Eriksson, Margareta Sollenberg and Håvard Strand. 2002. "Armed Conflict 1946–2001: A New Dataset." *Journal of Peace Research* 39(5): 615–637.

Global Justice Center. 2020. "Myanmar's Proposed Prevention of Violence Against Women Law—A Failure to Meet International Human Rights Standards." Factsheet, July. Available at: 20200710_MyanmarPOVAWlawAnalysis.pdf (globaljusticecenter.net).

GoP (Government of the Philippines). 2009. "The Philippine National Action Plan on UNSCRS 1325 & 1820: 2010–2016." Draft, 18 March. Available at: https://www.peacewomen.org/assets/file/NationalActionPlans/philippines_nap.pdf

GoP (Government of the Philippines). 2016. *Philippine National Action Plan on Women Peace and Security*. Report, Office of the Presidential Adviser on the Peace Process, Pasig City. Available at: https://1325naps.peacewomen.org/wp-content/uploads/2020/12/Philippines_20172022NAP.pdf

Gowrinathan, Nimmi and Zachariah Mampilly. 2019. "Resistance and Repression under the Rule of Rebels: Women, Clergy, and Civilian Agency in LTTE-Governed Sri Lanka." *Comparative Politics* 52(1): 1–20.

Gray, Harriet and Maria Stern. 2019. "Risky Dis/Entanglements: Torture and Sexual Violence in Conflict." *European Journal of International Relations* 25(4): 1035–1058.

Gray, Harriet, Maria Stern and Chris Dolan. 2020. "Torture and Sexual Violence in War and Conflict: The Unmaking and Remaking of Subjects of Violence." *Review of International Studies* 46(2): 197–216.

Greig, J. Michael. 2015. "Nipping Them in the Bud: The Onset of Mediation in Low-Intensity Civil Conflicts." *Journal of Conflict Resolution* 59(2): 336–361.

Grey, Rosemary and Laura J. Shepherd. 2013. "'Stop Rape Now?' Masculinity, Responsibility, and Conflict-Related Sexual Violence." *Men and Masculinities* 16(1): 115–135.

Guanzon, Rowena V. 2008. "Laws on Violence against Women in the Philippines." Expert paper presented at the United Nations Expert Group Meeting on Good Practices in Legislation on Violence Against Women, United Nations Office, Vienna, Austria, 26–28 May. Available at: http://www.un.org/womenwatch/daw/egm/vaw_legislation_2008/expertpapers/EGMGPLVAW%20Paper%20(Rowena%20Guanzon).pdf.

Guarnieri, Eleonora and Ana Tur-Prats. 2023. "Cultural Distance and Conflict-Related Sexual Violence." *The Quarterly Journal of Economics*, online view 138(3): 1817–1861.

REFERENCES 185

Guruge, Sepali, Vathsala Jayasuriya-Illesinghe and Nalika Gunawardena. 2015. "A Review of the Sri Lankan Health-Sector Response to Intimate Partner Violence: Looking Back, Moving Forward." *WHO South-East Asia Journal of Public Health* 4(1): 6–11.

Guruge, Sepali et al. 2017. "Intimate Partner Violence in the Post-War Context: Women's Experiences and Community Leaders' Perceptions in the Eastern Province of Sri Lanka." *PLOS ONE* 12(3): e0174801.

Haacke, Jürgen. 2009. "Myanmar, the Responsibility to Protect, and the Need for Practical Assistance." *Global Responsibility to Protect* 1(2): 156–184.

Hasanat, Fayeza. 2022. *The Voices of War Heroines: Sexual Violence, Testimony, and the Bangladesh Liberation War*. Leiden: Brill.

Hashim, Salamat. 2001. *The Bangsamoro People's Struggle against Oppression and Colonialism*. Mindanao Island: Agency for Youth Affairs, MILF (Moro Islamic Liberation Front).

Hata, Ikuhiko. 2018. *Comfort Women and Sex in the Battle Zone*. Lanham, MD: Rowman and Littlefield.

Heathcote, Gina. 2012. "Naming and Shaming: Human Rights Accountability in Security Council Resolution 1960 (2010) on Women, Peace and Security." *Journal of Human Rights Practice* 4(1): 82–105.

Hedström, Jenny. 2015. "Myanmar." In *Women in Conflict and Peace*, edited by Jenny Hedström and Thiyumi Senarathna. Stockholm: IDEA, 61–87.

Hedström, Jenny. 2016. "A Feminist Political Economy Analysis of Insecurity and Violence in Kachin State." In *Conflict in Myanmar: War, Politics, Religion*, edited by Nick Cheesman and Nicholas Farrelly. Singapore: ISEAS Publishing, 67–90.

Hedström, Jenny. 2017. "The Political Economy of the Kachin Revolutionary Household." *The Pacific Review* 30(4): 581–595.

Hedström, Jenny. 2022. "Militarized Social Reproduction: Women's Labour and Parastate Armed Conflict." *Critical Military Studies* 8(1): 58–76.

Hedström, Jenny and Elisabeth Olivius. 2021. "The Politics of Sexual Violence in the Kachin Conflict in Myanmar." *International Feminist Journal of Politics* 23(3): 374–395.

Heise, Lori L. and Andreas Kotsadam. 2015. "Cross-National and Multilevel Correlates of Partner Violence: An Analysis of Data from Population-Based Surveys." *Lancet* 3(6): e332–e340.

Henry, Nicola. 2011. *War and Rape: Law, Memory and Justice*. London: Routledge.

Henry, Nicola. 2016. "Theorizing Wartime Rape: Deconstructing Gender, Sexuality, and Violence." *Gender & Society* 30(1): 44–56.

Hilsdon, Anne-Marie. 2009. "Invisible Bodies: Gender, Conflict and Peace in Mindanao." *Asian Studies Review* 33(3): 349–365.

Ho, Tamara C. 2015. *Romancing Human Rights: Gender, Intimacy, and Power between Burma and the West*. Honolulu: University of Hawai'i Press.

Høiby, Marte. 2020. "Covering Mindanao: The Safety of Local vs. Non-local Journalists in the Field." *Journalism Practice* 14(1): 67–83.

Hongxi, Li. 2020. "The Extreme Secrecy of the Japanese Army's 'Comfort Women' System." *Chinese Studies in History* 53(1): 28–40.

Hoover Green, Amelia. 2018. "'Mind the Gap': Measuring and Understanding Gendered Conflict Experiences." In *The Oxford Handbook of Gender and Conflict*, edited by Fionnuala Ní Aoláin, Naomi Cahn, Dina Francesca Haynes and Nahla Valji. Oxford: Oxford University Press, 316–327.

Hoover Green, Amelia and Dara Kay Cohen. 2021. "Centering Human Subjects: The Ethics of 'Desk Research' on Political Violence." *Journal of Global Security Studies* 6(2): ogaa029.

HRW (Human Rights Watch). 2010. *"I Want to Help My Own People": State Control and Civil Society in Burma after Cyclone Nargis*. Report, April. Available at: https://reliefweb.int/report/myanmar/i-want-help-my-own-people-state-control-and-civil-society-burma-after-cyclone-nargis.

HRW (Human Rights Watch). 2012. "UN: Act on Failings in Sr Lanka: Appoint Independent Inquiry into Violations by Government and Tamil Tigers." 14 November. Available at: https://www.hrw.org/news/2012/11/14/un-act-failings-sri-lanka.

HRW (Human Rights Watch). 2013. *"We Will Teach You a Lesson": Sexual Violence against Tamils by Sri Lankan Security Forces*. Report, 26 February. Available at: https://www.hrw.org/report/2013/02/26/we-will-teach-you-lesson/sexual-violence-against-tamils-sri-lankan-security-forces.

HRW (Human Rights Watch). 2015. *Iraq: ISIS Escapees Describe Systematic Rape*. Report, 14 April. Available at: https://www.hrw.org/news/2015/04/14/iraq-isis-escapees-describe-systematic-rape#:~:text=The%2011%20women%20and%209,and%20by%20several%20ISIS%20fighters.

HRW (Human Rights Watch). 2020. Submission by Human Rights Watch to the UN Human Rights Committee in Advance of Its Review of Iraq. 7 August. Available at: https://www.hrw.org/news/2020/08/07/submission-human-rights-watch-un-human-rights-committee-advance-its-review-iraq.

HRW (Human Rights Watch). 2021. *"I Thought Our Life Might Get Better"—Implementing Afghanistan's Elimination of Violence Against Women Law*. Report, August. Available at: https://www.hrw.org/report/2021/08/05/i-thought-our-life-might-get-better/implementing-afghanistans-elimination.

Hudson, Valerie M. and Hilary Matfess. 2017. "In Plain Sight: The Neglected Linkage between Brideprice and Violent Conflict." *International Security* 42(1): 7–40.

Human Security Report Project. 2012. *Human Security Report 2012: Sexual Violence, Education, and War: Beyond the Mainstream Narrative*. Vancouver: Human Security Press.

Hutchinson, Susan. 2020. "Financing Da'esh with Sexual Slavery: A Case Study in Not Gendering Conflict Analysis and Intervention." *Journal of Global Security Studies* 5(2): 379–386.

ICG (International Crisis Group). 2011a. "Myanmar's Post-Election Landscape." Asia Briefing No. 118. Jakarta/Brussels, 7 March. Available at: https://www.refworld.org/country,COI,,,MMR,4562d8cf2,4d75e0c12,0.html.

ICG (International Crisis Group). 2011b. *Sri Lanka: Women's Insecurity in the North and East*. Asia Report No. 217, 20 December. Available at: https://www.crisisgroup.org/asia/south-asia/sri-lanka/sri-lanka-women-s-insecurity-north-and-east.

ICG (International Crisis Group). 2014. "The Forever War?: Military Control in Sri Lanka's North." Commentary, 25 March. Available at: https://www.crisisgroup.org/asia/south-asia/sri-lanka/forever-war-military-control-sri-lanka-s-north.

ICG (International Crisis Group). 2015. "Myanmar's Peace Process: A Nationwide Ceasefire Remains Elusive." Briefing No. 146, Yangon/Brussels, 16 September. Available at: https://www.crisisgroup.org/asia/south-east-asia/myanmar/myanmar-s-peace-process-nationwide-ceasefire-remains-elusive.

REFERENCES

ICG (International Crisis Group). 2016. *The Philippines: Renewing Prospects for Peace in Mindanao*. Asia Report No. 281, Brussels, July 6. Available at: https://www.crisisgroup.org/asia/south-east-asia/philippines/philippines-renewing-prospects-peace-mindanao.

ICG (International Crisis Group). 2017. *Sri Lanka's Conflict-Affected Women: Dealing with the Legacy of War*. Asia Report No. 289, Brussels, 28 July. Available at: https://www.crisisgroup.org/asia/south-asia/sri-lanka/289-sri-lankas-conflict-affected-women-dealing-legacy-war.

ICG (International Crisis Group). 2019. *The Philippines: Militancy and the New Bangsamoro*. Asia Report No. 301, Brussels, 27 June. Available at: https://www.crisisgroup.org/asia/south-east-asia/philippines/301-philippines-militancy-and-new-bangsamoro.

ICTJ (International Centre for Transitional Justice). 2014. *Navigating Paths to Justice in Myanmar's Transition*. Report, June. Available at: ICTJ-Myanmar-Development-Report-2014.pdf.

IDMC (Internal Displacement Monitoring Centre). 2022. "2021 Internal Displacement." Global Internal Displacement Database, Geneva. Available at: Global Internal Displacement Database | IDMC (internal-displacement.org).

IFRC (International Federation of Red Cross and Red Crescent Societies). 2011. "Myanmar: Cyclone Nargis 2008 Facts and Figures." Available at: https://reliefweb.int/report/myanmar/myanmar-cyclone-nargis-2008-facts-and-figures.

IHRC (International Human Rights Clinic). 2014. "Policy Memorandum: Preventing Indiscriminate Attacks and Willful Killings of Civilians by the Myanmar Military." Harvard Law School, Cambridge.

Imtiyaz, A.R.M. 2020. "The Easter Sunday Bombings and the Crisis Facing Sri Lanka's Muslims." *Journal of Asian and African Studies* 55(1): 3–16.

Ingram, Kiriloi M. 2023. "'Boulders of Strength and Pillars of Hope': Exploring Gender and Violent Extremism in Southeast Asia." AIIA (Australian Institute of International Affairs), 17 January. Available at: "Boulders of Strength and Pillars of Hope": Exploring Gender and Violent Extremism in Southeast Asia—Australian Institute of International Affairs—Australian Institute of International Affairs. https://www.internationalaffairs.org.au/australianoutlook/boulders-of-strength-and-pillars-of-hope-exploring-gender-and-violent-extremism-in-southeast-asia/

International Alert. 2021. "Conflict Alert 2020: Enduring Wars. Davao City: International Alert Philippines." https://www.international-alert.org/app/uploads/2021/07/Philippines-Conflict-Alert-2020-Enduring-Wars-EN-2021.pdf

International Alert. 2014. "Rebellion, Political Violence and Shadow Crimes in the Bangsamoro—The Bangsamoro Conflict Monitoring System (BCMS), 2011–2013." August. Available at: https://www.international-alert.org/app/uploads/2021/08/Philippines-Bangsamoro-Conflict-Monitoring-System-EN-2014.pdf.

Irrawaddy, The. 2022. "Myanmar Regime Forces Accused of Serial Sexual Assaults." 26 April. Available at: Myanmar Regime Forces Accused of Serial Sexual Assaults (irrawaddy.com).

ITJP (International Truth and Justice Project). 2015. *A Still Unfinished War: Sri Lanka's Survivors of Torture and Sexual Violence 2009–2015*. Report, July. Available at: stoptorture_report_v4_online.pdf (tamilrefugeecouncil.org.au).

ITJP (International Truth and Justice Project). 2016. *"Silenced"—Survivors of Sexual Violence and Torture in 2015*. Report, January. Available at: STOP_report_3_v5.1-2.pdf (tamilnet.com).

Jacobs, Rachel P. 2020. "Married by the Revolution: Forced Marriage as a Strategy of Control in Khmer Rouge Cambodia." *Journal of Genocide Research* 24(3): 357–379.

Jayasundere, Ramani and Craig Valters. 2014. "Women's Experiences of Local Justice: Community Mediation in Sri Lanka." JSRP Paper 10, Theory in Practice series. International Development Department, London School of Economics and Political Science, January.

Jayawardena, Kumari. 2016. *Feminism and Nationalism in the Third World*. London: Verso.

Jayawickrama, Nihal. 2015. "The Hybrid Court." *Colombo Telegraph*, 26 September. Available at: https://www.colombotelegraph.com/index.php/the-hybrid-court/.

Jeffery, Renée. 2018. "Amnesties and Intractable Conflicts: Managed Impunity in the Philippines' Bangsamoro Peace Process." *Journal of Human Rights* 17(4): 436–452.

Johansson, Karin and Mehwish Sarwari. 2019. "Sexual Violence and Biased Military Interventions in Civil Conflict." *Conflict Management and Peace Science* 36(5): 469–493.

Johnston, Melissa, Jacqui True, Eleanor Gordon, Yasmin Chilmeran and Yolanda Riveros-Morales. 2020. "Building a Stronger Evidence Base: The Impact of Gender Identities, Norms and Relations on Violent Extremism (a Case Study of Bangladesh, Indonesia and the Philippines)." Asia Regional Brief, April. Available at: https://asiapacific.unwomen.org/en/digital-library/publications/2020/05/building-a-stronger-evidence-base-the-impact-of-gender-identities-norms

Jordal, Malin, Kumudu Wijewardena and Pia Olsson. 2013. "Unmarried Women's Ways of Facing Single Motherhood in Sri Lanka—A Qualitative Interview Study." *BMC Women's Health* 13(1): 1–12.

Ju, Changwook. 2023. "Determinants of Conflict-Related Sexual Violence: A Meta-Reanalysis Distinguishing Two Classes of Zero Observations." *International Studies Quarterly* 67(3): 1–17.

Kamler, Erin M. 2015. "Women of the Kachin Conflict: Trafficking and Militarized Femininity on the Burma-China Border." *Journal of Human Trafficking* 1(3): 209–234.

Kamler, Erin M. 2019. "Towards a Feminist Foreign Policy in Myanmar." Heinrich Böll Stiftung, 22 February.

Kasumi, Nagakawa. 2008. *Gender-Based Violence during the Khmer Rouge Regime: Stories of Survivors from the Democratic Kampuchea (1975–1979)*. Cambodian Defenders Project, Phnom Pehn.

Kirby, Paul. 2013. "How Is Rape a Weapon of War? Feminist International Relations, Modes of Critical Explanation and the Study of Wartime Sexual Violence." *European Journal of International Relations* 19(4): 797–821.

Kirby, Paul. 2015. "Ending Sexual Violence in Conflict: The Preventing Sexual Violence Initiative and Its Critics." *International Affairs* 91(3): 457–472.

Kishi, Roudabeh. 2020. "Placing Peacekeeping Prevention of Conflict-Related Sexual Violence in the Context of Political Violence Targeting Women." In Peacekeeping Prevention: Strengthening Efforts to Preempt Conflict-Related Sexual Violence. With Louise Olsson, Angela Muvumba Sellström, Stephen Moncrief, Elisabeth Jean Wood, Karin Johansson, Walter Lotze, Chiara Ruffa, Amelia Hoover Green, Ann Kristin Sjöberg and Roudabeh Kishi. *International Peacekeeping* 27(4): 517–585, at 567–574.

Kivimäki, Timo. 2014. "Can the Pragmatic East Asian Approach to Human Security Offer a Way for the Deepening of the Long Peace of East Asia?" *Journal of Human Security* 10(1): 76–88.

Kochanski, Adam. 2020. "The Missing Picture: Accounting for Sexual and Gender-Based Violence during Cambodia's 'Other' Conflict Periods." *International Journal of Transitional Justice* 14(3): 504–523.

Kodikara, Chulani. 2014. "Good Women and Bad Women of the Post-War Nation." *Groundviews*, 22 May. Available at: https://groundviews.org/2014/05/22/good-women-and-bad-women-of-the-post-war-nation/.

Kodikara, Chulani. 2016. "Justice and Accountability for War-Related Sexual Violence in Sri Lanka." *Open Democracy*, 15 August. Available at: https://www.opendemocracy.net/en/5050/justice-and-accountability-for-war-related-sexual-violence-in-sri-lanka/.

Koens, Celeste and Samanthi Gunawardana. 2021. "A Continuum of Participation: Rethinking Tamil Women's Political Participation and Agency in Post-War Sri Lanka." *International Feminist Journal of Politics* 23(3):463–484.

Koos, Carlo. 2017. "Sexual Violence in Armed Conflicts: Research Progress and Remaining Gaps." *Third World Quarterly* 38(9): 1935–1951.

Korac, Maja. 1998. "Ethnic-Nationalism, Wars and the Patterns of Social, Political and Sexual Violence Against Women: The Case of Post-Yugoslav Countries." *Identities* 5(2): 153–181.

Kreft, Anne-Kathrin. 2020. "Civil Society Perspectives on Sexual Violence in Conflict: Patriarchy and War Strategy in Colombia." *International Affairs* 96(2): 457–478.

Kreft, Anne-Kathrin. 2023. "'This Patriarchal, Machista and Unequal Culture of Ours': Obstacles to Confronting Conflict-Related Sexual Violence." *Social Politics: International Studies in Gender, State & Society*, online view 30(2): 654–677.

Kreft, Anne-Kathrin and Philipp Schulz. 2022. "Political Agency, Victimhood, and Gender in Contexts of Armed Conflict: Moving beyond Dichotomies." *International Studies Quarterly* 66(2): sqac022.

Krüger, Jule and Ragnhild Nordås. 2020. "A Latent Variable Approach to Measuring Wartime Sexual Violence." *Journal of Peace Research* 57(6): 728–739.

Kubota, Makiko and Nami Takashi. 2016. "Case Study on Mindanao, the Philippines: Women's Participation and Leadership in Peacebuilding." JICA (Japan International Cooperation Agency) and the Georgetown Institute for Women, Peace and Security. Available at: JICA_MindanaoLO.pdf.

KWO (Karen Women Organization) et al. 2004. *Shattering Silences: Karen Women Speak Out about the Burmese Military Regime's Use of Rape as a Strategy of War in Karen State*. Report, with the collaboration of the Committee for Internally Displaced Karen People (CIDKP), the Karen Information Center (KIC), the Karen Human Rights Group (KHRG), the Mergui-Tavoy District Information Department. April.

Lake, Milli. 2014. "Ending Impunity for Sexual and Gender-Based Crimes: The International Criminal Court and Complementarity in the Democratic Republic of Congo." *African Conflict and Peacebuilding Review* 4(1): 1–32.

Larsen, Lise Wessel, Win Thuzar Aye and Espen Bjertness. 2021. "Prevalence of Intimate Partner Violence and Association with Wealth in Myanmar." *Journal of Family Violence* 36(4): 417–428.

Latt, Shwe Shwe Sein, Kim N. B. Ninh, Mi Ki Kyaw Myint and Susan Lee. 2017. *Women's Political Participation in Myanmar: Experiences of Women Parliamentarians 2011–2016.*

Report, The Asia Foundation, April. Available at: Womens-Political-Participation-in-Myanmar-MP-Experiences_report-1.pdf (asiafoundation.org).

Lawson, Jacqueline E. 1989. "'She's a Pretty Woman... for a Gook': The Misogyny of the Vietnam War." *Journal of American Culture* 12(3): 55–65.

Leatherman, Janie L. 2011. *Sexual Violence in Armed Conflict*. London: Polity Press.

Lei Win, Thin. 2013. "Cambodians Confront Taboo on Khmer Rouge Sex Crimes." Thomson Reuters, 3 December. Available at: https://news.trust.org/item/20131202171147-rwyuf.

Leiby, Michele. 2012. "The Promise and Peril of Primary Documents: Documenting Wartime Sexual Violence in El Salvador and Peru." In *Understanding and Proving International Sex Crimes*, edited by Morten Bergsmo, Alf Butenschøn Skre and Elisabeth J. Wood. Beijing: Torkel Opsahl Academic EPublisher, 315–366.

Lewis, Chloé. 2014. "Systemic Silencing: Addressing Sexual Violence against Men and Boys in Armed Conflict and Its Aftermath." In *Rethinking Peacekeeping, Gender Equality and Collective Security*, edited by Gina Heathcote and Dianne Otto. New York: Palgrave Macmillan, 203–247.

Lewis, Dustin A. 2019. "The Notion of 'Protracted Armed Conflict' in the Rome Statute and the Termination of Armed Conflicts under International Law: An Analysis of Select Issues." *International Review of the Red Cross* 101(912): 1091–1115.

Liebowitz, Debra J. and Susanne Zwingel. 2014. "Gender Equality Oversimplified: Using CEDAW to Counter the Measurement Obsession." *International Studies Review* 16(3): 362–382.

Lintner, Bertil. 2020. *Why Burma's Peace Efforts Have Failed to End Its Internal Wars*. Report No. 169, USIP (United States Institute of Peace), October. Available at: 20201002-pw_169-why_burmas_peace_efforts_have_failed_to_end_its_internal_wars-pw.pdf (usip.org).

Loken, Meredith. 2017. "Rethinking Rape: The Role of Women in Wartime Violence." *Security Studies* 26(1): 60–92.

Loong, Shona. 2022. "The Karen National Union in Post-coup Myanmar." Stimson Centre, 7 April. Available at: https://www.stimson.org/2022/the-karen-national-union-in-post-coup-myanmar/.

Lotze, Walter. 2020. "The Evolving United Nations Approach to Preventing and Addressing Conflict-Related Sexual Violence: Experiences from the Democratic Republic of the Congo." In *Peacekeeping Prevention: Strengthening Efforts to Preempt Conflict-related Sexual Violence*. With Louise Olsson, Angela Muvumba Sellström, Stephen Moncrief, Elisabeth Jean Wood, Karin Johansson, Walter Lotze, Chiara Ruffa, Amelia Hoover Green, Ann Kristin Sjöberg and Roudabeh Kishi. *International Peacekeeping* 27(4): 517–585, at 536–543.

Lozada, David. 2021. "How Duterte's 'War on Drugs' Is Being Significantly Opposed within the Philippines." *Melbourne Asia Review*, 12 July. Available at: https://melbourneasiareview.edu.au/how-dutertes-war-on-drugs-is-being-significantly-opposed-within-the-philippines/.

LSE (Centre for Women, Peace + Security). 2019. "WPS National Action Plans. With the University of Sydney." Available at: LSE—WPS National Action Plans (wpsnaps.org).

Lubina, Michal. 2021. *A Political Biography of Aung San Suu Kyi: A Hybrid Politician*. London: Routledge.

Lwin, Khaing Zar and Sureeporn Punpuing. 2022. "Determinants of Institutional Maternity Services Utilization in Myanmar." *PLOS ONE* 17(4): e0266185.

Ma, Agatha and Kyoko Kusakabe. 2015. "Gender Analysis of Fear and Mobility in the Context of Ethnic Conflict in Kayah State, Myanmar." *Singapore Journal of Tropical Geography* 36(3): 342–356.

Macgregor, Fiona. 2015. "Dozens of Rapes Reported in Northern Rakhine State." *Myanmar Times*, 27 October.

Mackinnon, Catherine. 1994. "Turning Rape into Pornography: Postmodern Genocide." In *Mass Rape: The War against Women in Bosnia-Herzegovina*, edited by Alexandra Stiglmayer. Lincoln: University of Nebraska Press, 73–81.

Mahderom, Saba. 2022. "Addressing Narratives Normalizing Weaponized Sexual Violence: The Case of Tigray." World Peace Foundation, 19 October. Available at: https://sites.tufts.edu/reinventingpeace/2022/10/19/addressing-narratives-normalizing-weaponized-sexual-violence-the-case-of-tigray/.

Maizland, Lindsay. 2022. "Myanmar's Troubled History: Coups, Military Rule, and Ethnic Conflict." Backgrounder, Council on Foreign Relations, 31 January. Available at: https://www.cfr.org/backgrounder/myanmar-history-coup-military-rule-ethnic-conflict-rohingya.

Malji, Andrea. 2021. "A Coup Can't Destroy an Ideology: The Future of Buddhist Nationalism in Myanmar." Berkley Forum, 12 March. Available at: https://berkleycenter.georgetown.edu/responses/a-coup-can-t-destroy-an-ideology-the-future-of-buddhist-nationalism-in-myanmar.

Manikkalingham, Ram. 2016. "The Politics of Punishing War Crimes in Sri Lanka." *Open Democracy*, 8 February. Available at: https://www.opendemocracy.net/en/openglobalrights-openpage/politics-of-punishing-war-crimes-in-sri-lanka/.

Manila Times. 2014. "ARMM Is Most Peaceful Philippine Region–PNP." 25 January. Available at: http://www.manilatimes.net/armm-is-most-peaceful-philippine-region-pnp/70675/.

Marsh, Nick. 2022. "Sri Lanka: The Divisions behind the Country's United Protests." *BBC News*, 4 May. Available at: https://www.bbc.com/news/world-asia-61295238.

Mcdonald, Joshua. 2020. "The Ampatuan Massacre: A Decade Long Fight for Justice." *The Diplomat*, 3 January. Available at: https://thediplomat.com/2020/01/the-ampatuan-massacre-a-decade-long-fight-for-justice/.

Medawatte, Danushka, Neloufer de Mel, Sandani N. Yapa Abeywardena and Ranitha Gnanaraj. 2022. *Conjunctures of Silence: Aphonias in the Prosecution of Conflict Related Sexual Violence in Sri Lanka—the Vishvamadu Case*. Report, The Gender, Justice and Security Hub, London. Available at: Conjunctures-of-Silence.pdf (thegenderhub.com).

Meger, Sara. 2016. *Rape Loot Pillage: The Political Economy of Sexual Violence in Armed Conflict*. Oxford: Oxford University Press.

Meger, Sara. 2021. "Sexual Violence in Times of War and Peace." In *Routledge Handbook of Feminist Peace Research*, edited by Tarja Väyrynen, Swati Parashar, Élise Féron and Catia Cecilia Confortini. London: Routledge, 115–125.

Menon, Ritu and Kamla Bhasin. 1998. *Borders & Boundaries: Women in India's Partition*. New Brunswick, NJ: Rutgers University Press.

Mibenge, Chiseche Salome. 2013. *Sex and International Tribunals: The Erasure of Gender from the War Narrative*. Philadelphia: University of Pennsylvania Press.

Min, Pyong Gap. 2021. *Korean "Comfort Women": Military Brothels, Brutality, and the Redress Movement*. New Brunswick, NJ: Rutgers University Press.

Minoletti, Paul. 2016. "Gender (In)Equality in the Governance of Myanmar: Past, Present, and Potential Strategies for Change." The Asia Foundation, April. Available at: 11.-mm-gender-paperen.pdf (opendevelopmentmyanmar.net).

Mintrom, Michael and Jacqui True. 2022. "COVID-19 as a Policy Window: Policy Entrepreneurs and the Prevention of Violence Against Women." *Policy and Society* 41(1): 143–154.

Mollica, Caitlin, Sara E. Davies, Jacqui True, Sri Wiyanti Eddyono, Bhavani Fonseka and Melissa Johnston. 2022. "Women and the Justice Divide in Asia Pacific: How Can Informal and Formal Institutions Bridge the Gap?" *Human Rights Quarterly* 44(3): 612–639.

Mookherjee, Nayanika. 2015. *The Spectral Wound: Sexual Violence, Public Memories, and the Bangladesh War of 1971*. Durham, NC: Duke University Press.

Myadar, Orhon and Ronald A. Davidson. 2020. "Remembering the 'Comfort Women': Geographies of Displacement, Violence and Memory in the Asia-Pacific and Beyond." *Gender, Place & Culture* 28(3): 347–369.

Myanmar Peace Monitor. 2019. "Prospect of Myanmar Peace Process through the Nationwide Ceasefire Agreement, 27 March." Available at: Prospect of Myanmar Peace Process through the Nationwide Ceasefire Agreement » Myanmar Peace Monitor (mmpeacemonitor.org).

Myint-U, Thant. 2019. *The Hidden History of Burma: A Crisis of Race and Capitalism*. London: Atlantic Books.

Myoe, Maung Aung. 2016. "Myanmar's Foreign Policy under the USDP Government: Continuities and Changes." *Journal of Current Southeast Asian Affairs* 35(1): 123–150.

Nagel, Robert U. 2021. "Conflict-Related Sexual Violence and the Re-Escalation of Lethal Violence." *International Studies Quarterly* 65(1): 56–68.

Nario-Galace, Jasmin. 2021. "Women Count for Peace and Security: A Story of Collaboration in the Philippines." *The Journal of Social Encounters* 5(2): 59–65.

Nesiah, Vasuki. 2012. "Uncomfortable Alliances: Women, Peace, and Security in Sri Lanka." In *South Asian Feminisms: Contemporary Interventions*, edited by Ania Loomba and Ritty Lukose. Durham, NC: Duke University Press Books, 139–161.

New Humanitarian, The. 2011. "Fewer 'I Dos' for Former Female Rebels." 23 February. Available at: https://www.thenewhumanitarian.org/report/92017/sri-lanka-fewer-i-dos-former-female-rebels.

Ní Aoláin, Fionnuala, Catherine O'Rourke and Aisling Swaine. 2015. "Transforming Reparations for Conflict-Related Sexual Violence: Principles and Practice." *Harvard Human Rights Journal* 28: 97–146.

Nordås, Ragnhild and Dara Kay Cohen. 2021. "Conflict-Related Sexual Violence." *Annual Review of Political Science* 24: 193–211.

Nowrojee, Bianfer. 1996. *Shattered Lives, Sexual Violence during the Rwandan Genocide and its Aftermath*. Report, Human Rights Watch, New York.

Nundakumar, Viruben. 2022. "In Sri Lanka, the Military Still Runs the Show." *Foreign Policy*, 4 August. Available at: Sri Lanka's Military Still Runs the Show (foreignpolicy.com). https://foreignpolicy.com/2022/08/04/sri-lanka-military-power-protests-history/

Oakland Institute, The. 2016. *Waiting to Return Home: Continued Plight of the IDPs in Post-War Sri Lanka*. Report. Available at: https://www.oaklandinstitute.org/sites/oaklandinstitute.org/files/SriLanka_Return_Home_final_web.pdf.

REFERENCES 193

Oatman, Annalise and Kate Majewski. 2020. "Rape as a Weapon of War in Myanmar/Burma." In *Women's Journey to Empowerment in the 21st Century: A Transnational Feminist Analysis of Women's Lives in Modern Times*, edited by Kristen Zaleski, Annalisa Enrile, Eugenia L. Weiss and Xiying Wang. Oxford: Oxford University Press, 266–284.

OCHA (Office for the Coordination of Humanitarian Affairs). 2015. "GenCap Contribution to the Global Study on SC Resolution 1325." Available at: https://www.humanitarianresponse.info/en/coordination.

OECD Development Centre. 2019. *SIGI 2019 Global Report: Transforming Challenges into Opportunities*. Social Institutions and Gender Index, OECD Publishing, Paris.

Office of the ICC Prosecutor. 2014. Policy Paper on Sexual and Gender-Based Crimes. International Criminal Court, Hague, June. Available at: https://www.icc-cpi.int/sites/default/files/iccdocs/otp/OTP-Policy-Paper-on-Sexual-and-Gender-Based-Crimes--June-2014.pdf.

OHCHR (Office of the High Commission for Human Rights). 2014. "OHCHR Investigation on Sri Lanka." United Nations. Available at: http://www.ohchr.org/EN/HRBodies/HRC/Pages/OISL.aspx.

OHCHR (Office of the High Commission for Human Right). 2015a. "Myanmar: UN Rights Experts Express Alarm at Adoption of First of Four 'Protection of Race and Religion' Bills." Press Release, United Nations, 27 May. Available at: https://www.ohchr.org/en/press-releases/2015/05/myanmar-un-rights-experts-express-alarm-adoption-first-four-protection-race.

OHCHR (Office of the High Commissioner for Human Rights). 2015b. *Report of the OHCHR Investigation on Sri Lanka*. Human Rights Council 30th session, United Nations, Geneva, A/HRC/30/62, 16 September. Available at: https://www.ohchr.org/en/hr-bodies/hrc/regular-sessions/session30/list-reports#:~:text=on%20Sri%20Lanka%20(OISL)-,English,-A/HRC/30/62.

OHCHR (Office of the High Commission for Human Rights). 2018a. "Myanmar: UN Fact-Finding Mission Releases Its Full Account of Massive Violations by Military in Rakhine, Kachin and Shan States." Press Release, United Nations, 18 September. Available at: https://www.ohchr.org/en/press-releases/2018/09/myanmar-un-fact-finding-mission-releases-its-full-account-massive-violations.

OHCHR (Office of the High Commission for Human Rights). 2018b. *Report of the Independent International Fact-Finding Mission on Myanmar*. A/HRC/39/64, United Nations, 12 September. Available at: https://www.ohchr.org/sites/default/files/Documents/HRBodies/HRCouncil/FFM-Myanmar/A_HRC_39_64.pdf.

OHCHR (Office of the High Commission for Human Rights). 2018c. *Report of the Special Rapporteur on the Situation of Human Rights in Myanmar*. A/HRC/37/70, United Nations, 24 May. OHCHR | A/HRC/37/70: Report of the Special Rapporteur on the Situation of Human Rights in Myanmar. https://www.ohchr.org/en/documents/country-reports/ahrc3770-report-special-rapporteur-situation-human-rights-myanmar

OHCHR (Office of the High Commission for Human Rights). 2019. "UN Fact-Finding Mission on Myanmar Exposes Military Business Ties, Calls for Targeted Sanctions and Armed Embargoes." Press Release, 5 August. Available at: UN Fact-Finding Mission on Myanmar Exposes Military Business Ties, Calls for Targeted Sanctions and Arms Embargoes | OHCHR. https://www.ohchr.org/en/press-releases/2019/08/un-fact-finding-mission-myanmar-exposes-military-business-ties-calls

Olsson, Louise, Angela Muvumba Sellström, Stephen Moncrief, Elisabeth Jean Wood, Karin Johansson, Walter Lotze, Chiara Ruffa, Amelia Hoover Green, Ann Kristin

Sjöberg and Roudabeh Kishi. 2020. "Peacekeeping Prevention: Strengthening Efforts to Preempt Conflict-Related Sexual Violence." *International Peacekeeping* 27(4): 517–585.

Oo, Phyu Phyu and Sara E. Davies. 2021. "Access to Whose Justice? Survivor-Centered Justice for Sexual and Gender-Based Violence in Northern Shan State." *Global Studies Quarterly* 1(3): ksab014.

Oostervald, Valerie. 2005. "The Definition of 'Gender' in the Rome Statute of the International Criminal Court: A Step Forward or Back for International Criminal Justice?" *Harvard Human Rights Journal* 18(1): 55–84.

Oostervald, Valerie. 2018. "The ICC Policy Paper on Sexual and Gender-Based Crimes: A Crucial Step for International Criminal Law." *William and Mary Journal of Race, Gender, and Society* 24(3): 443–457.

Palermo, Tia, Jennifer Bleck and Amber Peterman. 2014. "Tip of the Iceberg: Reporting and Gender-Based Violence in Developing Countries." *American Journal of Epidemiology* 179(5): 602–612.

Palik, Júlia, Siri Aas Rustad and Fredrik Methi. 2020. "Conflict Trends in Asia, 1989–2019." Peace Research Institute (PRIO), Oslo.

Palmer, Emma and Sarah Williams. 2017. "A 'Shift in Attitude'? Institutional Change and Sexual and Gender-Based Crimes at the Extraordinary Chambers in the Courts of Cambodia." *International Feminist Journal of Politics* 19(2): 1–17.

Pangalangan, Raul C. 2022. *Philippine Materials in International Law*. Leiden: Koninklijke Brill NV.

Parks, Thomas, Nat Coletta and Ben Oppenheim. 2013. *The Contested Corners of Asia: Subnational Conflict and International Development Assistance*. San Francisco: The Asia Foundation.

Parpart, Jane L. and Swati Parashar. 2019. "Introduction: Rethinking the Power of Silence in Insecure and Gendered Sites." In *Rethinking Silence, Voice and Agency in Contested Gendered Terrains*, edited by Jane L. Parpart and Swati Parashar. New York: Routledge, 1–15.

Pasimio, Judy A. 2020. "A Snapshot of the Lives of Indigenous Women. With LILAK (Purple Action for Indigenous Women's Rights)." In *Philippine NGO Beijing + 25 Report*, edited by Rosalinda Pineda Ofreneo and Jeanne Frances I. Illo. UP Center for Women's and Gender Studies and Oxfam. Quezon City, 15 September, 405–417. Available at: Philippine NGO Beijing + 25 Report (2020).pdf—Google Drive. https://www.researchgate.net/profile/Naomi-Fontanos/publication/346474713_Struggling_from_the_Margins_to_the_Intersectionalities_of_Power_The_State_of_Lesbian_Gay_Bisexual_Transgender_Intersex_Queer_LGBTIQ_Filipinos_from_2015_to_2020/links/5fc44e91299bf104cf93e625/Struggling-from-the-Margins-to-the-Intersectionalities-of-Power-The-State-of-Lesbian-Gay-Bisexual-Transgender-Intersex-Queer-LGBTIQ-Filipinos-from-2015-to-2020.pdf

Patrick, Andrew. 2015. "Ending Sexual Violence in Conflict." *The Irrawaddy*, 11 August. Available at: https://www.irrawaddy.com/news/military/ending-sexual-violence-in-conflict-time-to-act.html.

Peace Support Fund. 2016. *The Women Are Ready: An Opportunity to Transform Peace in Myanmar*. Report. Available at: https://www.jointpeacefund.org/sites/jointpeacefund.org/files/documents/the_women_are_ready_english_1.pdf.

PEARL (People for Equality and Relief in Lanka). 2022. "No Trials, Only Tribulations for Tamil Victims of Sri Lanka's Conflict-Related Sexual Violence." Washington, DC,

August. Available at: https://pearlaction.org/wp-content/uploads/2022/08/No-Trials-Only-Tribulations-for-Tamil-Victims-of-Sri-Lankas-CRSV-August-2022.pdf.

Pepper, Mollie. 2018. "Ethnic Minority Women, Diversity, and Informal Participation in Peacebuilding in Myanmar." *Journal of Peacebuilding & Development* 13(2): 61–75.

Perempuan, Komnas. 2007. Kejahatan Terhadap Kemanusiaan Berbasis Jender, Mendengarkan Suara Perempuan Korban Peristiwa 1965 [Gender-based crimes against humanity, listening to the women's voices of the 1965 tragedy]. Jakarta: Komnas Perempuan. Available at: https://www.komnasperempuan.go.id/reads-laporan-pem antauan-hamperempuan-kejahatan-terhadap-kemanusiaan-berbasis-jender-mende ngarkan-suaraperempuan-korban-peristiwa-1965.

Peterman, Amber, Dara Kay Cohen, Tia Palermo and Amelia Hoover Green. 2011. *Rape Reporting during War*. Council on Foreign Relations, 1 August.

Pohlman, Annie. 2015. *Women, Sexual Violence and the Indonesian Killings of 1965–66*. London: Routledge.

Progressive Voice. 2020. "Denying the Irrefutable: Women, Justice and the POVAW Law." 23 July. Available at: https://progressivevoicemyanmar.org/2020/07/23/denying-the-irrefutable-women-justice-and-the-povaw-law/.

PSA (Philippine Statistics Authority). 2016. "Official Poverty Statistics of the Philippine— 2015 Full Year." Republic of the Philippines, Quezon City, October 27. Available at: 2015 Full Year Official Poverty Statistics of the Philippines Publication_0.pdf (psa.gov.ph).

PSA (Philippine Statistics Authority). 2017. "Poverty Statistics in ARMM." January. Available at: ARMM Poverty Statistics.pdf (psa.gov.ph).

PSA (Philippine Statistics Authority). 2018. "Philippines National Demographic and Health Survey 2017. Republic of the Philippines, Quezon City, with the DHS Program ICF." Rockville, Maryland, October. Available at: Philippines National Demographic and Health Survey 2017 [FR347] (dhsprogram.com).

Quijano, Alejandra A. and Jocelyn Kelly. 2012. "A Tale of Two Conflicts: An Unexpected Reading of Sexual Violence in Conflict through the Cases of Colombia and Democratic Republic of Congo." In *Understanding and Proving International Sex Crimes*, edited by Morten Bergsmo, Alf Butenschøn Skre and Elisabeth J. Wood. Beijing: Torkel Opsahl Academic EPublisher, 437–494.

Rubio-Martin, Ruth, ed. 2006. *What Happened to the Women? Gender and Reparations for Human Rights Violations*. New York: Social Science Research Council.

Ryan, Sophie. 2020. "When Women Become the War Zone: The Use of Sexual Violence in Myanmar's Military Operations." *Global Responsibility to Protect* 12: 37–63.

Rydstrom, Helle. 2015. "Politics of Colonial Violence: Gendered Atrocities in French Occupied Vietnam." *European Journal of Women's Studies* 22(2): 191–207.

Saikia, Yasmin. 2011. "War as History, Humanity in Violence: Women, Men, and Memories of 1971, East Pakistan/Bangladesh." In *Sexual Violence in Conflict Zones: From the Ancient World to the Era of Human Rights*, edited by Elizabeth D. Heineman. Philadelphia: University of Pennsylvania Press, 152–172.

Salter, Mark. 2015. *To End a Civil War: Norway's Peace Engagement in Sri Lanka*. London: Hurst.

Salween Institute for Public Policy and WLB (Women's League of Burma). 2018. "Strategies to Promote Gender Equality." Policy Paper, January. https://www.women ofburma.org/policy-papers/strategies-promote-gender-equality

Salzman, Todd A. 1998. "Rape Camps as a Means of Ethnic Cleansing: Religious, Cultural, and Ethical Responses to Rape Victims in the Former Yugoslavia." *Human Rights Quarterly* 20(2): 348–378.

Santiago, Irene M. 2015. "The Participation of Women in the Mindanao Peace Process." Research paper prepared for the United Nations Global Study on 15 Years of Implementation of UN Security Council Resolution 1325 (2000). UN Women, New York, October. Available at: https://wps.unwomen.org/pdf/research/Santiago.pdf.

Santos, Ana P. 2020. "Women of the Eastern Caliphate Part 2: By Blood and Marriage." Pulitzer Center, 2 January. Available at: Women of the Eastern Caliphate Part 2: By Blood and Marriage | Pulitzer Center. https://pulitzercenter.org/stories/women-eastern-caliphate-part-2-blood-and-marriage

Sarvananthan, Muttukrishna. 2016. *The Pains of Labor in the Post–Civil War Development in the City of Jaffna, Northern Province, Sri Lanka*. Report prepared for the Solidarity Center in Sri Lanka, March. Available at: https://www.researchgate.net/publication/306031406_The_Pains_of_Labor_in_the_Post-Civil_War_Development_in_the_City_of_Jaffna_Northern_Province_Sri_Lanka.

Schmitt-Degenhardt, Stephan. 2013. *A Regional Perspective on Poverty in Myanmar*. Report, UNDP (UN Development Programme), August. Available at: Report_A_Regional_Perspective_on_Poverty_in_Myanmar_UNDP_August2013.pdf (themimu.info).

Schopper, Doris. 2014. "Responding to the Needs of Survivors of Sexual Violence: Do We Know What Works?" *International Review of the Red Cross* 96(894): 585–600.

Schott, Robin May. 2011. "War Rape, Natality and Genocide." *Journal of Genocide Research* 13(1–2): 5–21.

Schulz, Philipp. 2020. "Examining Male Wartime Rape Survivors' Perspectives on Justice in Northern Uganda." *Social & Legal Studies* 29(1): 19–40.

Schulz, Philipp and Heleen Touquet. 2020. "Queering Explanatory Frameworks for Wartime Sexual Violence against Men." *International Affairs* 96(5): 1169–1187.

Schwartz, Stephen. 1994. "Rape as a Weapon of War in the Former Yugoslavia." *Hastings Women's Law Journal* 5(1): 69–88.

Seatzu, Francesco. 2021. "The Standardized Monitoring, Analysis and Reporting Arrangements (MARA): An Effective Tool for Ending Armed Conflict-Related Sexual Violence?" *Florida Journal of International Law* 33(1): 41–73. Available at: https://scholarship.law.ufl.edu/fjil/vol33/iss1/2.

Selth, Andrew. 2019. "Aung San Suu Kyi: Why Defend the Indefensible?" *The Interpreter*, Lowy Institute, 12 December. Available at: Aung San Suu Kyi: Why Defend the Indefensible? | Lowy Institute.

Senanayake, Lakshmen. 2021. *Sexual and Gender-Based Violence in Sri Lanka: An Analysis of the Available Literature & Annotated Bibliography*. Report, UNFPA (United Nations Population Fund), Sri Lanka. Available at: https://srilanka.unfpa.org/en/publications/sexual-and-gender-based-violence-sri-lanka-analysis-available-literature-annotated.

Sepali, Guruge, Marilyn Ford-Gilboe, Colleen Varcoe, Vathsala Jayasuriya-Illesinghe, Mahesan Ganesan et al. 2017. "Intimate Partner Violence in the Post-war Context: Women's Experiences and Community Leaders' Perceptions in the Eastern Province of Sri Lanka." *PLOS ONE* 12(3):1–16.

Shivji, Salimah. 2022. "'We Must Not Lose Hope': Activists, Victims Seek War Crimes Charges against Ex-Sri Lankan President." *CBC News*, 26 August. Available at: https://www.cbc.ca/news/world/sri-lanka-gotabaya-rajapaksa-war-crimes-1.6561580.

REFERENCES 197

SHRF (Shan Human Rights Foundation) and SWAN (Shan Women's Action Network). 2002. *License to Rape: The Burmese Military Regime's Use of Sexual Violence in the Ongoing War in Shan State*. Report, May. Available at: https://shanhumanrights.org/wp-content/uploads/2021/02/Licence_to_rape-English.pdf.

Shwe Shwe Sein Latt, Kim N. B. Ninh, Mi Ki Kyaw Myint and Susan Lee. 2017. *Women's Political Participation in Myanmar: Experiences of Women Parliamentarians 2011–2016*. Report, The Asia Foundation, Yangon, April. Available at: Womens-Political-Participation-in-Myanmar-MP-Experiences_report-1.pdf (asiafoundation.org).

Sifris, Ronli and Maria Tanyag. 2019. "Intersectionality, Transitional Justice, and the Case of Internally Displaced Moro Women in the Philippines." *Human Rights Quarterly* 41(2): 399–420.

Sivenasen, Anupama. 2011. "Gender Violence as Insecurity: Research Trends in South Asia." New Voices Series No. 9, Global Consortium on Security Transformation, February. http://retro.prajnya.in/anugcst.pdf.

Sjoberg, Laura. 2016. *Women as Wartime Rapists: Beyond Sensation and Stereotyping*. New York: New York University Press.

Skjelsbæk, Inger. 2001. "Sexual Violence and War: Mapping Out a Complex Relationship." *European Journal of International Relations* 7(2): 211–237.

Skjelsbæk, Inger. 2011. *The Political Psychology of War Rape: Studies from Bosnia and Herzegovina*. London: Routledge.

Skjelsbæk, Inger. 2018. "Silence Breakers in War and Peace: Research on Gender and Violence with an Ethics of Engagement." *Social Politics: International Studies in Gender, State & Society* 25(4): 496–520.

Smith, Julia, Sara E. Davies, Karen A. Grépin, Sophie Harman, Asha Herten-Crabb, Alice Murage, Rosemary Morgan and Clare Wenham. 2022. "Reconceptualizing Successful Pandemic Preparedness and Response: A Feminist Perspective." *Social Science & Medicine* 315: 1–7.

Solamo-Antonio, Isabelita. 2015. "The Philippine Shari'a Courts and the Code of Muslim Personal Laws." In *The Sociology of Shari'a: Case Studies from around the World*, edited by Adam Possamai, James T Richardson and Bryan S. Turner. Cham: Springer, 83–101.

Solangon, Sarah and Preeti Patel. 2012. "Sexual Violence Against Men in Countries Affected by Armed Conflict." *Conflict, Security & Development* 12(4): 417–442.

Sooka, Yasmin, the Bar Human Rights Committee of England and Wales (BHRC), and the International Truth & Justice Project. 2014. *An Unfinished War: Torture and Sexual Violence in Sri Lanka 2009–2014*. Report, Sri Lanka, March. Available at: https://barhumanrights.org.uk/wp-content/uploads/2014/03/an_unfinihsed_war._torture_and_sexual_violence_in_sri_lanka_2009-2014_0-compressed.pdf.

Sooka, Yasmin and the International Truth & Justice Project. 2015. *A Still Unfinished War: Sri Lanka's Survivors of Torture and Sexual Violence 2009–2015*. Report, Sri Lanka, July. Available at: https://sangam.org/wp-content/uploads/2015/08/Stop-Torture-Report.pdf.

South, Ashley. 2018. "'Hybrid Governance' and the Politics of Legitimacy in the Myanmar Peace Process." *Journal of Contemporary Asia* 48(1): 50–66.

South, Ashley and Christopher M. Joll. 2016. "From Rebels to Rulers: The Challenges of Transition for Non-State Armed Groups in Mindanao and Myanmar." *Critical Asian Studies* 48(2): 168–192.

Southgate, Laura. 2019. *ASEAN Resistance to Sovereignty Violation: Interests, Balancing and the Role of the Vanguard State*. Bristol: Bristol University Press.

Staniland, Paul. 2021. *Ordering Violence: Explaining Armed Group-State Relations from Conflict to Cooperation*. Ithaca, NY: Cornell University Press.

Stanton, Gregory H. 2014. "Could the Rwanda Genocide Have Been Prevented?" *Journal of Genocide Research* 6(2): 211–228.

Stephens, Matthew. 2011. "Islamic Law in the Philippines: Between Appeasement and Neglect." Background Paper Series, ARC Federation Fellowship Islam, Syari'ah and Governance. Centre for Islamic Law and Society, Melbourne Law School, University of Melbourne. Available at: https://law.unimelb.edu.au/__data/assets/pdf_file/0011/1547795/Stephens_web2.pdf.

Stern, Maria. 2019. "Courageously Critiquing Sexual Violence: Responding to the 2018 Nobel Peace Prize." *International Affairs* 95(6): 1235–1249.

Stetz, Margaret D. 2019. "Reframing the 'Comfort Women' Issue: New Representations of an Old War Crime." In *Genocide and Mass Violence in Asia: An Introductory Reader*, edited by Frank Jacob. Berlin: de Gruyter, 61–77.

Sundar, Vaishnavi. 2022. "Crisis in Sri Lanka Brings Dire Consequences for Women." 5 April. Available at: https://4w.pub/crisis-in-sri-lanka-brings-dire-consequences-for-women/.

Swaine, Aisling. 2015. "Beyond Strategic Rape and between the Public and Private: Violence against Women in Armed Conflict." *Human Rights Quarterly* 37(3): 755–786.

Swaine, Aisling. 2017. "Furthering Comprehensive Approaches to Victims/Survivors of Conflict-Related Sexual Violence: An Analysis of National Action Plans on Women, Peace and Security in Indonesia, Nepal, Philippines, and Timor-Leste." In *Conflict-Related Sexual Violence in Asia-Pacific: Putting Victims/Survivors First*. Report, UN Women, 9–58.

SWAN (Shan Women's Action Network). 2015. *Upholding the Rights of Women and Children*. Report. Available at: SWAN (shanwomen.org).

Swe, Lei Mon. 2019. "Ceasefire Signatories Discuss Holding Next Peace Talks This Year." *Myanmar Times*, 8 July. Available at: https://www.mmtimes.com/news/ceasefire-signatories-discuss-holding-next-peace-talks-year.html.

Szablewska, Natalia and Olga Jurasz. 2019. "Sexual and Gender-Based Violence: The Case for Transformative Justice in Cambodia." *Global Change, Peace & Security* 31(3): 263–282.

Tameshnie, Deane. 2016. "Historical and Political Background to the Erosion of the Rule of Law and Human Rights during Sri Lanka's Civil War and the Way Forward." *Small Wars & Insurgencies* 27(6): 971–995.

Tanyag, Maria. 2018. "Resilience, Female Altruism, and Bodily Autonomy: Disaster-Induced Displacement in Post-Haiyan Philippines." *Signs: Journal of Women in Culture and Society* 43(3): 563–585.

Thant, Htoo. 2015. "New Idea Floated to Allow NLD Leader to Assume Presidency." *Myanmar Times*, 10 December. Available at: https://opendevelopmentmekong.net/news/new-idea-floated-to-allow-nld-leader-to-assume-presidency/.

The Asia Foundation. 2017. *The State of Conflict and Violence in Asia*. San Francisco: The Asia Foundation.

TJRC (Transitional Justice and Reconciliation Commission). 2016. *Report of the Transitional Justice and Reconciliation Commission*. Makati City, February. Available at: https://asiapacific.unwomen.org/sites/default/files/Field%20Office%20ESEAsia/Docs/Publications/2016/10/TJRC%20Report.pdf.

REFERENCES 199

TNI (Transnational Institute). 2017. "Beyond Panglong: Myanmar's National Peace and Reform Dilemma." Myanmar Policy Briefing 21, 19 September. Available at: https://www.tni.org/en/publication/beyond-panglong-myanmars-national-peace-and-reform-dilemma.

TNI (Transnational Institute). 2020. "Myanmar: Ethnic Politics and the 2020 General Election." Policy Briefing, 24 September. Available at: https://www.tni.org/en/publication/myanmar-ethnic-politics-and-the-2020-general-election.

TNI (Transnational Institute). 2023. *The Nationwide Ceasefire Agreement in Myanmar—Promoting Ethnic Peace or Strengthening State Control?* Report, 20 April. Available at: https://www.tni.org/en/publication/the-nationwide-ceasefire-agreement-in-myanmar.

Totani, Yuma. 2011. "Legal Responses to World War II Sexual Violence: The Japanese Experience." In *Sexual Violence in Conflict Zones: From the Ancient World to the Era of Human Rights*, edited by Elizabeth D. Heineman. Philadelphia: University of Pennsylvania Press, 217–231.

Touquet, Heleen and Philipp Schulz. 2021. "Navigating Vulnerabilities and Masculinities: How Gendered Contexts Shape the Agency of Male Sexual Violence Survivors." *Security Dialogue* 52(3): 213–230.

Traunmüller, Richard, Sara Kijewski and Markus Freitag. 2019. "The Silent Victims of Sexual Violence during War: Evidence from a List Experiment in Sri Lanka." *Journal of Conflict Resolution* 63(9): 2015–2042.

Tripon, Ma. Olivia H. and Lisa Garcia. 2020. "Women and the Media." In *Philippine NGO Beijing + 25 Report*, edited by Rosalinda Pineda Ofreneo and Jeanne Frances I. Illo. UP Center for Women's and Gender Studies and Oxfam. Quezon City, 15 September, 252–289. Available at: Philippine NGO Beijing + 25 Report (2020).pdf—Google Drive. https://www.researchgate.net/profile/Naomi-Fontanos/publication/346474713_Struggling_from_the_Margins_to_the_Intersectionalities_of_Power_The_State_of_Lesbian_Gay_Bisexual_Transgender_Intersex_Queer_LGBTIQ_Filipinos_from_2015_to_2020/links/5fc44e91299bf104cf93e625/Struggling-from-the-Margins-to-the-Intersectionalities-of-Power-The-State-of-Lesbian-Gay-Bisexual-Transgender-Intersex-Queer-LGBTIQ-Filipinos-from-2015-to-2020.pdf

Trojanowska, Barbara K. 2019. "'Courage Is Very Important for Those Who Wage Peace': Conversation with Jasmin Nario-Galace, Peace Educator, on the Implementation of the UN's Women, Peace and Security Agenda in Conflict-Ridden Philippines." *International Feminist Journal of Politics* 21(2): 317–325.

True, Jacqui. 2012. *The Political Economy of Violence against Women*. Oxford: Oxford University Press.

True, Jacqui. 2013. "Gendered Violence in Natural Disasters: Learning from New Orleans, Haiti and Christchurch." *Aotearoa New Zealand Social Work* 25(2): 78–89.

True, Jacqui. 2020. "Sexual and Gender-Based Violence Reporting and Terrorism in Asia." In *Conflicting Identities: The Nexus between Masculinities, Femininities and Violent Extremism in Asia*, edited by UNDP/UN Women. United Nations, Bangkok, Thailand, 75–96.

Tun, Chit Min. 2019. "Govt Suggests KNPP Signs Ceasefire This Fall." *The Irrawaddy*, 18 July. Available at: https://www.irrawaddy.com/news/burma/govt-suggests-knpp-sign-ceasefire-fall.html.

Tyner, James A. 2017. *Memory, Landscape, and Post-Violence in Cambodia*. London: Rowman and Littlefield.

Tyner, James A. 2018. "Gender and Sexual Violence, Forced Marriages, and Primitive Accumulation during the Cambodian Genocide, 1975–1979." *Gender, Place and Culture* 25(9): 1305–1321.

UCDP and PRIO. 2014. UCDP/PRIO Armed Conflict Dataset Codebook Version 4-2014a. UCPD (Uppsala Conflict Data Program) and PRIO (International Peace Research Institute, Oslo). Available at: 1 Introduction (uu.se). https://ucdp.uu.se/downloads/old/ucdpprio/ucdp-prio-acd-4a-2014.pdf

Umel, Richel V. and Ryan D. Rosauro. 2023. "Marawi Body Sets Rules for Claims." *Inquirer*, 26 May. Available at: Marawi Body Sets Rules for Claims | Inquirer News.

UN (United Nations). 2022a. *Framework for the Prevention of Conflict-Related Sexual Violence*. Office of the Special Representative of the Secretary-General on Sexual Violence in Conflict and Stop Rape Now: UN Action against Sexual Violence in Conflict, August. Available at: https://www.un.org/sexualviolenceinconflict/wp-content/uploads/2022/09/auto-draft/202209-CRSV-Prevention-Framework.pdf.

UN (United Nations). 2022b. "Significant Progress Being Made in Evidence Collection of ISIL/Da'esh's Crimes in Iraq, Investigating Team Head Tells Security Council." SC/14928, 8 June. Available at: Significant Progress Being Made in Evidence Collection of ISIL/Da'esh's Crimes in Iraq, Investigating Team Head Tells Security Council | UN Press. https://press.un.org/en/2022/sc14928.doc.htm

University of Edinburgh, the. 2015. Peace Agreements Database: Myanmar. October. Available at: https://www.peaceagreements.org/wsearch?WggSearchForm%5Bregion%5D=3&WggSearchForm%5Bcountry_entity%5D=92&WggSearchForm%5Bname%5D=&WggSearchForm%5Bcategory_mode%5D=any&WggSearchForm%5Bagreement_text%5D=&s=Search+Database.

UNDP (UN Development Programme). 2015. *Women and Local Leadership: Leadership Journeys of Myanmar's Female Village Tract/Ward Administrators*. Report, November. Available at: Report_Women_and_Local_Leadership_UNDP_Nov2015.pdf (themimu.info).

UNDP (UN Development Programme). 2016. *Gender Equality and Women's Rights in Myanmar—A Situation Analysis*. Report with the Asian Development Bank, United Nations Population Fund, and the United Nations Entity for Gender Equality and the Empowerment of Women. New York. Available at: Gender Equality and Women's Rights in Myanmar: A Situation Analysis (adb.org). https://www.adb.org/documents/gender-equality-and-womens-rights-myanmar-situation-analysis

UNDP (UN Development Programme). 2021. "Myanmar Urban Poverty Rates Set to Triple, New United Nations Survey Finds." 1 December. Available at: Myanmar Urban Poverty Rates Set to Triple, New United Nations Survey Finds | United Nations Development Programme (undp.org). https://www.undp.org/asia-pacific/press-releases/myanmar-urban-poverty-rates-set-triple-new-united-nations-survey-finds#:~:text=Yangon%2C%20Myanmar%2C%201%20December%202021,Development%20Programme%20(UNDP)%20finds

UNFPA (UN Population Fund). 2016a. *Keeping the Promise to Women*. Report, 1 January. Available at: https://srilanka.unfpa.org/en/publications/keeping-promise-women.

UNFPA (UN Population Fund). 2016b. *G2G UNFPA Inter-generational Policy Dialogues: Bringing Generations Together for Our Sri Lanka*. Report, UNFPA Inter-generational Dialogues, Colombo, March. Available at: https://srilanka.unfpa.org/sites/default/files/pub-pdf/G2G%20Voices.pdf.

UNFPA (UN Population Fund). 2018. "Women Come Together to Address Gender-Based Violence in Marawi, Philippines." News, Philippines, 20 November. Available at: UNFPA Philippines | Women Come Together to Address Gender-Based Violence in Marawi, Philippines. https://philippines.unfpa.org/en/news/women-come-together-address-gender-based-violence-marawi-philippines

UNFPA (UN Population Fund). 2022. "Violence Against Women—Regional Snapshot (2022)—kNOwVAWdata." Fact Sheet, August. Available at: UNFPA Asiapacific | Violence Against Women—Regional Snapshot (2022)—kNOwVAWdata. https://asiapacific.unfpa.org/en/resources/violence-against-women-regional-snapshot-2022-knowvawdata

UNGA (UN General Assembly). 1993. "Declaration on the Elimination of Violence Against Women." A/RES/48/104, 85th Plenary Meeting, 20 December. Available at: Microsoft Word—Document1 (un.org). https://www.ohchr.org/en/instruments-mechanisms/instruments/declaration-elimination-violence-against-women

UNGA (UN General Assembly). 2006. "Report of the Special Rapporteur on the Situation of Human Rights in Myanmar." A/61/369, 21 September.

UNGA (UN General Assembly). 2007. "Situation of Human Rights in Myanmar." A/HRC/6/14, 7 December.

UNHCR (UN High Commissioner for Refugees). 2019. "Zamboanga City—Five Years after the Siege." Press Release, 28 June. Available at: https://www.protectionclusterphilippines.org/?p=1866.

UNHCR (UN High Commissioner for Refugees). 2023. "Myanmar Situation." Available at: https://data.unhcr.org/en/situations/myanmar.

UNHRC (UN Human Rights Council). 2017. "Observations by the Special Rapporteur on the Promotion of Truth, Justice, Reparation and Guarantees of Non-Recurrence, Mr. Pablo De Greiff, on the Conclusion of His Recent Visit to Sri Lanka." Statement, 23 October. Available at: https://www.ohchr.org/en/statements/2017/10/observations-special-rapporteur-promotion-truth-justice-reparation-and.

UNHRC (UN Human Rights Council). 2021. "Promoting Reconciliation, Accountability and Human Rights in Sri Lanka." 46th Session, A/HRC/46/20, 25 February. Available at: https://daccess-ods.un.org/tmp/154788.717627525.html.

UNHRC (UN Human Rights Council). 2022a. *Report of the Special Rapporteur on the Situation of Human Rights in Myanmar, Thomas H. Andrews*. 49th Session, A/HRC/49/76, 16 March. Available at: Report of the Special Rapporteur on the Situation of Human Rights in Myanmar, Thomas H. Andrews (A/HRC/49/76) (Advance Unedited Version)—Myanmar | ReliefWeb. https://www.ohchr.org/en/documents/country-reports/ahrc4976-report-special-rapporteur-situation-human-rights-myanmar-thomas

UNHRC (UN Human Rights Council). 2022b. *Situation of Human Rights in Sri Lanka*. Comprehensive Report of the United Nations High Commissioner for Human Rights, A/HRC/51/5, 6 September. Available at: Situation of Human Rights in Sri Lanka—Comprehensive Report of the United Nations High Commissioner for Human Rights (A/HRC/51/5) (Advance Unedited Version)—Sri Lanka | ReliefWeb. https://www.ohchr.org/en/documents/reports/ahrc515-situation-human-rights-sri-lanka-comprehensive-report-united-nations-high

UNHRC (UN Human Rights Council). 2022c. "Sri Lanka: Criminalisation of Same-Sex Sexual Activity Breached Rights of a LGBTI Activist, UN Women's Rights Committee Finds." Press Release, 23 March. Available at: https://www.ohchr.org/en/press-releases/2022/03/sri-lanka-criminalisation-same-sex-sexual-activity-breached-rights-lgbti.

UNHRC (UN Human Rights Council). 2022d. *Promoting Reconciliation, Accountability and Human Rights in Sri Lanka*. Report of the United Nations High Commissioner for Human Rights, 49th Session, A/HRC/49/9, 18 March. Available at: A_HRC_49_9-EN.pdf.

UNSC (UN Security Council). 2004. *The Rule of Law and Transitional Justice in Conflict and Post-conflict Societies—Report of the Secretary General.* S/2004/616, United Nations, New York, 23 August. Available at: https://www.securitycouncilreport.org/atf/cf/%7B65BFCF9B-6D27-4E9C-8CD3-CF6E4FF96FF9%7D/PCS%20S%202004%20616.pdf

UNSC (UN Security Council). 2011. *Report of the Secretary-General's Panel of Experts on Accountability in Sri Lanka*. Report, United Nations, New York, 31 March. Available at: https://www.securitycouncilreport.org/atf/cf/%7B65BFCF9B-6D27-4E9C-8CD3-CF6E4FF96FF9%7D/POC%20Rep%20on%20Account%20in%20Sri%20Lanka.pdf.

UNSG (UN Secretary-General). 2009. *Report of the Secretary General—Implementing the Responsibility to Protect*. A/63/677, United Nations, New York, 12 January. Available at: https://daccess-ods.un.org/tmp/1495319.00882721.html.

UNSG (UN Secretary-General). 2012a. Conflict Related Sexual Violence: Report of the Secretary-General. S/2012/33 United Nations, New York, 13 January. Available: https://www.securitycouncilreport.org/atf/cf/%7B65BFCF9B-6D27-4E9C-8CD3-CF6E4FF96FF9%7D/WPS%20S%202012%2033.pdf

UNSG (UN Secretary-General). 2012b. *Report of the Secretary-General's Internal Review Panel on United Nations Action in Sri Lanka*. United Nations, New York, November. Available at: https://digitallibrary.un.org/record/737299/files/The_Internal_Review_Panel_report_on_Sri_Lanka.pdf?ln=en

UNSG (UN Secretary-General). 2013. *Report of the Secretary-General on Conflict-Related Sexual Violence*. S/2013/149, United Nations, New York, 14 March. Available at: *https://www.securitycouncilreport.org/atf/cf/%7B65BFCF9B-6D27-4E9C-8CD3-CF6E4FF96FF9%7D/s_2013_149.pdf.*

UNSG (UN Secretary-General). 2014. *Report of the Secretary-General on Conflict-Related Sexual Violence*. S/2014/181, United Nations, New York, 13 March. Available at: https://www.securitycouncilreport.org/atf/cf/%7B65BFCF9B-6D27-4E9C-8CD3-CF6E4FF96FF9%7D/s_2014_181.pdf.

UNSG (UN Secretary-General). 2015. *Report of the Secretary-General on Conflict-Related Sexual Violence*. S/2015/203, United Nations, New York, 23 March. Available at: https://www.securitycouncilreport.org/atf/cf/%7B65BFCF9B-6D27-4E9C-8CD3-CF6E4FF96FF9%7D/s_2015_203.pdf

UNSG (UN Secretary-General). 2016. *Report of the Secretary-General on Conflict-Related Sexual Violence*. S/2016/361, United Nations, New York, 20 April. Available at: https://reliefweb.int/report/world/conflict-related-sexual-violence-report-secretary-general-s2016361-enar.

UNSG (UN Secretary-General). 2017. *Report of the Secretary-General on Conflict-Related Sexual Violence*. United Nations, New York, S/2017/249, 15 April. Available at: https://www.securitycouncilreport.org/atf/cf/%7B65BFCF9B-6D27-4E9C-8CD3-CF6E4FF96FF9%7D/s_2017_249.pdf

UNSG (UN Secretary-General). 2018. *Report of the Secretary-General on Conflict-Related Sexual Violence*. United Nations, New York, S/2018/250, 25 March. Available: https://www.securitycouncilreport.org/atf/cf/%7B65BFCF9B-6D27-4E9C-8CD3-CF6E4FF96FF9%7D/s_2018_250.pdf

UNSG (UN Secretary-General). 2019. *Conflict-Related Sexual Violence—Report of the Secretary-General.* S/2019/280, 29 March. Available at: https://www.securitycouncilreport.org/atf/cf/%7B65BFCF9B-6D27-4E9C-8CD3-CF6E4FF96FF9%7D/s_2019_280.pdf

UNSC (UN Security Council). 2020. *Conflict-Related Sexual Violence—Report of the Secretary General.* S/2020/487, United Nations, New York, 3 June. Available at: https://www.securitycouncilreport.org/atf/cf/%7B65BFCF9B-6D27-4E9C-8CD3-CF6E4FF96FF9%7D/s_2020_487.pdf

UNSG (UN Secretary-General). 2021. *Conflict-Related Sexual Violence—Report of the Secretary-General.* S/2021/312, United Nations, New York, 30 March. Available at: https://www.securitycouncilreport.org/atf/cf/%7B65BFCF9B-6D27-4E9C-8CD3-CF6E4FF96FF9%7D/s_2021_312.pdf

UNSG (UN Secretary-General). 2022a. *Women and Peace and Security—Report of the Secretary-General.* S/2022/740, United Nations, New York, 5 October. Available at: https://www.securitycouncilreport.org/atf/cf/%7B65BFCF9B-6D27-4E9C-8CD3-CF6E4FF96FF9%7D/S-2022-740.pdf

UNSG (UN Secretary-General). 2022b. *Conflict-Related Sexual Violence—Report of the Secretary-General.* S/2022/272, United Nations, New York, 29 March. Available at: https://www.securitycouncilreport.org/atf/cf/%7B65BFCF9B-6D27-4E9C-8CD3-CF6E4FF96FF9%7D/s-2022-272.pdf

UNSG (UN Secretary-General). 2023. *Conflict-Related Sexual Violence—Report of the Secretary-General.* S/2023/413, United Nations, New York, 22 June. Available at: https://www.securitycouncilreport.org/atf/cf/%7B65BFCF9B-6D27-4E9C-8CD3-CF6E4FF96FF9%7D/S_2023_413.pdf

UN Women. 2019. "The Marawi Siege: Women's Reflections Then and Now." Briefing Note, April. Available at: https://asiapacific.unwomen.org/en/digital-library/publications/2019/04/the-marawi-siege.

UN Women and UNHCR. 2018. *A Gender Analysis of the Right to a Nationality in Myanmar.* Report, in collaboration with NRC and SNAP, March. Available at: https://asiapacific.unwomen.org/en/digital-library/publications/2019/01/a-gender-analysis-of-the-right-to-a-nationality-in-myanmar.

Utne, Kelsey J. 2021. "The Commemorative Continuum of Partition Violence." In *Post-Conflict Memorialization: Missing Memorials, Absent Bodies*, edited by Olivette Otele, Luisa Gandolfo and Yoav Gala. Cham: Palgrave Macmillan, 151–169.

Veloso, Diana Therese M. 2017. "Multiple Marginalization and Gender-Based Violence in Post-conflict Settings: The Experiences of IDPs in Zamboanga City." Paper presented at the 10th DLSU Arts Congress De La Salle University, Manila, Philippines, 16 February. https://www.researchgate.net/publication/315896141_Multiple_Marginalization_and_Gender-Based_Violence_in_Post-Conflict_Settings_The_Experiences_of_IDPs_in_Zamboanga_City

Verite Research. 2016. *The President's Pledges to Women: A Review of the Promises and Progress Made in President Sirisena's Pledge: "A New Sri Lanka for Women."* Report, January. Available at: https://www.veriteresearch.org/wp-content/uploads/2018/05/The-President_s-Pledges-to-Women.pdf.

Verite Research. 2018. "Sri Lanka: Resolution 30/1 Implementation Monitor." Statistical and Analytical Review No. 3, February. Available at: https://www.veriteresearch.org/wp-content/uploads/2018/02/Verite-Research_UNHRC-Monitor-No3-February-2018.pdf.

Von Joeden-Forgey, Elise. 2012. "Gender and the Future of Genocide Studies and Prevention." *Genocide Studies and Prevention* 7(1): 89–107.

Waller, Emily, Emma Palmer and Louise Chappell. 2014. "Strengthening Gender Justice in the Asia-Pacific through the Rome Statute." *Australian Journal of International Affairs* 68(3): 356–373.

Walmsley, Roy. 2017. "World Prison Population List." 12th ed. WPB (World Prison Brief) and ICPR (Institute for Crime and Justice Policy Research). Available at: wppl_12.pdf (prisonstudies.org).

Walton, Matthew J., Melyn McKay and Daw Khin Mar Mar Kyi. 2015. "Women and Myanmar's 'Religious Protection Laws.'" *The Review of Faith & International Affairs* 13(4): 36–49.

Wamsley, Laurel. 2022. "Rape Has Reportedly Become a Weapon in Ukraine." NPR, 30 April. Available at: War in Ukraine: How Rape Has Reportedly Become a Weapon: NPR. https://www.npr.org/2022/04/30/1093339262/ukraine-russia-rape-war-crimes

Wansai, Sai. 2017. "Jump-Starting the Stalled Peace Process—Is Revitalization of the 1961 Federal Amendment Proposal the Way to Go?" TNI (The Transnational Institute), 4 May. Available at: Jump-Starting the Stalled Peace Process | Transnational Institute (tni.org). https://www.tni.org/en/article/jump-starting-the-stalled-peace-process

WEF (World Economic Forum). 2017. *Global Gender Gap 2017*. Insight Report. Written by Klaus Schwab, Richard Samans, Saadia Zahidi, Till Alexander Leopold, Vesselina Ratcheva, Ricardo Hausmann and Laura D. Tyson. Geneva. Available at: WEF_GGGR_2017.pdf (weforum.org).

Wenham, Clare, Julia Smith, Sara E. Davies, Huiyun Feng, Karen A. Grépin, Sophie Harman, Asha Herten-Crabb and Rosemary Morgan. 2020. "Women Are Most Affected by Pandemics—Lessons from Past Outbreaks." *Nature* 583(7815): 194–198.

Whitaker, Beth Elise, James Igoe Walsh and Justin Conrad. 2019. "Natural Resource Exploitation and Sexual Violence by Rebel Groups." *Journal of Politics* 81(2): 702–706.

WHO (World Health Organization). 2008. *National Report on Violence and Health in Sri Lanka*. With the Ministry of Healthcare and Nutrition (Sri Lanka). Colombo, April. Available at: https://docplayer.net/99267124-Ministry-of-healthcare-and-nutrition-national-report-on-violence-and-health-in-sri-lanka.html.

Wickramasinghe, Maithree and Chulani Kodikara. 2012. "Representation in Politics: Women and Gender in the Sri Lankan Republic." In *The Sri Lankan Republic at 40: Reflections on Constitutional History, Theory and Practice*, edited by Asanga Welikala. Colombo: Centre for Policy Alternatives and Friedrich Naumann Stiftung für die Freiheit (FNF), 772–820. Available at: http://republicat40.org/wp-content/uploads/2013/01/Representation-in-Politics1.pdf.

Wickremesinghe, Ramil. 2014. *Report of the Leader of the Opposition's Commission on the Prevention of Violence Against Women and the Girl Child*. Report, December. Available at: http://gbvforum.lk/r-library/document/Report%20of%20the%20Leader.pdf.

Wijayatilaka, Kamalini. 2004. *Study on Sexual and Gender-Based Violence in Selected Locations in Sri Lanka*. Colombo: Centre for Women's Research (CENWOR).

Willis, Christopher P. 2021. "Sexual Violence by the State: The Role of Political Institutions in Sexual Violence Perpetration." *International Studies Quarterly* 65(3): 768–781.

Wilson, Trevor. 2010. "The Use of Normative Processes in Achieving Behaviour Change in Myanmar." In *Ruling Myanmar: From Cyclone Nargis to National Elections*, edited by Nick Cheesman, Monique Skidmore and Trevor Wilson. Singapore: ISEAS, 294–318.

Win, Aye Aye. 2015. "Burma President Signs Off on Contested Population Law." *The Irrawaddy*, 24 May. Available at: Myanmar President Signs Off on Contested Population Law (irrawaddy.com). https://www.irrawaddy.com/news/burma/burma-president-signs-off-on-contested-population-law.html

Win, Chit and Thomas Kean. 2017. "Communal Conflict in Myanmar: The Legislature's Response, 2012–2015." *Journal of Contemporary Asia* 47(3): 413–439.

WIN (Women in Need). 2019. *Why Accessing Justice Is Challenging for Victims of Sexual and Gender Based Violence?* June. Available at: Sri-Lanka_-Inside-Justice-Summary-Report.pdf (think-asia.org).

WLB (Women's League of Burma) and AJAR (Asia Justice and Rights). 2017. "Access to Justice for Women Survivors of Gender-Based Violence Committed by State Actors in Burma (2016)." Available at: https://www.womenofburma.org/sites/default/files/2018-06/2016_Nov_VAW_BriefingPaper_Eng.pdf.

WLHRB (Women's Legal and Human Rights Bureau). 2015. "Engendering the Barangay Justice System." 20 October. Available at: Engendering the Barangay Justice System (EBJS)—Women's Legal & Human Rights Bureau (wlbonline.org). https://wlbonline.org/engendering-the-barangay-justice-system-ebjs/

Wood, Elisabeth Jean. 2006. "Variation in Sexual Violence during War." *Politics & Society* 34(3): 307–342.

Wood, Elisabeth Jean. 2008a. "Sexual Violence during War: Toward an Understanding of Variation." In *Order, Conflict and Violence*, edited by Stathis Kalyvas, Tarek Masoud and Ian Shapiro. Cambridge: Cambridge University Press, 323–351.

Wood, Elisabeth Jean. 2008b. "The Social Processes of Civil War: The Wartime Transformation of Social Networks." *Annual Review of Political Science* 11: 539–561.

Wood, Elisabeth Jean. 2009. "Armed Groups and Sexual Violence: When Is Wartime Rape Rare?" *Politics & Society* 37(1): 131–161.

Wood, Elisabeth Jean. 2014. "Conflict-Related Sexual Violence and the Policy Implications of Recent Research." *International Review of the Red Cross* 96(894): 457–478.

Wood, Elisabeth Jean. 2015. "Social Mobilization and Violence in Civil War and Their Social Legacies." *The Oxford Handbook of Social Movements*, edited by Donatella Della Porta and Mario Diani. Oxford: Oxford University Press, 452–466.

Wood, Elisabeth Jean. 2018. "Rape as a Practice of War: Toward a Typology of Political Violence." *Politics & Society* 46(4): 513–537.

Wood, Elisabeth. 2020. "Understanding Conflict-Related Sexual Violence: What Peacekeepers Should Know." With Stephen Moncrief. International Peacekeeping, 2020. In *FORUM. Peacekeeping Prevention: Strengthening Efforts to Preempt Conflict-related Sexual Violence*, edited by Louise Olsson, Angela Muvumba Sellström, Stephen Moncrief, Elisabeth Jean Wood, Karin Johansson, Walter Lotze, Chiara Ruffa, Amelia Hoover Green, Ann Kristin Sjöberg and Roudabeh Kishi International Peacekeeping, 27(4): 517–585.

WPB (World Prison Brief). 2022. "Philippines." ICPR (Institute for Crime and Justice Policy Research) and Birbeck. Available at: https://www.prisonstudies.org/country/philippines

Yadav, Punam and Denise M. Horn. 2021. "Continuums of Violence Feminist: Peace Research and Gender-Based Violence." In *Routledge Handbook of Feminist Peace Research*, edited by Tarja Väyrynen, Swati Parashar, Elise Féron and Catia Cecilia Confortini. London: Routledge, 2–11.

Yamahata, Chosein. 2022. "Myanmar at a 'Point of No Return': Unity Reborn Despite Junta's Terrorization." In *Demystifying Myanmar's Transition and Political Crisis*, edited by Chosein Yamahata and Bobby Anderson. Singapore: Palgrave Macmillan, 321–344.

Ye Mon. 2017. "Govt Eyes Meeting with Northern Alliance Ahead of Next 21CPC." *Democratic Voice of Burma (DVB)*, 17 August. Available at: http://www.dvb.no/news/govt-eyes-meeting-northern-alliance-ahead-next-21cpc/76926.

Yoshimi, Yoshiaki. 2002. *Comfort Women: Sexual Slavery in the Japanese Military during World War II*. New York: Columbia University Press.

Zalewski, Marysia, Paula Drumond, Elisabeth Prügl and Maria Stern. 2018. "Introduction: Sexual Violence against Men in Global Politics." In *Sexual Violence Against Men in Global Politics*, edited by Marysia Zalewski, Paula Drumond, Elisabeth Prügl and Maria Stern. New York: Routledge, 1–19.

Zartman, William. 2015. *Preventing Deadly Conflict*. Cambridge: Polity Press.

Zin, Min. 2015. "Anti-Muslim Violence in Burma: Why Now?" *Social Research* 82(2): 375–397.

Index

For the benefit of digital users, indexed terms that span two pages (e.g., 52–53) may, on occasion, appear on only one of those pages.

Note: Tables and figures are indicated by an italic t and f following the page number.

abductions, 10, 30–31, 32, 90, 95–96, 112–14, 146, 164–65
Alliance for Gender Inclusion in Peace Processes (AGIPP), 63
Amnesty International, 25–26, 39
Arakan Rohingya Salvation Army (ARSA), 59
Armed Conflict Location and Event Data (ACLED) project, 32, 39
Asal, Victor, 15–16, 20–21, 27
ASEAN Regional Action Plan on Women, Peace and Security, 41
The Asia Foundation, 1, 14, 63
Association of South East Asian Nations (ASEAN), 57–58, 162–63
atrocity crimes, 29, 69–70, 71
Autonomous Region of Muslim Mindanao (ARMM), 10–11, 87–88, 89, 146

Baaz, Maria Eriksson, 2–3, 5–6, 15–16, 19, 22, 27, 37
Bangladesh Liberation War, 30–31
Bangladesh war, 1
Bangsamoro Autonomous Region in Muslim Mindanao (BARMM), 87, 89, 90–91, 97, 152–53, 160–61
Bangsamoro Ceasefire (1997), 10
Bangsamoro Comprehensive Peace Agreement, 155
Bangsamoro Islamic Freedom Fighters (BIFF), 88–89
Bangsamoro Organic Law, 88–89, 172–73n.1
battle deaths, 4, 30, 32–33, 38–39, 48, 49–52, 139–40
Boesten, Jelke, 22, 28, 44–45, 47

Buddhist Women's Special Marriage Law, 73–74
Burmese SGBV reporting
  analysis of, 81–83
  background on conflicts, 55–60, 57f
  ceasefire attempts and, 10, 55, 58–60, 63, 65–68, 82–83, 154
  civil conflict abuses, 60–62
  conflict endings and, 154
  culture of impunity, 67–74
  current trends, 159
  data trends, 74–81, 76f, 77f, 78f, 79f, 80f, 145–46
  domestic violence, 40, 63, 65, 68, 73–74, 82, 145, 154
  nonstate armed actors, 149–50, 151f
  Tatmadaw soldiers, 10, 69–74
  women's role in peace process, 62–67

Cambodian war, 30–31
Campbell, Kirsten, 35
ceasefire attempts
  in Afghanistan, 32
  brokering of, 153–54
  in Burma, 10, 55, 58–60, 63, 65–68, 82–83, 154
  in Philippines, 10, 84, 87–88, 103
  in Sri Lanka, 11, 111
CEPA (Centre for Poverty Analysis, Sri Lanka), 121–22
civil society activism, 7–8
civil society organizations (CSOs), 65, 67, 96–97
clan violence, 10, 146
Code of Muslim Personal Laws, 90
Cohen, Dara Kay, 20–21, 25–26

combatant socialization theory, 25–26
comfort women, 1, 12
Commission of Inquiry, Sri Lanka, 116
Committee for Internally Displaced Karen People (CIDKP), 62
Communist Party of Burma, 56
Comprehensive Bangsamoro Agreement (CBA), 84–85
conflict-related SGBV (CRSV)
  case studies, 32–34
  evolution of, 16–20
  examining methodologies for, 36–44
  future research on, 165–68
  gender analyses bias, 42–44
  gendered norms and, 164–65
  limited awareness of, 40–41
  in low-intensity conflict, 30–31
  political conditions of, 162–64
  reframing of, 14–16
  regional case comparisons, 47–48
  rethinking methodologies for, 35
  theories and patterns, 20–30
Consultation Task Force on Reconciliation Mechanisms (CTF), Sri Lanka, 125, 147, 161
Convention on the Elimination of all Forms of Discrimination Against Women (CEDAW), 89, 105, 125–26, 167, 169n.1
COVID-19 pandemic, 162, 167–68
CPA (Centre for Policy Alternatives, Sri Lanka), 117, 118, 120, 124, 125–27
crimes against humanity, 16–17, 20–21, 98, 113–14, 126–27, 159, 160, 162
culture of opportunity, 72

D'Costa, Bina, 22, 30–31, 32
Democratic Republic of Congo, 6, 20–21
Department of Interior and Local Government (DILG), 97–98
discrimination
  gendered discrimination, 9, 28–29, 35, 40, 41, 49–52, 53–54, 81–83, 92–93, 112, 126, 137, 140, 158, 163–64, 165–66
  gender inequality, 2, 25–26, 28–29, 33–34, 55, 89, 95–96, 119, 157
displacement camps, 37, 81, 83, 106–7, 114–15, 123–24, 132, 147–48

Dolan, Chris, 2–3, 65
domestic violence
  in Burma, 40, 63, 65, 68, 73–74, 82, 145, 154
  coding reports on, 49
  conflicting reports on, 142
  in Philippines, 41, 89, 146
  reporting levels, 146
  in Sri Lanka, 117–18
  WHO global studies of, 41–42
Duriesmith, David, 94

economic justice, 136
elimination of violence against women (EVAW) law, 146
ethnic armed organizations (EAOs), 59, 65–66
ethnic cleansing, 14–15, 20–21, 25, 32, 59, 67, 69–71, 82, 159
ethnic targeting, 23–24, 70–71, 82
ethnonationalism, 47–48, 111–12, 134–36, 137, 166
extreme war rape, 23

Farr, Kathryn, 23–25
female-headed households (FHH), 121–22
feminism
  Burmese conflicts and, 62, 67, 73–74
  civil society activism, 7–8
  gender discrimination and, 35
  male victims-survivors and, 28
  reporting silence and, 8, 44–45, 53–54, 164, 165–66
  Sri Lankan conflicts and, 138
  violence against women, 5–6, 15
feminist methodology, 44, 165
FOKUS Women, 115, 117, 119–20, 121–22, 126, 143–45
forced marriages, 1, 12, 75–77, 81, 90, 96, 109–10, 113–14, 137, 146, 152–53, 160–61

gang rape, 25–26, 31, 71–72, 74–75, 98–99, 118, 174n.1
gender-based violence (GBV), defined, 169n.1
gender codes, 4
gendered bias, 2–3, 5

gendered discrimination, 9, 28–29, 35, 40, 41, 49–52, 53–54, 81–83, 92–93, 112, 126, 137, 140, 158, 163–64, 165–66
gendered norms
  amongst displaced populations, 146
  Burmese SGBV and, 24, 65, 70, 73–74
  causal nature of, 27
  of conflict-related SGBV, 39–40, 43, 44–45, 164–65
  Philippine SGBV and, 94, 95–96, 98, 109–10
  SGBV crime and, 2–3, 158–61, 162, 164, 168
  transitional justice systems and, 155
gendered political violence, 4, 12, 15–16, 27, 35, 43, 119, 140
gender equality, 28–29, 33–34, 63–64, 66–67, 89, 92–93, 136
gender inequality, 2, 25–26, 28–29, 33–34, 53–54, 55, 89, 95–96, 119, 134–36, 157
gender norms, 3, 24, 27, 39–40, 43, 44–45, 65, 73–74, 146, 155, 160–61, 162, 164, 168
gender security, 136
gender stereotypes, 29, 64, 72–73, 83
GEN (Gender Equality Network), 141–42
genocide
  Bangladesh Liberation War, 30–31
  in Burma, 59–61
  Cambodian war, 30–31
  Rohingya genocide, 30, 60–61
  Rwandan genocide, 20–21, 30
Gleditsch, Nils Petter, 14–15
Global Gender Gap report, 90
Gray, Harriet, 2–3, 35

Hedström, Jenny, 27, 32, 39, 45, 64, 67–68, 73–74, 152–53, 165
Henry, Nicola, 5–6, 22, 28, 47
high-intensity conflicts, 14–16, 33–34, 112, 139–40
homosexuality, 3, 4, 26, 118, 125–26
Hoover Green, Amelia, 2–3, 14–15, 19, 20–21, 33–34, 42–43, 70
human rights violations, 30, 64, 112–13, 115, 120–21, 122–23, 125–26, 135–36, 139–40, 145

Human Rights Watch, 25–26, 39, 114, 123

ICG (International Crisis Group), 58, 59, 86–89, 119–20, 124–25, 134–35
ideal victim analysis, 46
impunity culture
  Burmese SGBV reporting, 67–74
  conflict endings and, 153–55
  future research on, 165–68
  political conditions of CRSV, 162–64
  Sri Lanka SGBV reporting, 122–27
  trends in Burma, 159
  trends in Philippines, 160–61
  trends in Sri Lanka, 161–62
impunity gap, 25–26, 120–21
Indochinese wars, 31
internally displaced persons (IDPs), 62, 67, 79–81, 95, 114
International Court of Justice (ICJ), 59–60
International Criminal Court (ICC), 1, 20, 49, 98, 160. *see also* Rome Statute of the International Criminal Court
International Criminal Tribunals on Former Yugoslavia and Rwanda, 7–8
international nongovernment organizations (INGOs), 105
International Truth and Justice Project (ITJP), 123, 126
intimate partner violence, 4–5, 37, 68, 89, 171n.4
Islamic State (IS), 84, 88–89, 170n.11
Islamophobia, 161–62

Jayawardena, Kumari, 119
Jeddah Accord, 87

Kamler, Erin M., 67, 71–72
Karen ethnic group, 56, 59–60
Karen Human Rights Group (KHRG), 62
Karen Information Center (KIC), 62
Karen Women's Organization (KWO), 62
Kirby, Paul, 22, 35
Komnas Perempuan, 31
Kreft, Anne-Kathrin, 2–3, 15–16, 35, 37, 39, 42

Lai massacre, 31

Lessons Learned and Reconciliation
    Commission (LLRC), Sri Lanka,
    119, 123–24
Liberation Tigers of Tamil Eelam (LTTE),
    11–12, 111–18, 120, 121, 150–52
low-intensity conflicts
    conflict-related SGBV in, 30–31
    defined, 170n.2
    gender analyses bias, 42–44
    prevalence and patterns, 36–44
    reframing knowledge and action, 14–16
    regional case comparisons, 47–48
low reporting, 12, 89, 140, 145–48,
    148f, 165

Magna Carta of Women (MCW), the
    Philippines, 92–93, 96–97
Manik Farm camp, 114
Marawi Siege Compensation Act, 160–61
marital rape, 169n.1
masculinized violence, 23, 25–26, 72–73
media reporting, 1, 14–15, 39, 48, 52–53,
    78–79, 82–83, 105, 108, 142–43
Meger, Sara, 14–16, 18, 32
Memorandum of Agreement on
    Ancestral Domain (MOA-AD), the
    Philippines, 87–88
militarized violence, 38, 55, 61, 72–73,
    114–20, 121–22, 136, 172n.10
minor conflicts, defined, 38
Moro Islamic Liberation Front (MILF),
    84–89, 91–92, 103
Moro National Liberation Front (MNLF),
    86–87, 95

Nagel, Robert U., 15–16, 20–22, 27
Nanking Massacre, 1, 30–31
National Action Plans on Women, Peace
    and Security, 41, 63, 93–94
National League of Democracy (NLD), 58
Nationwide Ceasefire Agreement (NCA),
    Burma, 58–59, 65–66, 82–83
Nationwide Peace Agreement, 159
Nesiah, Vasuki, 135–36
Ní Aoláin, Fionnuala, 2–3, 19
nongovernment organizations
    (NGOs), 126
nonrecognition of conflict, 38–39

nonreporting problems, 1, 12, 14, 27–28,
    36, 40, 43–44, 48, 53, 140, 148, 153–
    54, 157. *see also* reporting silence;
    under-reporting
nonstate armed actors, 149–53, 149f, 150f,
    151f, 152f, 153f

Office of the High Commissioner for
    Human Rights (OHCHR), 49, 61,
    112–14, 116, 123–24
official reporting, 42–43, 44–45, 105, 111,
    142–43, 150–52, 153–54, 157
Olsson, Louise, 18–19, 136
online violence, 167–68
Oostervald, Valerie, 16–17
opportunistic rape, 24, 32
Organization of Islamic Cooperation
    (OIC), 87

participatory justice, 136
patriarchal state, 43, 73–74, 91–92,
    117, 136
patterns and trends in SGBV reporting
    conflict endings and, 153–55
    escalation of reports, 141–45, 141f,
        143f, 144f
    introduction to, 139–41
    justice and transitional justice, 155–57
    low reporting, 140, 145–48, 148f
    nonstate armed actors, 149–53, 149f,
        150f, 151f, 152f, 153f
peace accords, 12–13, 154–55
Peace Agreement (2014), 10
peaceful Asia narrative, 38–39
Philippine Commission on Women, 92–93
Philippine peace and SGBV reporting
    background on conflicts, 85–89
    ceasefire attempts and, 10, 84, 87–
        88, 103
    civil conflict abuses, 90–91
    conflict endings and, 154
    current trends, 160–61
    data trends, 99–108, 100f, 101f, 102f,
        104f, 105f, 106f, 107f, 146
    domestic violence, 41, 89, 146
    existing explanations for SGBV, 92–99
    introduction to, 84–85
    nonstate armed actors, 150, 151f

women's role in, 91–92
Philippines Demographic and Health Survey (DHS), 97
Philippines Women, Peace, and Security National Action Plan (NAP), 84–85
political bias, 5, 157
Population Control Healthcare Law, Burma, 73–74
postconflict crimes in Sri Lanka, 115, 119–27, 137–38

rape
  background on, 2–3
  in Burma, 73–75, 82, 143–45
  in civil conflicts, 25
  extreme war rape, 23
  gang rape, 25–26, 31, 71–72, 74–75, 98–99, 118, 174n.1
  of Indigenous women by migrant colonizers, 3
  marital rape, 169n.1
  perpetrator dynamics and, 29
  in Philippines, 89, 93–103, 146, 160–61
  retribution rape, 3
  in Sri Lanka, 113–18, 123–24, 164–65
  wartime vs. peacetime, 6
rape, as weapon of war
  by American soldiers, 31
  in Burma, 71–72
  opportunistic component, 24, 32
  as recognition of crime, 20–21
  Tatmadaw soldiers, 10
Rape of Nanking. see Nanking Massacre
rebel groups, 24, 59–60
reparative justice, 64, 92, 136, 138
reporting events, 6
reporting silence. see also nonreporting problems; under-reporting
  data connections in, 47
  feminism and, 8, 44–45, 53–54, 164, 165–66
  future research needs, 13
  gendered norms and, 164
  gender inequality and, 2
  identification of, 44–47
  impact of, 36–37, 54, 83
  interrogation of, 48–53
  regional case comparisons, 47–48, 50*t*

retribution rape, 3
Rohingya genocide, 30, 60–61
Rome Statute of the International Criminal Court, 1, 7–8
  definition of SGBV, 139–40
  genocide and, 20–21
  introduction of, 32–33
  lack of ratification, 41
  overview of, 16–20
  war crimes and, 39–40
Rwandan genocide, 20–21, 30

Schulz, Philipp, 2–3, 15–16, 27, 28, 35, 37
sex tourism, 92–93, 98–99
sexual slavery, 1, 16–17, 30–31, 32, 66, 160–61
sexual violence against men and boys, 28, 37, 114–15, 118, 124
Shan Human Rights Foundation (SHRF), 61
Shan Women's Action Network (SWAN), 61
Sjoberg, Laura, 2–3, 26, 27, 35
Skjelsbæk, Inger, 5–6, 15–16
social reproduction roles, 73–74, 95–96
socioeconomic power, 27
Sooka, Yasmin, 28, 113–14, 116, 117, 123–24, 126
Sri Lanka Civil War (1983-2009), 32, 112–18
Sri Lanka SGBV reporting
  background on civil war, 112–18
  ceasefire attempts and, 11, 111
  conflict endings and, 153–54
  conflict patterns, 114–18
  culture of impunity, 122–27
  current trends, 161–62
  data trends, 127–33, 128*f*, 129*f*, 131*f*, 132*f*, 133*f*, 147
  domestic violence, 117–18
  ethnonationalism, 111–12, 134–36, 137
  gender inequality and, 119, 120–22, 134–36
  introduction to, 111–12
  militarized violence, 114–20, 121–22, 134–36
  nonstate armed actors, 149–52, 152*f*
  postconflict crimes, 115, 119–27, 137–38

State Peace and Development Council
    (SPDC), 58
Stern, Maria, 2-3, 5-6, 15-16, 19,
    22, 27, 37
stigmatization of victims-survivors
  gendered norms and, 2-3
  impact of, 5-6, 26, 89, 119-20, 143-45
  impunity culture and, 137
  judicial system and, 125-26, 136
  medical assistance and, 96, 120, 121-
    22, 135
  in Philippines, 109
  reporting silence and, 36-37, 123-24,
    147, 155-56
  risk of, 97, 109-10
  transitional justice and, 156
  under-reporting, 36-37, 40-42, 116-18
strip searches, 31, 71-72, 75-77, 160-61
Swaine, Aisling, 2-3, 19, 22, 39

Tatmadaw soldiers, 10, 69-74
torture
  by American soldiers, 31
  background on, 2-3
  Burmese SGBV, 71-72
  Cambodian genocide and, 30-31
  Philippine SGBV, 98-99
  psychological torture, 23
  Sri Lankan SGBV, 114-18, 123
  by state security forces, 24
trafficking, 81, 89, 91, 93-94, 95-96, 101-
    2, 146
transitional justice
  gender inequalities and, 138
  lack of in Burma, 64, 146
  lack of in Philippines, 85
  lack of in Sri Lanka, 11, 112, 115-16,
    124-25, 126, 135-37, 153-54
  patterns and trends in SGBV
    reporting, 155-57
Transitional Justice and Reconciliation
    Commission (TJRC), the
    Philippines, 101-2
Tripoli Agreement, 87
Tyner, James A., 1, 30-31

UK Preventing Sexual Violence Initiative
    (PSVI), 143-45

UN Committee on the Elimination of
    Discrimination against Women
    (CEVAW), 135-36
under-reporting. *see also* nonreporting
    problems; reporting silence
  cultural sensitivities, 116
  human rights defenders, 36
  impunity from crimes, 147-45
  lack of data and, 41-44
  in low-intensity conflicts, 48
  by male victims-survivors, 37, 118
  problems with, 1, 3-5, 33-34, 42
  stigmatization of victims-survivors,
    36-37, 40, 116
  transitional justice and, 135-36
UN Framework on the Prevention of
    Conflict-Related Sexual Violence, 37
UN General Assembly (UNGA), 56-
    57, 61, 69
UN Human Rights Council
    Resolution, 123-24
Union Peace Dialogue Joint Committee
    (UPDJC), Burma, 65-66
Union Solidarity Development Party
    (USDP), 58, 159
United Nations Human Rights Council
    (UNHRC), 61, 69, 125, 147, 162, 167
UN Office of the Special Representative on
    Sexual Violence in Armed Conflict,
    18-20, 85
unofficial reporting, 1, 4, 78-79, 81, 82-83,
    105, 127, 130-32, 139-40, 142-43,
    157, 171n.6
UN peacekeeping missions, 18-19, 20-21,
    36, 170n.7
UN Security Council, 38-39, 61, 115-
    16, 139
UN Security Council Resolution 1325
    (2002), 1, 7-8, 17-18
UN Security Council Resolution 1820
    (2002), 7-8, 17-18
Uppsala Conflict Data Program (UCDP),
    25-26, 38, 56-57, 112-13, 169n.1

vanguard state theory, 38-39
violence against civilians, 22, 160
violence against women (VAW), 5-6, 15,
    44-45, 63, 75-77, 97-98

Wars of Partition, 1, 12
war tactics, 70, 71–72, 74
welfare needs and services, 75–77, 88–89, 101–2
women
   activism by, 134–36
   comfort women, 1, 12
   empowerment movements, 11–12
   role in Burmese SGBV reporting, 62–67
   role in Philippine peace and SGBV reporting, 91–92
Women's League of Burma (WLB), 61
Women Under Siege, 39
Wood, Elizabeth, 23

Printed in the USA/Agawam, MA
November 1, 2024

875500.009